MICHAEL FORSTER

BUMPER BOOK OF ASSEMBLIES 2

50 ready-made assemblies for Key Stage 2

First published in 2004 by
KEVIN MAYHEW LTD
Buxhall, Stowmarket, Suffolk, IP14 3BW
E-mail: info@kevinmayhewltd.com

Bumper Book of Assemblies 2 is a compilation of material
previously published in *God's Wonderful Ways,*
God's Wonderful People and *Wonderful World.*

9 8 7 6 5 4 3 2 1 0

ISBN 1 84417 306 2
Catalogue No 1500731

Front cover by Angela Selfe
Printed in Great Britain

Contents

Foreword

Virtually all the assemblies in this book are directly about relationships – relationships with God and with one another. For Christians, those two can never be neatly separated; many biblical texts point out that how we relate to each other – including those who are very obviously different – is the real measure of our relationship with God. Even without specific texts to quote, we should still see this as the natural consequence of the Incarnation: the God who comes to us in human form and invites us to recognise and relate to him.

In the worlds of education and religion, the ongoing debate about what children need to learn is always live. Without wishing to be a reductionist, I don't think it takes much imagination to see relationship issues affecting every level of society. Whether we're concerned about playground bullying, discipline, 'hate crime', or suicide bombers and the strangely conceived 'war on terror', we are actually thinking about relationships. How do we 'teach' our children about those?

I don't think there's any substitute for experience, which is why these assemblies all seek to involve children alongside teachers, both in the preparation and the presentation. Of course, doing things *with* people always involves more effort, time and risk than doing things *for* them, but it really is so worthwhile!

Indeed, the distinction between 'teacher' and 'learner' is blurred here. Whatever a particular person's principal role may be, everyone is both a learner and an enabler of others' learning.

The assemblies are based on storytelling, the activity that for countless ages has helped bond families and communities together. The story can be read either by one person in a narrative form or by several in its dramatised version. The prayers and other activities can also be shared between a number of people – and what about getting the children to write their own prayers, sharing their concerns and together searching for the words to express them?

I take great joy in the thought that if the same assembly were done in a thousand schools, each following the format given, there would be a thousand unique assemblies as each group made the work their own. More than that, because listening and watching are activities too, there would be tens or hundreds of thousands of unique *experiences* as each person received the material through the unique 'filters' of their own background, culture and experience. The ability to be part of that kaleidoscope of experience, and relate to others who share it differently – and not feel threatened by it or want to make it 'the same for everyone' – is one of the God-given treasures of our humanity.

So, let these assemblies be not just learning tools but celebrations of our infinite, mysterious God, and of the wonderful, diverse humanity through which that infinite mystery only just begins to be expressed.

Most of the songs mentioned in this book appear in *The Children's Hymn Book* (Kevin Mayhew Publishers). Those marked (SS) can be found in the Song Section on page 207.

MICHAEL FORSTER

Let It Be

Based on Genesis 1

Get the children involved *together* in something creative. You could make up a large sheet of paper and get them to co-operate on a painting. Or is there an area of the school or grounds that they could brighten up? If so, take some photographs while they're doing it, to make a display for the assembly.

- Think about the actions for all the children to join in during the story.

ON THE DAY

Introduction

Today we're going to hear the story about how God created the world. We've been getting creative, too, but more of that later. First, we're going to say our 'Thank you' prayer.

'Thank you' Prayer

Thank you, God, for all you give us,
thank you for the earth and sea;
thank you, God, for special people,
thank you, God, for making me.

God's Story

Before God made the world, it was very, very dark. The universe was shapeless and had no life in it, except for God. In the silence, the only sound was of God breathing. Then God spoke.

'Let there be light!'

And suddenly, there was light everywhere. Just imagine having all the lights in your street burning in your bedroom. It was brilliant! The trouble was, there was no one there to see it, except God. But he was working on that.

God looked at the light, and said, 'That's pretty good, but it wouldn't do to have it always. I know. I'll create time.' So he divided up light from darkness. 'There,' he said. 'That's the day, and I'll call *that* the night.' So the evening came, and then the morning, and that completed the very first day. But things were still in a pretty disordered state – a bit like most children's bedrooms, only a million times worse! So God decided it was time to do some sorting out. 'There,' he said, when he had finished, 'I'll call this part "heaven".' By that time it was evening, and after that came another morning: the second day had gone.

Well, there was an awful lot of water sloshing about in the world, and God decided that was the next bit to be tidied up. 'Let's get all the water together,' he said, 'and make a bit of dry land. I'll call the dry bits "earth" and the watery bits "sea". My Word, that looks good!' Then God really started to get going! 'Now, let's see what this earth can produce!' he said. 'Give me some plants!' And it happened. 'Give me some seeds,' said God. And it happened. 'Give me some fruit!' And before long, the earth was covered with wonderful green plants, and brightly coloured fruit: red strawberries, yellow bananas – what else can you think of? 'Well, bless me!' thought God. 'This is really good!' But by now – yes, you've guessed it – the evening had come again. Then came the morning, and that was the third day taken care of.

Well, the earth was looking pretty spectacular. So God looked around at the sky and thought, 'Perhaps I should spruce this up a bit. Let's have some stars, and planets around here. And they'd better move round in circles to mark the seasons – otherwise we'll end up with May blossom in November or something equally silly.' And d'you know, people still use them for that, all these centuries later. So God provided a bright light for the day, and a dimmer one at night – just enough to stop it being too frightening. By then it was evening again, and God said, 'Well upon my Word – that's a good day's work!' Then he waited for morning. The fourth day had gone.

Now there were all kinds of plants and flowers on the earth, wonderful stars in the sky, but the sea was looking a bit empty. So God spoke to the sea. 'Let's see what you can do,' he said. 'Give me lots of animals – great big sea monsters, and whales and sharks, and octopuses. And let's have some birds in the air as well.' And before you could say – well, you couldn't say anything because people hadn't happened yet – but anyway, there were fish and birds all over the place.

- The fish *swam*
- the eels *wriggled*
- and the birds *flapped their wings*

God said, 'That's right – make yourselves at home, and let's have lots of you – I want plenty of life in the world!' And then what do you think? That's right – it was evening again and the fifth day was over.

When morning came, God looked at the earth, and said, 'Come on – let's have some life around here! Don't leave it all to the sea.' And that's exactly what happened. Every kind of wild animal – everything from dinosaurs to dingoes! And God was pleased – but not *that* pleased! 'What would really top it off,' he said, 'would be people. Human beings, made like me, able to love and be loved, who would be my special friends. They'd be able to help me – we could do things together. They would be the best of all the things I've made.' So God made men and women; he made them able to love, and able to think, and said, 'Come and be my special friends and helpers. Share my work of making this creation a wonderful place to be. Look, I've given you great things – plants and fruit and rocks, wonderful colours, and everything you could ever need. Look after it well, and work with me to make it even better.'

And so it was. God looked at everything he had made, and thought, 'Even though I say it myself, it's pretty terrific!' The sixth day had passed.

Then the morning came again: the seventh day. And what do you think God did then? He had a rest!

Our Story

Show the assembly what the class has done, and describe how it relates to the story: how they had to work together, arrange things in proper order, separate things out, etc.

Prayers

We're Sad

We're sorry, God,
for all the things that spoil your world.
Sometimes we forget just how beautiful
and how fragile it is.
Forgive us, and help us
to care for your creation.

We're Glad

The world's a wonderful place:
full of colour, and light and life.
Thank you for making it beautiful
in so many ways.
And thank you especially
for letting us help you.

Let's Pray for People

There are some people who can't see or hear
the beautiful things in the world.
And some just don't notice,
because they're too busy.
Please God, help all people
to enjoy your creation
in lots of different ways.

Songs

God's love is deeper
God turned darkness into light
Let it be (SS)
Morning has broken
Think of a world without any flowers
We can plough and dig the land

Let It Be

God's Story

Narrator	Before God made the world, it was very, very dark.
God	Let there be light!
Narrator	And suddenly, there was light everywhere.
God	That's pretty good, but it wouldn't do to have it always. There. That's the day, and I'll call *that* the night.
Narrator	So the evening came, and then the morning, and that completed the very first day. But things were still pretty messy! So God did some sorting out.
God	There, I'll call this part 'heaven'.
Narrator	By that time it was evening, and after that came another morning: the second day had gone. But there was an awful lot of water sloshing about in the world.
God	Let's make a bit of dry land. I'll call the dry bits 'earth' and the watery bits 'sea'. My Word, that's good! Now, let's see what this earth can produce! Give me some plants! Give me some seeds! Give me some fruit!
Narrator	Before long, the earth was covered with wonderful green plants and brightly coloured fruit: red strawberries, yellow bananas – all sorts of things.
God	Well, bless me! This is really good!
Narrator	The evening had come again. Then came the morning, and that was the third day taken care of. The earth was looking pretty spectacular. So God looked around at the sky.
God	I'll spruce this up a bit. Let's have some stars, and planets around here. And they'd better move round in circles to mark the seasons – otherwise we'll end up with May blossom in November or something equally silly. We'll have bright light for the day, and a dimmer one at night. Well upon my Word – that's a good day's work!

Narrator	Now the fourth day had gone. The earth looked great, but the sea was looking a bit empty.
God	Let's see what the sea can do. Give me lots of animals – great big sea monsters, and whales and sharks, and octopuses. And let's have some birds in the air as well.
Narrator	Straight away, there were fish and birds everywhere.

- The fish *swam*
- the eels *wriggled*
- and the birds *flapped their wings*

God	That's right – make yourselves at home, and let's have lots of you – I want plenty of life in the world!
Narrator	Now the fifth day was over. When morning came, God looked at the earth again.
God	Come on – let's have some life around here! Don't leave it all to the sea.
Narrator	And so there were animals – everything from dinosaurs to dingoes! And God was pleased – but not *that* pleased!
God	What would really top it off would be people. Human beings, made to be like me, able to love and be loved, to be my special friends. We could do things together. They would be the best of all the things I've made.
Narrator	So God made men and women; he made them able to love, and able to think.
God	Come and be my special friends. Look, I've given you great things – plants and fruit and rocks, wonderful colours, and everything you could ever need. Look after it well, and work with me to make it even better.
Narrator	The sixth day had passed and God was pleased with everything he had made.
God	Even though I say it myself, it's pretty terrific! A good week's work by any standards. Bless me! Is that the time? I think I'll have a day off.

Oh, Brother!

Based on Genesis 4:1-12

BEFORE THE DAY

Think about ways of belonging and caring. Are any of the children Cubs or Brownies, or perhaps in the Boys' or Girls' Brigade? Get them to collect badges, logos etc. from any appropriate organisations they can think of, and make a display. Don't limit them unnecessarily. Greenpeace or WWF, for example, give a creation-wide dimension to this.

• Think about the actions for all the children to join in during the story.

ON THE DAY

Introduction

Today we're going to think about belonging, caring and taking responsibility. First, we're going to say our 'Thank you' prayer.

'Thank you' Prayer

Thank you, God, for all you give us,
thank you for the earth and sea;
thank you, God, for special people,
thank you, God, for making me.

God's Story

Adam and Eve had two sons. The first one's name was Cain, and when he was born Eve was really proud. Then about a year later they had another baby, and called him Abel. The two boys were very much like ordinary children, really. They sometimes played together, and at other times they would argue and fight. Most children grow out of this kind of silliness, but still, Eve was anxious.

'I worry about those two,' she said. 'One of these days one of them's going to get badly hurt in their arguments.'

'Oh don't exaggerate!' Adam replied. 'You worry too much. It's just the way children are. We were young once, you know.'

'No we weren't,' said Eve. 'That's the problem with being the first people God made.'

'There you are, then!' retorted Adam. 'What d'you know about children? Leave them alone.'

That wasn't very helpful of Adam, was it? Well, Cain and Abel grew up from children into young men and they were still quarrelling and getting jealous of each other. Eve got really worried. 'They'll never survive if they carry on like this,' she said. Then Adam had an idea.

'I know. We'll teach Abel to be a shepherd and Cain to be a gardener,' he said. 'Then they won't be able to get jealous of one another because they'll be doing such different things.'

- Cain learned to *scatter seeds*
- and to *clip hedges*
- Abel learned to *shear sheep*

Eve thought that was a wonderful idea, and decided that everything was going to be all right after all. She didn't realise how wrong she was!

The boys grew into men, and still they didn't learn not to fight all the time. Eventually, Eve's worst fears came true.

When Abel's sheep had their first lambs, he said, 'I must give some of them to God, as a way of saying thank you.'

Well of course Cain immediately decided that he should give some of his crops as well. If Abel was going to give God a wonderful present, then Cain would make jolly sure he gave God a better one! So Cain went and got the best crops he had grown. 'I'll make God like me more than he likes Abel,' he thought slyly.

So the day for the offering came and Abel brought some beautiful young lambs and offered them to God. Just as he was doing it, he heard a voice behind him say, 'Come on, God – get a load of this, then!' Abel turned round and there was Cain staggering along pushing a great big barrow loaded with all the fruit and vegetables you can imagine (*such as . . .*)

Cain staggered up to where Abel was, dropped the handles of the barrow and gasped, 'There! Better than a few silly little lambs, eh!'

God did not like this one little bit. 'Abel just wanted to give me a present,' he said, 'but you did it because you were jealous of him. So it's Abel's gift that pleases me most.'

Now I've seen some spoilt children in my time, but when it came to throwing tantrums Cain could have been a gold medallist! He jumped up and down; he waved his arms in the air; he threw himself on the ground and hammered the earth with his fists. After a little while, God said, 'Why are you so angry?'

'Why am I so angry?' Cain spluttered. 'I bring you barrowloads of food, and Abel brings a few scruffy little lambs, and you prefer his present to mine – and then you ask why I'm angry!'

'Look,' said God, 'if you're going to get like this every time you lose then you're going to end up in real trouble. I'd watch that temper if I were you.'

Cain didn't like that, but he hadn't got an answer so he just bottled it all up and plotted to get his own back on Abel. One day he suggested a nice walk in the country. Abel thought that must mean they were friends again, so he said, 'That's a good idea,' and off they went.

As soon as they got out of sight of the house, Cain pretended to have cramp in his foot and got behind Abel. He picked up a big sharp stone and he attacked Abel from behind, bringing the stone down on his head as hard as he could. Poor old Abel didn't stand a chance; he went down and lay very still. Cain knew that he was dead.

It's strange how things that seemed like a good idea at first often don't look so good afterwards. What was Cain to do? He couldn't bring Abel back to life, and he really wished he hadn't got so carried away. But there was nothing to be done, now.

As Cain was going back towards his house, he heard God speaking to him: 'Cain, where's your brother?'

Cain made what he thought was a very clever reply. 'Who am I,' he asked, 'his keeper?'

'That's a silly question,' said God. 'Abel's never needed a keeper, but he's often wanted a brother.'

'I'm his brother,' replied Cain.

'Exactly,' said God. 'Now where's Abel?'

Cain was really frightened now. 'Um – er – I – ah,' he gabbled.

'Don't try to fool me,' said God. 'You've killed him. I warned you to watch that temper of yours. You know what you've done, don't you? You can't face your parents now, so you're going to have to go and live somewhere else. And for the rest of your life you'll be a guilty person, on the run.'

So that's how it turned out. How Cain wished he'd listened to God and learnt to control his temper!

Our Story

Show the children the display, and get them to identify some of the logos and say how those particular organisations fit into today's theme. Could joining one of these be a way of taking on a little more responsibility?

Prayers

We're Sad

Please, God, forgive us
when we feel jealous of other people's success.
Help us to be glad for them,
to share their happiness,
and to learn from them.

We're Glad

Thank you, God,
for making us all brothers and sisters
to one another.
Thank you for all the joy we get
from sharing our lives.

Let's Pray for People

All over the world,
people are finding things to fight about.
Please God, bless the people
who are trying to find answers
and to bring peace.

Songs

Make me a channel of your peace
Thank you, O God, for all our friends (SS)
We are one family together
When I needed a neighbour

Oh, Brother!

God's Story

Narrator	Adam and Eve had two sons, called Cain and Abel. Sometimes the boys played together, and at other times they would argue and fight, and they often used to get jealous of one another.
Eve	I worry about those two. One of these days one of them's going to get badly hurt in their arguments.
Adam	Oh don't exaggerate! You worry too much. It's just the way children are. We were young once, you know.
Eve	No we weren't! That's the problem with being the first people God made.
Adam	There you are, then! What d'you know about children? Leave them alone.
Narrator	That wasn't very helpful of Adam, was it? Well, Cain and Abel grew up from children into young men and they were still quarrelling and getting jealous of each other.
Eve	They'll never survive if they carry on like this.
Adam	I know. We'll teach them separate trades, so they can't compete.
Narrator	So that's what they did.

- Cain learned to *scatter seeds*
- and to *clip hedges*
- Abel learned to *shear sheep*

Narrator	Even when they grew up into men, the boys wouldn't stop fighting. The real trouble happened when Abel's sheep had their first lambs.

Abel	I'll give some of the lambs to God, to say thank you.
Narrator	Straight away, Cain had a bad thought.
Cain	I'll make God like me more than he likes Abel.
Narrator	Abel brought some beautiful young lambs and offered them to God. Then he heard a mean voice behind him.
Cain	Come on, God – get a load of this, then! I've brought you some wheat, some bread, carrots, potatoes, apples, pears – better than a few silly little lambs, eh!
Narrator	God did not like this one little bit.
God	Abel just wanted to give me a present, but you did it to get one up on him. So I like Abel's gift best.
Cain	*(Aside)* I'll get Abel for this! Just see if I don't. *(To Abel)* How about a nice walk in the country?
Narrator	As soon as they got out of sight of the house, Cain picked up a big sharp stone, and killed Abel with it. Then he turned to go home.
God	Cain, where's your brother?
Cain	Who am I – his keeper?
God	That's a silly question. Abel's never needed a keeper. But he's often wanted a brother.
Cain	I'm his brother.
God	Exactly. Now where's Abel? You've killed him, haven't you? Well, you can't face your parents now, so you're going to have to go and live somewhere else. And for the rest of your life you'll be a guilty person, on the run.
Narrator	So that's how it turned out. How Cain wished he'd learnt to control his temper!

Rabbles and Babbles

Based on Genesis 11:1-9

BEFORE THE DAY

Think with the children about great human achievements: obvious ones with child appeal like computers and space travel, but other ones as well: transplant surgery and penicillin (children once used to die from what are now much less serious illnesses); social reforms (how would the children like to have to clean chimneys by climbing up them?) Perhaps the children themselves could research one of these subjects and draw some pictures. You could also teach the children to say a simple phrase in various languages, and then let them shout them out together where indicated.

• Think about the actions for all the children to join in during the story.

ON THE DAY

Introduction

Soon, we're going to hear about some people who tried to be too clever, but first we're going to say our 'Thank you' prayer.

'Thank you' Prayer

Thank you, God, for all you give us,
thank you for the earth and sea;
thank you, God, for special people,
thank you, God, for making me.

God's Story

A long, long time ago, in a land called Shinar, some people had what they thought was a great idea. They believed that all they had to do was work together, and they could do anything. And since everybody spoke the same language, working together should have been easy. 'Why,' said Barnaby, 'with our combined knowledge and skills, we could climb right up to heaven!'

Barnaby's friend, Johnny, wasn't so sure. 'To begin with,' he said, 'how do you know exactly where heaven is?

'Oh, don't be stupid!' said Barnaby, crossly. 'Heaven's got to be up there; it's not down here, so that's the only place left.'

'I know it looks that easy,' said Johnny, 'but things might not be quite as they seem.'

Barnaby was impatient. 'Look,' he said, 'it's very simple. What you see is what there is. Don't make things complicated by asking unnecessary questions. This is earth, and heaven's up there. That's how it looks, and that's how it is.'

Johnny didn't like arguing with Barnaby, but he couldn't resist saying, 'Perhaps God doesn't want us to climb up to heaven – if that's where it is. Perhaps that's why we can't see it.'

Barnaby thought this was the silliest idea he'd heard so far. 'Of course God wants us to do it!' he said, scornfully. 'Would he have made us so wonderfully clever, and taught us how to build towers and things if he didn't want us to do it?'

Johnny opened his mouth to speak, but Barnaby held up his hand. 'No more!' he said. 'We have a duty to use all the knowledge we have. That's what God expects. So whatever we're capable of doing must be right.'

Johnny thought, 'I'm capable of punching you on the nose, but it wouldn't be right to do it!' But he didn't say that, because he knew Barnaby would have an answer. Barnaby always did!

So everyone set to work – everyone except Johnny and Barnaby, that is.

• The designers *drew the plans*
• the stone masons *hammered and chiselled*
• the carpenters *sawed the wood*

God wasn't happy about it, though. He hadn't put people on earth so that they could spend all their time trying to get back to heaven! He could see what was really happening, and he didn't like it. The people who were building the tower were so obsessed with it that they forgot about everything else. They never played with their children, or looked after their elderly relations. They started to think that the tower was all that mattered. Some people even died from neglect. All the workers were interested in doing was trying to get to heaven! So God got very angry. 'I'm going to teach them a lesson,' he thought.

So it was that, one morning, Barnaby got up and went out as usual to find a very unwelcome surprise awaiting him. He'd have known about it earlier if he'd listened to his wife that morning, but he never did that. As he got near to the tower, he heard the most amazing sound – a loud babbling of lots of people all shouting at one another at the tops of their voices. So Barnaby went up and tried to silence them, but he had to get a whistle and blow it before they noticed him. When they did, he started telling them off.

'You're supposed to be building this tower,' he shouted at them, 'not gossiping amongst yourselves – now get on with it!'

Barnaby couldn't understand why the people were looking at him in such a strange, bewildered way. Then the foreman came up and spoke to him, and it was Barnaby's turn to look amazed. He couldn't understand anything the foreman was saying. 'What's the matter with you?' he yelled at the foreman. 'Talk properly so that I can understand you.'

The foreman couldn't make out what Barnaby was saying, and realised that Barnaby couldn't understand him either. So he tried again – but louder. Barnaby still couldn't understand and he shouted back – louder still. Then all the others joined in, and before long everyone was shouting at everyone else, and nobody was listening.

You know what had happened, don't you? They were all speaking different languages! Everything everybody said made sense – but only to them! No one could understand anybody else at all!*

So the tower never got finished.

And it won't be. God is still trying to teach us that heaven isn't in the sky; the way to find heaven is to care about other people, and learn to understand each other.

And all this time later, we're still not very good at it!

* If prepared, the children shout their phrases here.

Our Story

God's got nothing against skills – it's what we do with them that's important. Show and tell the whole assembly what the class has learnt.

Prayers

We're Sad

Sometimes we think we're more important than anyone else in the world.
Then it ends up with us all shouting at each other and nobody listening to anyone else.
We're sorry, God.
Please teach us to be good listeners.

We're Glad

Loving God,
everyone matters to you.
We don't need to work at it.
You don't mind if we're not clever.
You just love us, as we are.
Thank you, God.

Let's Pray for People

We pray for people who get forgotten,
people who are in trouble but don't get noticed;
people whose voices get lost
in all the noise others are making.
Please God, help us to hear them,
so that we can show them
how important they really are.

Songs

I'm black, I'm white, I'm short, I'm tall
Peace, perfect peace is the gift
Rabbles, babbles (SS)
Thank you, O God, for all our friends (SS)

Rabbles and Babbles

God's Story

Narrator   A long, long time ago, everyone in the world spoke the same language – until Barnaby had his bright idea.

Barnaby   You know, Johnny, if we all worked together we could do anything – even climb right up to heaven!

Johnny   That's ridiculous. How do you know heaven's up there? It might be more complicated than you think.

Barnaby   Oh, don't be stupid! Heaven's got to be up there; it's not down here, so that's the only place left. And where d'you think all that light comes from?

Johnny   I know – but things aren't always as they seem.

Barnaby   You're a philosopher.

Johnny   That's a rotten thing to say!

Barnaby   Look, it's very simple. This is earth, and heaven's up there. That's how it looks, and that's how it is.

Narrator   Johnny didn't like arguing with Barnaby, because he always felt so inferior; Barnaby seemed to know so much, and to be so confident, and Johnny always ended up feeling silly. Still, he tried again.

Johnny   Perhaps God doesn't want us to climb up to heaven. Perhaps that's why we can't see it.

Barnaby   Don't be stupid – if God didn't want us to do it we wouldn't be able to.

Johnny   (*Aside to audience*) I'm *able* to punch him on the nose, but that doesn't mean God would want me to do it!

Narrator   So *nearly* everyone set to work. Johnny didn't join in because he thought it was wrong, and Barnaby thought *he* was too important.

Barnaby   I'm an ideas man. I must save my creative energy, and let less important people do the actual work.

Narrator   Surprisingly, most of the other people joined in. They were very impressed by Barnaby's confidence, and thought Johnny was a very silly man.

- So the designers *drew the plans*
- the stone masons *hammered and chiselled*
- the carpenters *sawed the wood*

Narrator   God knew what was happening, and he didn't like it.

God   I didn't put people on earth so that they could spend all their time trying to get back to heaven! These people are obsessed! They never play with their children, or look after their elderly relations. I'll teach them a lesson and give them something else to think about.

Narrator   So it was that, one morning, Barnaby got up and went out as usual to find an unwelcome surprise awaiting him. He'd have known about it earlier if he'd listened to his wife, but he never did that – he just used to get up and rush straight out to see how the tower was getting on. As he got near to the tower, he heard a loud babbling – lots of people all shouting and yelling at one another.

Barnaby   You're supposed to be building this tower, not gossiping amongst yourselves – now get on with it!

Narrator   Soon, they were all shouting at one another and getting nowhere because they were all speaking different languages! No one could understand anybody else at all! Just imagine it*.

Barnaby   Now the tower will never get finished.

Narrator   God is still trying to teach us that heaven isn't in the sky; the way to find heaven is to care about other people, and learn to understand each other. And all this time later, we're still not very good at it!

* If prepared, the children shout their phrases here.

Not a Lot of Brotherly Love

Based on Genesis 37:1-28

BEFORE THE DAY

What different kinds of clothes do the children wear, and why? Do they play in the garden in their best clothes? Why not? Could they make some simple 'mannequins' and dress them in different clothes, for working, for school etc? Perhaps you could get some local factories to contribute some more specialised clothing: safety helmets, gloves and so on.

• Think about the actions for all the children to join in during the story.

ON THE DAY

Introduction

Do you know the story of Joseph's special coat? We'll hear it in a minute, but first we'll say our 'Thank you' prayer.

'Thank you' Prayer

Thank you, God, for all you give us,
thank you for the earth and sea;
thank you, God, for special people,
thank you, God, for making me.

God's Story

Joseph had eleven brothers. Can you imagine that! I bet they had trouble remembering each other's names! Anyway, I'm not going to tell you all of them, or you'll be as confused as they probably were! Now I'd like to tell you what a wonderful boy Joseph was, and how much his brothers loved him. I'd like to. But I can't. The truth is that he was not really a very nice person at all, when he was young – although he improved as he got older. As a boy, he was always telling tales about his brothers – and his father believed him. Now

his father was Jacob, and he'd been no angel when he was Joseph's age. So he should have known better than to believe what Joseph was saying. Anyway, Joseph's brothers gradually got more and more fed up with the trouble Joseph caused. Then, one day, they decided they'd had enough.

'He got me into trouble again today,' said Reuben, 'saying I'd neglected the sheep; and I hadn't.'

'Well,' said Levi, who was older than Joseph but younger than Reuben, 'it wouldn't be so bad if he did any work himself, but he doesn't. And Dad's bought him a new coat. It's got *long sleeves!* He can't work in that, can he?' That was true, of course. It's not easy to work in posh clothes, is it?

• He couldn't *milk the cows*
• He couldn't *clean the windows*
• He couldn't *paint the fences*

'That's nothing,' said Reuben. 'What about all these dreams he's been telling us about – dreaming that he's the greatest, and we're all going to bow and scrape to him? I'm the eldest, and I'll tell you this: I bow and scrape to nobody!'

They decided they'd have to teach Joseph a lesson. Then, one day, when they had taken the sheep a long way away looking for some grass, they jumped on Joseph and were going to kill him.

Reuben was very worried. 'Joseph might be a stuck-up little so-and-so,' he thought, 'but he's still our brother.' So he said to the others, 'Don't kill him – just put him into one of these dried-up wells, and scare him.' He thought he could go back later and rescue Joseph.

So that's what they did. Can you imagine how Joseph felt, being left in a deep hole in the ground? He wasn't tough and brave, like his brothers, because he'd been spoilt all his life. So he was really frightened, and angry. 'You come and get me out of here!' he kept shouting out, and, 'You just wait until I tell Dad what you've done!'

'I've had enough of this!' said one of the brothers. 'The very next camel that comes along, he's on it. I don't care where it's going.'

Very soon, they saw some Egyptian traders coming across the desert on camels. They ran and got Joseph out of the hole and took him to meet them. 'Look,' they said, 'we've got something for you – a slave. Thirty pounds and he's yours.'

The trader said, 'You must be joking – he doesn't look as if he could survive a good day's work. Thirty pounds indeed! I'll take him off your hands for ten!'

'Twenty-five,' said Dan.

'No way,' said the trader. 'Twenty pounds, take it or leave it. I can't hang around here all day.'

So Joseph was sold for twenty pounds to an Egyptian trader, and soon disappeared over the horizon. The problem then was, what were his brothers going to tell their father?

'I know,' said Dan, 'let's say a wolf got him.'

And do you know – that is just what they did. Jacob was terribly upset, because he thought he would never see his favourite son again.

But of course, he was wrong.

Joseph, as we know, was still alive, although very frightened. What no-one knew at that time was that he was going to have great adventures in Egypt.

But we'll have to hear about that another time.

Our Story

Ask the children to look at the display and work out what the different kinds of clothes are for. Get the children thinking and talking about the different kinds of work that happen in their house and what their part is in it.

Prayers

We're Glad

Dear God,
thank you for our families and friends;
thank you for the things we do together.
Thank you for the fun we have,
for the games we play,
(*and especially for . . .*)

We're Sad

Loving God,
some people don't like us,
and sometimes we don't like them.
We get unhappy,
cross,
selfish,
but you still love us.
Thank you for loving us,
and please help us to love one another.

Let's Pray for People

Let's pray for people we don't see very often.
Thank you, God,
for our friends and relatives
who live far away.
Keep them safe,
and let them know
that we love them.

Songs

God's love is deeper
Kum ba yah
We can plough and dig the land
When I needed a neighbour

Not a Lot of Brotherly Love

God's Story

Narrator Joseph had eleven brothers. Can you imagine that! I bet they had trouble remembering each other's names! Anyway, I'm not going to tell you all of them, or you'll be as confused as they probably were!

Now I'd like to tell you what a wonderful boy Joseph was, and how his brothers loved him. I'd like to. But I can't. The truth is that he was not a very nice person at all, when he was young – although he improved as he got older. As a boy, he was always telling tales about his brothers – and his father believed him. Now his father was Jacob, and he'd been no angel when he was Joseph's age. So he should have known better than to believe what Joseph was saying.

Anyway, one day, Reuben told Levi he'd had enough.

Reuben That brother of ours got me into trouble again today, saying I'd neglected the sheep; and I hadn't.

Levi It wouldn't be so bad if he did any work himself, but he doesn't. And now Dad's bought him a new coat. It's got *long* sleeves! He can't work in that, can he?

Narrator That's true. Joseph couldn't do hard work wearing fancy clothes, could he?

- He couldn't *milk the cows*
- He couldn't *clean the windows*
- He couldn't *paint the fences*

No wonder the brothers were angry. They were going to have to do Joseph's share of the work!

Reuben That's nothing! What about all these dreams he's been telling us about – dreaming that he's the greatest, and we're all going to bow and scrape to him? I'm the eldest, and I'll tell you this: I bow and scrape to nobody!

Narrator	The brothers got together and decided to teach Joseph a lesson. Then, one day, when they had taken the sheep a long way away looking for some grass, they jumped on Joseph and were going to kill him. Reuben was very worried.
Reuben	Joseph might be a stuck-up little so-and-so, but he's still our brother. Don't kill him – just put him into one of these dried-up wells, and scare him.
Narrator	Can you imagine how Joseph felt, being left in a deep hole in the ground? He wasn't tough and brave, like his brothers, because he'd been spoilt all his life. So he was really frightened and angry and he wouldn't stop shouting.
Joseph	You come and get me out of here! You just wait until I tell Dad what you've done!
Levi	I've had enough of this! The very next camel that comes along, he's on it. I don't care where it's going.
Narrator	Very soon, they saw some Egyptian traders coming across the desert on camels. They ran and got Joseph out of the hole, and took him to meet them. They wanted thirty pounds for him but the traders beat them down to twenty. They handed Joseph over to the traders and watched as their camels disappeared over the horizon. Then they had another problem.
Reuben	What are we going to tell Dad?
Levi	I know. Let's say a wolf got him.
Narrator	And do you know – that is just what they did. Jacob was terribly upset, because he thought he would never see his favourite son again. But of course, he was wrong. Joseph, as we know, was still alive, although very frightened. What no-one knew at that time was that he was going to have great adventures in Egypt. But we'll have to hear about that another time.

Joseph's Adventures

Based on Genesis 40-41

BEFORE THE DAY

Have the children visited interesting places (perhaps on a school trip)? Could they draw pictures about them? Perhaps they have some snapshots or souvenirs they could bring to display in the assembly.

• Think about the actions for all the children to join in during the story.

ON THE DAY

Introduction

We're going to hear about some of Joseph's adventures in Egypt, but first we'll say our 'Thank you' prayer.

'Thank you' Prayer

Thank you, God, for all you give us,
thank you for the earth and sea;
thank you, God, for special people,
thank you, God, for making me.

God's Story

This is a story about Joseph, who was taken to Egypt as a slave. He was soon in trouble again and finished up in prison. It wasn't his fault – someone who didn't like him very much told lies about him. That's what he used to do about his brothers, and he learnt that it wasn't funny when it happened to him! But while he was in prison his adventures started.

Anthony, the palace barman, was there as well. 'What have you done?' asked Joseph.

'Mind your own business!' replied Anthony, which wasn't very friendly. Joseph kept quiet after that, as he had learnt not to upset people if he could help it. But next morning, Anthony was very quiet and thoughtful. He didn't say a word! He sat in a corner of the cell and . . .

• He *scratched* his head
• He *stroked* his chin
• He *shook* his head from side to side

'What's the matter?' asked Joseph, expecting to get told to mind his own business again. But Anthony was much nicer.

'I've had a funny dream,' he said. 'I was standing beside this grapevine with three branches. While I was there, grapes grew on the branches.'

'What did you do?' asked Joseph.

'What I'm here to do,' replied Anthony. 'I squeezed the grapes, and made some wine for the king.'

'Well, that's easy to understand,' said Joseph, 'each branch is like one day. So you'll be out of here and back in your job in three days.'

Anthony couldn't believe it when that came true! Of course, he could have told the king and perhaps got Joseph released, but he forgot. He was not at all grateful.

Two years later, the king had strange dreams which no-one in the palace could explain. Then the barman remembered. He went to the king and said, 'I'm terribly sorry – I forgot to tell you – I had a dream when I was in prison.'

'Don't come bothering me with your dreams!' the king snapped. 'I'm too worried about my own.'

'That's just it, Your Majesty,' answered Anthony. 'There was a prisoner called Joseph – foreign chap – and he told me what the dream meant.' So Joseph was sent for.

'It's like this,' said the king. 'I dreamt that I was standing by the river when seven fat cows came up from the water and stood on the bank.'

Anthony interrupted, 'Er . . . what kind of cows were they, Your Majesty – were they brown or black?'

'Don't interrupt!' said the king. 'Or you'll find yourself back in prison.'

'Well!' thought Anthony. 'I only asked!'

'As I was saying,' the king went on, 'there were these seven fat cows. Then up came seven thin cows, and ate all the fat ones! Now what could that mean?'

'That's easy!' said Joseph. 'The cows are like years. There will be seven good years – plenty of food, people will have jobs, and no-one will go hungry. But then there'll be seven bad years, without any rain. The crops won't grow, there'll be no water, people will lose their jobs, and a lot of people will go hungry. And it will be just as if the seven good years had never happened.'

'That's terrible!' said the king. 'What can we do?'

'You need some help, Your Majesty,' said Joseph. 'Put someone who's really wise and clever in charge of the country. You've got to save as much as you can in the good years, to see you through the bad.'

'Well,' said the king, 'I can't think of anyone wiser or cleverer than you. So it looks as though you've got the job.'

That was how Joseph became a very important person in Egypt. For the first seven years, he made sure that as much food as possible was saved. Then the bad years came. No food was growing anywhere, not in Egypt and not in the countries round about, either. But no-one starved in Egypt, because Joseph had done his job so well.

Our Story

Draw attention to the 'travel' display. Joseph was in a foreign country. He met some very interesting people and had wonderful adventures. And they found out that 'foreign chaps' bring their own special gifts with them, as well.

Prayers

We're Glad

Wonderful God,
you give us so much.
Thank you for the things we see and hear,
thank you for the people we meet.
(*Especially* . . .)

We're Sad

Sometimes, we're so happy
that we don't notice other people
who aren't.
Sometimes, we're so full of ourselves
that we forget to say 'Thank you'.
We're sorry.
Help us to notice other people,
and to love them.

Let's Pray for People

Let's say 'thank you' to God
for people who are nice to us.
Loving God,
we remember our friends
and people who help us.
Thank you for them.
Thank you for all the things we like about them:
let them know how we appreciate them,
and help us to show it more ourselves.

Songs

God knows me
Just imagine
We can plough and dig the land
When I needed a neighbour

Joseph's Adventures

God's Story

Narrator	This is a story about Joseph, who was taken to Egypt as a slave. He was soon in trouble again, and finished up in prison. Someone told lies about him. That's what he used to do about his brothers, and he learnt that it wasn't funny, when it happened to him! But then his adventures started. Anthony, the palace barman, was there as well. So Joseph tried to make polite conversation.
Joseph	What have you done to get put in here?
Anthony	Mind your own business!
Narrator	Joseph, kept quiet after that, as he had learnt not to upset people if he could help it. But next morning, Anthony was very thoughtful. He just sat in the corner of his cell, and . . .

- He *scratched* his head
- He *stroked* his chin
- He *shook* his head from side to side

Joseph couldn't contain his curiosity any longer.

Joseph	What's the matter? I hope you don't mind me asking!
Anthony	No – sorry about yesterday – I've had a funny dream. I was standing beside this grapevine with three branches. While I was there, grapes grew on the branches.
Joseph	What did you do?
Anthony	What I'm here to do – I squeezed the grapes, and made some wine for the king.
Joseph	Well, that's easy to understand. In your dream, each branch is like one day. So you'll be out of here and back in your job in three days.
Narrator	Anthony couldn't believe it when that came true! Of course, he could have told the king and perhaps got Joseph released, but he forgot. He was not at all grateful.
	Two years later, the king had strange dreams, which no-one in the palace could explain. Then the barman remembered.

Anthony I'm terribly sorry – I forgot to tell you – I had a dream, when I was in prison.

King Don't come bothering me with your dreams! I'm too worried about my own.

Anthony That's just it, Your Majesty. There was a prisoner called Joseph – foreign chap – and he told me what the dream meant.

Narrator So Joseph was sent for.

King It's like this: I dreamt that I was standing by the river, when seven fat cows came up from the water, and stood on the bank.

Anthony Er . . . what kind of cows were they, Your Majesty – were they brown or black?

King Don't interrupt, or you'll find yourself back in prison.

Anthony Well! I only asked!

King As I was saying, there were these seven fat cows. Then up came seven thin cows, and ate all the fat ones! Now what could that mean?

Joseph That's easy! The cows are like years. There will be seven good years – plenty of food, and no-one will go hungry. But then there'll be seven bad years, without any rain, and in the end it will be just as if the seven good years had never happened.

King That's terrible! What can we do?

Joseph You need some help, Your Majesty. Put someone who's really wise and clever in charge of the country. You've got to save as much as you can in the good years, to see you through the bad.

King Well I can't think of anyone wiser or cleverer than you. So it looks as though you've got the job.

Narrator That was how Joseph became a very important person in Egypt. For the first seven years, he made sure that as much food as possible was saved. Then the bad years came. No food was growing anywhere, not in Egypt and not in the countries round about, either. But no-one starved in Egypt, because Joseph had done his job so well.

Baby in the Bulrushes

Based on Exodus 2:1-10

BEFORE THE DAY

Ask the children whether they have ever had a nice surprise. Perhaps they expected to be told off, and were praised instead; maybe they thought they had lost something, and it turned out to be safe; or possibly they were worried about someone who was ill, who unexpectedly got better.

• Think about the actions for all the children to join in during the story.

ON THE DAY

Introduction

We all love nice surprises. Sometimes, just when we expect things to go wrong, something happens to put them right. It doesn't always work out of course, but it's wonderful when it does. First, we'll say our 'Thank you' prayer.

'Thank you' Prayer

Thank you, God, for all you give us,
thank you for the earth and sea;
thank you, God, for special people,
thank you, God, for making me.

God's Story

A very long time ago, in a place called Egypt, lived a really bad king. He made all the foreign people in his country into slaves. They had to work all day long in the hot sun, making bricks, moving heavy stones about and doing all the jobs that the king didn't want his own people to have to do.

Then the king got frightened. He didn't like the children in slave families especially the little boys. 'Little boys grow up into men,' he thought, 'and men fight. What if one day they get fed up with being slaves, and attack me?' So he did a horrible thing. He tried to kill all the boy babies.

There was a little girl called Miriam in one of the slave families. She was really pleased because she had a new baby brother. But her parents were very worried, because they knew what the king would do if he found out. What do you think they did? They put the little baby boy into a special waterproof basket, and hid it in the bulrushes with Miriam hiding nearby and watching.

Imagine how horrified she was when a princess from the king's palace came along to swim in the river! 'Oh dear!' thought Miriam, 'I hope they don't find the baby!'

But of course the princess soon noticed the basket in the reeds. She opened it, and cried out, 'Oh what a beautiful baby! But he's crying. He must be frightened, poor little thing!'

So what do you think the princess did?

• She *lifted* him up
• She *hugged* him
• She *rocked* him

'What should I do now?' thought Miriam. 'I know – I'll pretend to be just passing by, and see if I can help.'

So she strolled along the river bank, humming a little tune to herself, until she accidentally-on-purpose bumped into the princess. 'Ooh! What a lovely baby!' she said, pretending never to have seen him before.

'Yes,' said the princess, 'I think he's a foreign baby. He's so beautiful and I would love to keep him. So, since no-one knows whose he is, I'll take him back to the palace.'

Then Miriam had a wonderful idea. 'Shall I get you a nurse for him?' she asked, 'After all, you wouldn't want to do everything yourself, Your Highness!'

'What a good idea!' said the princess. 'Go and find a woman from among the foreign slave people, who can nurse him for me.'

Well, Miriam raced home as fast as she could, and went bursting into her home, gasping for breath. 'Really, Miriam!' said her father. 'How many times must I tell you to be more ladylike? Charging around like that, anyone would think something exciting was happening!'

Miriam could hardly talk, she was so out of breath. All she could do was point towards the river, while gasping for air! 'What on earth's the matter?' asked Mum, 'It isn't the baby, is it?' and she began to get very agitated indeed.

By now, Miriam was getting her breath back. 'A princess . . .' she spluttered, 'by . . . river . . . found . . . baby . . . needs a nurse.'

They all hurried back to the river. There they found the princess still holding the baby. Taking a deep breath, Miriam went up to her and said, 'I've found someone who can nurse the baby for you.'

'Good!' smiled the princess, who was nowhere near as horrible as her father; in fact she was rather nice, 'You realise you'll have to live at the palace?'

'Of course,' said Mum. The princess handed over the baby. 'He's a lovely little thing,' she said. 'I wish I knew who his parents are.'

Of course, no-one told her, because that would have been too dangerous. But they all set off to the palace together. Miriam was really excited about living in a real palace, with a real live princess – nearly as excited as she was about having a baby brother.

'What are you going to call the baby?' she asked.

'I think I'll call him Moses,' answered the princess.

So the baby was taken to the palace, along with the 'nurse' who was really his mother, and the princess treated him just like one of the royal family.

Our Story

Tell the school about the stories you shared in preparation. Perhaps some of the children in other classes have something to add? Things don't always work out as well as they did for Miriam's family, but life does have its nice surprises.

Prayers

We're Glad

Amazing God!
Life can be so exciting!
We never know what might happen!
Sometimes, people are nice to us,
when we don't expect it.
Lovely things happen,
which we haven't planned.
Thank you for a wonderful world,
full of surprises.

We're Sad

We're sorry, God,
for letting people down.
We're sorry for not being
as good as we could be.
Help us to give people nice surprises,
not nasty shocks.

Let's Pray for People

God, our friend,
we pray for happy people
(especially . . .)
Thank you for their happiness.
Help us to show them
that we're happy, too.
And we pray for unhappy people
(especially . . .)
Let them know that we care,
and that we're sad for them.

Songs

He's got the whole world in his hands
Kum ba yah
Morning has broken
Out to the great wide world we go
Water of life

Baby in the Bulrushes

God's Story

Narrator   A very long time ago, in a place called Egypt, lived a really bad king. In his country were some people of another race, and he hated them. He made them work as slaves. Then he did something very evil, and decided to kill all their boy babies. So when a little girl called Miriam found she had a new baby brother she was very pleased, but also very frightened.

Miriam   Mum, I've got an idea. Why don't we hide the baby in a basket? If we cover it in tar, it will float, and then we can hide it in the rushes at the side of the river.

Narrator   So that's what they did. They put the little baby boy into the basket, and hid it in the bulrushes. Miriam decided to hide nearby and keep an eye on it, just in case. Imagine how horrified she was when a princess from the king's palace came along to swim in the river! The princess went into the water and began to swim, and then noticed the basket in the reeds. She opened it and saw the baby.

Princess   Oh what a beautiful baby! But he's crying. He must be frightened, poor little thing!

Narrator   So, what do you think the princess did?

- She *lifted* him up
- She *hugged* him
- She *rocked* him

Miriam was very worried. So she strolled along the river bank, humming a little tune to herself, until she accidentally-on-purpose bumped into the princess.

Miriam   Ooh! What a lovely baby! Is he yours?

Princess   No, I think he's a foreign baby. He's so beautiful, and I would love to keep him. So, since no-one knows whose he is, I'll take him back to the palace.

Miriam   Er, would you like me to try and find a nurse for him? After all, you wouldn't want to do *everything* yourself, Your Highness!

Princess   What a good idea. Go and find a woman from among the foreign slave people who can nurse him for me.

Narrator   Well, Miriam raced home as fast as she could and went bursting into her home, gasping for breath.

Mum   What on earth's the matter? It isn't the baby, is it?

Miriam   *(Breathlessly)* It's a princess . . . by the river . . . found the baby . . . wants a nurse!

Narrator   So Miriam and Mum hurried back to the river, and found the princess still there, holding the baby.

Miriam   Er . . . Your Highness, I've found a woman who can act as a nurse for you.

Princess   That's fine. *(Turns to Mum)* You don't mind coming to live at the palace?

Mum   Not at all. Um . . . can I ask what you're going to call him?

Princess   I think I'll call him Moses.

Narrator   So the baby was taken to the palace, along with the 'nurse' who was really his mother, and the princess treated him just like one of the royal family.

Don't Ask Me!

Based on Exodus 3:1-4:16

Let the children imagine being asked to do something they didn't want to do (*that* will not be difficult!) What excuses might they use to avoid it? Write them down in large letters on the left-hand side of a flip chart. Now let them imagine that they want to do something, but have to persuade you to let them. What might they say, then? Write those arguments down in the right-hand column. Make it a game, and enjoy a good laugh with them, thus encouraging them to think of more outlandish answers. Note when they run out and start to repeat themselves!

• Think about the actions for all the children to join in during the story.

ON THE DAY

Introduction

You wouldn't make excuses if you didn't want to do something, would you? We're going to see some very interesting examples in a few minutes, but first we'll say our 'Thank you' prayer.

'Thank you' Prayer

Thank you, God, for all you give us,
thank you for the earth and sea;
thank you, God, for special people,
thank you, God, for making me.

God's Story

Moses was having a nice quiet life. The rest of the Hebrew people were terribly unhappy, because they were slaves in Egypt, but Moses had escaped from that and he was working as a shepherd. Apart from chasing the odd wolf away, life didn't get very exciting; he just walked from place to place finding grass for the sheep to eat. Mind you, that was hard work, but Moses never complained because most of the time it was safe, even if it was a little boring.

One day, he was out minding the sheep when he noticed something strange. A bush nearby seemed to be on fire, except that it wasn't going all black and shrivelled the way bushes normally do when they burn. So he thought he'd take a closer look. Then he had the shock of his life – he heard a voice.

'Hey! Moses!'

'What!' exclaimed Moses, looking all round. 'Where did that come from?'

'I'm over here!' said the voice.

Surely, it couldn't be the bush talking, could it? It was really scary! Moses was about to run away when the voice came again.

'Come over here, Moses. I want to talk to you. But take your shoes off, first, because this is holy ground.'

Holy ground! Of course! It was God who was speaking. Mind you, it might have been better if it had been the bush; when God gives people visions he usually has a job for them! Moses did as he was told; he took off his shoes and went closer.

'That's better,' said God. 'Now we can talk properly. I've been watching what's been going on in Egypt.'

'Lucky you,' thought Moses. 'I haven't seen a good cabaret dancer in years.' But that wasn't what God was talking about. God was very unhappy about the way the Hebrew slaves were being treated, and had decided to set them free. Moses got worried.

'I hope you're not going to ask me to get involved in politics,' he said, 'because I don't think it mixes with religion.'

'Oh, not that cop-out again!' sighed God. 'If you had any idea how often I've heard that! Look, people are suffering, and I want to do something about it. And you're going to help me.' This was getting a bit heavy, and Moses really felt he would prefer to talk to the bush, but it wasn't to be. Then he heard the words he'd been dreading.

'You're to go and see Pharaoh,' said God, 'and tell him to let the people go.'

'Go and see who? And tell him what?' squeaked Moses, who was very frightened by now. 'I can't do that! It's all right for you, but I have to live in this world! Anyway, you need a good orator – an experienced politician. I just know what'll happen when I get in front of the king: I'll get all tongue tied – that's if he doesn't cut it out first.'

God wasn't going to listen to that kind of talk. 'Come on, Moses,' he said, 'trust me. I'll be right with you the whole time.'

Things weren't going Moses' way. So he decided to try another approach.

- He *scratched his head*
- and then he *shook it from side to side* and
- suddenly he *snapped his fingers*. Got it!

He put on his most reasonable and worldly-wise voice – the way people do when they know they are wrong. 'Well of course, God, the reality is,' he said, 'that these people have never heard of you. They've been in slavery all their lives, and I'm afraid we need to face up to the situation as it really is – they've forgotten you. I mean, what am I going to say if they ask who you are? Have you got a name?'

God wasn't falling for that. 'Oh no you don't, Moses!' he said. 'You can't put a label on me, like a plant or an animal. I'm greater than any name you could think of. *I* decide who and what I am, and I will be whoever I choose – you go to the slaves and tell them that! And say that I'm going to set them free!'

Moses was getting desperate by now, and he started to repeat himself: 'But no one's going to listen to me!' he wailed. 'I'm a terrible speaker – you ask my wife about that, she'll tell you! No one will take notice of me. Look, I've got a nice home, a lovely wife, and a good, steady job. That's the kind of bloke I am. I'm not into . . .'

'If you mention politics again, you'll regret it!' said God, and the bush seemed to burn more fiercely than before. 'I care about people – and if you're a friend of mine you will as well. Stop trying to wheedle out of it and do as I ask.' Then the voice got gentler again. 'Look, Moses, I know you're frightened, but I wouldn't ask you to do it if I wasn't going to back you up. If it makes you feel better, you can take Aaron with you – he can talk.'

'That's true!' said Moses. 'He could talk the humps off a camel, could Aaron.'

'That's settled then,' said God. 'Now go and find Aaron, and let's get cracking. We're going to set the people free!'

And that is exactly what they did. But that's a much longer story.

Our Story

Show the children the flip chart, and tell them about the fun you had making it. You can see Moses going through the same process in the story, and eventually starting to repeat himself. You might speculate as to how he would have tried to persuade God, if the boot had been on the other foot.

Prayers

We're Sad

We're sorry God.
Sometimes we say, 'I can't'
when we mean 'I won't'.
When people are in trouble,
we make excuses for not helping them.
Show us what we can do,
and help us to trust you.
Oh, and don't take 'No' for an answer!

We're Glad

Thank you, God, for not giving up,
even when we do.
Thank you for helping us
to be good friends to one another.

Let's Pray for People

We know that some people are unhappy,
perhaps because other people are cruel to them,
or because they are poor, or ill.
Please show us what we can do to help,
and then give us the faith to do it.

Songs

Lead my people to freedom!
One more step
The voice from the bush
We're all going to the Promised Land (SS)

Don't Ask Me!

God's Story

Narrator   Moses was having a nice quiet life. The rest of the Hebrew people were terribly unhappy, because they were slaves in Egypt, but Moses had escaped from that and he was working as a shepherd. One day, he was out minding the sheep when he noticed something strange. A bush nearby seemed to be on fire, except that it wasn't going all black and shrivelled the way bushes normally do when they burn. So he took a closer look. Then he had the shock of his life – he heard a voice.

God   Hey! Moses! Over here.

Moses   What's that? Surely, not the bush talking!

God   Come over here, Moses. I want to talk to you. But take your shoes off, first, because this is holy ground.

Narrator   Holy ground! Of course! It was God who was speaking. Mind you, it might have been better if it had been the bush; when God gives people visions he usually has a job for them to do! Moses did as he was told; he took off his shoes and went closer.

God   That's better. Now we can talk properly. I've been watching what's been going on in Egypt.

Moses   *(Aside)* Lucky him! I haven't seen a cabaret in years.

God   Not that! I'm going to set the slaves free – and you're going to help me.

Moses   I hope you're not going to ask me to get involved in politics, because I don't think it mixes with religion.

God   Oh, not that cop-out again! If you had any idea how often I've heard that! Look, people are suffering, and I care! Go and see Pharaoh and tell him to let them go.

Moses   Go and see who? And tell him what? I can't do that! It's all right for you, but I have to live in this world!

Anyway, you need a good orator – an experienced politician. I just know what'll happen when I get in front of the king: I'll get all tongue-tied – that's if he doesn't cut it out first.

God   Trust me, Moses. I'll be right with you the whole time.

Narrator   Things weren't going Moses' way. So he tried to think of another approach.

- He *scratched his head*
- and then he *shook his head* and
- suddenly he *snapped his fingers.* Got it!

Moses put on his most reasonable and worldly-wise voice – the way people do when they know they are wrong.

Moses   Well of course, God, the reality is that these people have never heard of you. They've been in slavery all their lives, and I'm afraid we need to face up to the situation as it really is – they've forgotten you. I mean, what am I going to say if they ask who you are? Have you got a name?'

God   Oh no you don't, Moses! You can't put a label on me, like a plant or an animal. I'm greater than any name you could think of. *I* decide who and what I am, and I will be whoever I choose – go and tell the slaves that!

Moses   But no one's going to listen to me! I'm a terrible speaker – you ask my wife about that, she'll tell you! No one will take notice of me. Look, I've got a nice home, a lovely wife, and a good, steady job. That's the kind of bloke I am. I'm not into . . .

God   If you mention politics again, you'll regret it! I care about people – and if you're a friend of mine you will as well. Take Aaron with you – he can talk.

Moses   That's true! He could talk the humps off a camel, could Aaron.

God   That's settled then. Now go and find Aaron, and let's get cracking. We're going to set the people free!

You Can't Get Water from a Stone

Based on Exodus 17:2-7

BEFORE THE DAY

Let the children have fun drawing some cartoons which show people complaining in opposite circumstances: in the heat and in the cold, in drought and in flood, becalmed sailors and someone with an umbrella in a gale, and so on. What examples can they think of themselves? Perhaps some could make up stories about 'Mr Never-Satisfied'!

• Think about the actions for all the children to join in during the story.

ON THE DAY
Introduction

Soon, we're going to hear about some people who were always complaining; but first, we'll say our 'Thank you' prayer.

'Thank you' Prayer

Thank you, God, for all you give us,
thank you for the earth and sea;
thank you, God, for special people,
thank you, God, for making me.

God's Story

You remember Moses, don't you? He was the man whom God used to lead the Israelites out of Egypt. The trouble was that the people thought he was going to solve all their problems in one go. They'd been slaves all their lives and they thought that Moses was going to make everything wonderful. Just like that. They didn't realise that that isn't the way God usually works.

Whatever happened, the people were never satisfied. If there was no breeze, they complained about the heat, and if there was one they whined about sand being blown in their faces. During the day, they moaned about the weight of their luggage; and then at night they complained that they hadn't got enough blankets to keep warm!

One day, Moses said to God, 'I'm fed up with this. Why couldn't you have left me alone? I enjoyed being a shepherd.'

'Oh, come on, Moses,' said God. 'Don't start all that again. I took you from being the leader of a few sheep and made you the leader of a nation.'

'I'd have preferred the sheep,' said Moses. 'On the whole they're probably more intelligent than this lot. And they never moaned at me.'

'If you want to be a great leader, you've got to cope with that,' God answered.

'But I *don't* want to be a great leader,' said Moses, in despair. 'I was happy as a shepherd, minding the sheep and my own business.'

'Were you?' asked God. 'You knew that your brother and sister, and all your people were slaves and were being ill treated – and you wanted to do something about it. You just didn't think you were capable of it.'

'And I'm not!' said Moses.

'I know you're not,' said God, 'but I am. And all you need to do is trust me. Anyway, stop arguing because you've got visitors.'

Moses looked round and, sure enough, an angry-looking crowd were approaching, and leading them was the chief agitator.

'Oh, no!' said Moses. 'It's that Simon character. He's been making trouble ever since we left Egypt.'

'Hey, Moses! shouted Simon. 'We want a word with you. We're thirsty.'

'Well, stop shouting, then,' said Moses, 'or you'll make it worse.'

Simon didn't like that at all. 'Don't you get clever with me,' he snarled at Moses. 'We're all fed up with your high and mighty ways.'

'Look,' said Moses, 'I told you we'd get to the Promised Land, and we will.'

'When?' asked Simon, aggressively.

'I don't know,' Moses answered.

'This year? Next year? Sometime? Never?' taunted Simon. 'All right, then – where is it?'

'What d'you mean?' asked Moses.

'Good grief!' said Simon. 'He doesn't even understand plain Hebrew. Watch my lips, Water-baby! WHERE IS THE PROMISED LAND?'

'How should I know?' said Moses.

'You're the one who's leading us there, yelled Simon. 'Of course you should know!'

'Don't be idiotic, Simon,' said Moses. 'D'you think I put that pillar of cloud and fire in the sky? God's the one who's leading us, and he knows where we're going.'

'Look,' said Simon, 'if you've got God on your side, what about a bit of water – that's not much to ask, is it?'

Then all the others started to join in.

(Have a few children primed to lead the barracking.)

- Simon: What do we want?
- Children: *Water!*
- Simon: When do we want it?
- Children: *Now!*
      (Repeat ad lib)

'OK, God,' said Moses. 'You told me to trust you. Now what do I do?'

'Simple,' said God. 'Get some water out of one or those rocks.'

Moses wondered whether the heat had got to God, as well! 'What!' he answered. 'Get water out of a stone? That's impossible.'

'Look, Moses,' said God, 'I could get blood out of a stone if I wanted to, but water will do for now. Stop arguing and do as I say. Hit one of those rocks with your stick.'

Moses was really angry, and he would rather have hit Simon, but instead he raised his stick and brought it down as hard as he could on the rock.

'Temper, temper!' scolded Simon.

He had hardy got the words out when he heard a strange gurgling sound and a trickle of water came out from the rock. Just as Simon and his friends ran forward excitedly, all fighting to get the first drink, there was a great, thunderous crash and the stone face split wide open as a rush of water came pouring out. Simon was knocked right off his feet, and ended up rolling around in a big puddle of muddy water. Everyone else thought it was really funny, and whenever Simon tried to stand up someone pushed him down again. He had wet sand in his clothes, in his shoes, in his hair, in his ears and in his mouth. And it tasted horrible!

'There you are, Simon,' laughed Moses. 'All the water you could want. That'll teach you not to complain.'

But it didn't.

Simon and his friends found lots more to complain about – but I'll have to tell you about that another time.

Our Story

Show the assembly the cartoons, and/or let the children tell their stories. How often are we like 'Mr Never-Satisfied'?

Prayers

We're Sad

Please forgive us, God,
for being so silly!
When we've got water we waste it,
then we complain about the shortage.
And after that, we moan about the rain!
Please help us to be sensible, and grateful.

We're Glad

God, you're full of surprises!
Just when we think we know everything,
you show us something new.
Thank you for this wonderful world,
and the exciting things that happen in it!

Let's Pray for People

It's a funny thing, water.
Sometimes we love it, sometimes we hate it!
But we always need it.
In some places people die of thirst,
and some people get ill drinking dirty water.
Help us to learn to help one another.

Songs

Sing a song of weather (SS)
Water of life
You can drink it, swim in it

You Can't Get Water from a Stone

God's Story

Narrator   Remember Moses? He was the man who helped God set the Israelites free. The trouble was that the people thought he was going to solve all their problems in one go. And when he didn't, they all moaned at Moses.

Moses   I'm fed up with this, God. I never wanted the job in the first place – I told you I wasn't up to it.

God   I know you're not, but I am – so trust me. Anyway, you've got visitors and they don't look very happy.

Moses   Oh, no! It's that Simon character. He's been making trouble ever since we left Egypt.

Simon   Hey, Moses! We want a word with you. We're thirsty.

Moses   Well, stop shouting, then, or you'll make it worse.

Simon   Don't you get clever – we've had enough of that.

Moses   Look, I said we'd find the Promised Land, and we will.

Simon   When?

Moses   I don't know.

Simon   All right, then – where is it?'

Moses   Don't ask me – how should I know?

Simon   Well you're the one who's leading us there!

Moses   Don't be idiotic, Simon. God's the one who's leading us, and as long as he knows where we're going that's all that matters.

Simon   You're mad, you are. Just because you hear strange voices, you think God's talking to you. All right, then – if you've got God on your side, what about a bit of water? That's not much to ask, is it?'

Narrator	Then all the others started to join in.

(Have a few children primed to lead the barracking.)

- Simon: What do we want?
- Children: *Water!*
- Simon: When do we want it?
- Children: *Now!*

(Repeat ad lib)

Moses	OK, God, you told me to trust you. Now what?
God	Simple – get some water out of one or those rocks.
Moses	What! Get water out of a stone? That's impossible.
God	Look, Moses, I could get blood out of a stone if I wanted to, but water will do for now. Stop arguing and do as I say. Hit one of those rocks with your stick.
Narrator	Moses was certainly ready to hit something! He raised his stick and brought it down hard on the rock.
Simon	Temper, temper! That won't get you anywhere.
Narrator	A tiny crack appeared in the rock, and a trickle of water came out. Everyone ran forward, fighting to get the first drink in case there wasn't enough to go round. Just as they got to the rock, there was a great, thunderous crash and it split wide open as a rush of water came pouring out. Simon was closest, and ended up rolling around in a big puddle of muddy water. Every time he tried to stand up someone pushed him down again. He had wet sand in his clothes, in his shoes, in his hair, in his ears and in his mouth. And it tasted horrible!
Moses	There you are, Simon – all the water you could want. That'll teach you not to complain.
Narrator	But it didn't.

A Little Yellow Idol

Based on Exodus 32:1-24

BEFORE THE DAY

Get the children to make models from scrap materials: computers from cardboard boxes, space rockets from kitchen roll cores, etc.

• Think about the actions for all the children to join in during the story, and if using the drama version rehearse the class to lead the assembly in the response.

ON THE DAY

Introduction

We're going to hear about some model makers who got a bit carried away. First, though, we're going to say our 'Thank you' prayer.

'Thank you' Prayer

Thank you, God, for all you give us,
thank you for the earth and sea;
thank you, God, for special people,
thank you, God, for making me.

God's Story

Moses was up a mountain, praying, and he had been there a very long time. He and God had a lot to talk about; the people weren't at all happy about being in the desert. They used to moan and grumble at Moses all the time, as though all the trouble were his fault. 'It's all very well,' Moses said to God, 'but I'm not really leading them, am I? You are. And yet they moan at me.'

'That's the way it is,' said God. 'They can't see me – and if they could they'd be too frightened to say anything – so they have a go at whoever they think is closest to me. Anyway, you'd better get to work. I've got a few rules to help you all live properly, and I want you to write them down on stone.'

'That's hard work, 'said Moses, 'Can't I use clay or something?'

'Stone,' said God, sternly. 'This has got to last.'

Meanwhile, down at the bottom of the mountain, Simon was stirring up trouble. But then, Simon always did. He'd always secretly thought that he would be a much better leader than Moses, so he kept on saying how useless Moses was. And at this particular moment, he'd got a crowd round him and was having the time of this life!

'We were better off as slaves!' he shouted. 'At least then we had our bed, board and guaranteed employment.'

'Yeah!' shouted everyone, forgetting that it wasn't actually *paid* employment!

'Moses is a fool!' Simon cried.

'Yeah!' responded all the people.

'Couldn't find his way along a straight line if it was signposted!' roared Simon.

'Yeah!' the people shouted, and then went all quiet and embarrassed because of course they should have shouted 'No'!

'How much longer are we going to go on following him?' asked Simon. Then he turned to Aaron. 'Well, you're Moses' brother, aren't you – what are you going to do about it?'

Aaron was getting very frightened; he could see the crowd were really worked up. So he thought to himself, 'It wouldn't do any harm – just to calm things down until Moses gets back.' Then out loud, he said, 'All right – collect all the people's earrings, bangles, bracelets, anything at all that's made of gold. While that's happening, I'll make a mould.'

Up at the mountain top, God said to Moses, 'I think you'd better get back down there. Things are getting out of hand.'

'Oh, Aaron will handle it,' said Moses, who didn't really want to go back down yet.

'That's what you think!' said God. 'Go on, before I help you on your way. And don't forget to take the commandments with you.'

So Moses went back down the mountain, and when he got near the bottom he couldn't believe his eyes! All the people were singing and dancing and having a real party.

- Some were *banging the drums*
- some were *blowing their trumpets*
- and some were *waving their arms about*

In the middle of it all was this strange looking statue which seemed to be a golden calf. Then, to his horror, he saw people bowing down to it and praying to it as though it were a god. He hurried down to where they were, and saw Aaron – his own brother – leading it all. Moses was really angry!

'Hey! Aaron!' he shouted. 'What's that thing?'

Aaron was frightened. 'Oh – well – er – it was the funniest thing,' he babbled. 'You'll laugh when I tell you.'

Moses didn't laugh.

'Well we just put our gold on the fire,' said Aaron, 'and out came this calf.'

Now you know and I know that it wasn't like that – Aaron gave it a lot of help!

'I'm not swallowing that,' said Moses. 'But you are.'

Moses strode to the altar, picked up the idol and started grinding it down. No one moved. They were wondering what Moses was going to do.

When the calf was just a heap of gold dust, Moses sent for some water, and poured out a cup for everyone present. Then he sprinkled the gold dust on the water.

'There you are,' he said. 'Drink it!'

The people were horrified. 'He doesn't mean it!' they said.

'Oh yes I do,' said Moses. 'If that thing was a god then it must be full of life and goodness. Now you can find out.'

And Moses made them drink every drop! They found out that it wasn't good at all.

Simon didn't say anything for a very long time after that. That was partly because he was so ashamed.

But it was mainly because his throat was sore.

Our Story

Show the children the models, and ask them to identify them. Then see if they work. Can the computer be switched on? Can the rocket rise under its own power? They're all very good models, no doubt, but they won't work like the real thing. Now what about the model of God? Oh, of course, there isn't one! We can't even begin to make that!

Prayers

Let's Chat

Having fun is important,
but do toys, video games or television
take up too much of our lives?

We're Glad

Thank you, God,
for the good things we have,
and especially for our family and our friends.
Help us to enjoy everything you give to us,
and always to put you and people first.

Let's Pray for People

Some people are unhappy
because they haven't got enough.
Other people are unhappy
because they worship money, or possessions.
Please God, teach us all to love each other
and to share the things that are really important.

Songs

All things bright and beautiful
God turned darkness into light
It's me, O Lord
Out to the great wide world we go!

A Little Yellow Idol

God's Story

Narrator   Moses was up a mountain, praying.

Moses   It's not fair, God. *You're* the boss, but *I* get moaned at.

God   That's the way it is. They can't see me, so they have a go at my friends. Anyway, you'd better get to work. I've got a few rules to help you all live properly, and I want you to write them down on stone.

Moses   That's hard work. Can't I use clay or something?

God   *(Sternly)* Stone. This has got to last.

Narrator   Meanwhile, down at the bottom of the mountain, Simon was stirring up trouble. But then, Simon always did. And at this particular moment, he'd got a crowd round him and was having the time of this life!

Simon   We were better off as slaves!

Children   Yeah!

Simon   Moses is a fool!

Children   Yeah!

Simon   Couldn't find his way along a straight line if it was signposted!

Children   Yeah!

Narrator   That got Simon confused, because he wasn't sure whether they should really have shouted 'No'!

Simon   Well, Aaron – you're Moses' brother, aren't you – what are you going to do about it?

Aaron   All right – collect all the people's earrings, bangles, bracelets, anything at all that's made of gold. While that's happening, I want two volunteers to help me make a mould. You and you will do.

Narrator Up the mountain, God had finished talking to Moses.

God I think you'd better go. Things are getting out of hand.

Narrator When Moses got down the mountain, he couldn't believe his eyes! There was a big party going on, round a golden statue of a calf.

- Some people were *banging their drums*
- some were *blowing their trumpets*
- and some were *waving their arms about*

Narrator Moses didn't mind that – or the dancing and singing. It was the statue he objected to.

Moses Hey! Aaron! What's that thing?

Aaron Oh – well – er – it was the funniest thing. You'll laugh when I tell you. We just put our gold on the fire, and out came this calf.

Moses I'm not swallowing that – but you are.

Aaron Eh?

Moses Grind it down into dust, mix it with water and drink it.

Aaron You don't mean it!

Moses Oh yes I do. If that thing was a god then it must be full of life and goodness. Now you can find out.

Narrator And Moses made them drink every drop! They found out that it wasn't good at all.

Moses Right! You can think about that while I'm gone. I've got some more praying to do.

Narrator And with that, Moses set off back up the mountain. Simon didn't say anything for a very long time. That was partly because he was so ashamed, but it was mainly because his throat was sore.

The Donkey's Tale

Based on Numbers 22-24

BEFORE THE DAY

Ask the children what they would like if they could wish for anything they wanted. Write up their wishes on a board, encouraging them to be as outrageous as they like, but be careful not to encourage false hopes!

• Think about the actions for all the children to join in during the story.

ON THE DAY

Introduction

In a few moments, we'll hear from a donkey whose owner wasn't very clever. First, we're going to say our 'Thank you' prayer.

'Thank you' Prayer

Thank you, God, for all you give us,
thank you for the earth and sea;
thank you, God, for special people,
thank you, God, for making me.

God's Story

I'm going to tell you a story, but you mustn't let on that it was me that told you. Why? Because we donkeys aren't supposed to know what's going on. It's a great life, being a donkey. Humans always think that they're the only ones who understand anything. So they talk about things in front of us and think it doesn't matter. Let me give you a tip: if you've got any secrets, don't talk about them in front of donkeys, because we've got long ears.

Anyway, I used to work for a man called Balaam. Yes, I know it's a funny name, but most people knew better than to laugh at it because it was said that Balaam could put a curse on you if he wanted to. Once he put a curse on his next-door neighbour – all over a misunderstanding. His neighbour used to call him Bally, and one day when he was talking about him somebody asked, 'Bally Who?' and everyone laughed. Balaam thought they were laughing at him and put a curse on his neighbour so that all his hair fell out. So now you know. Don't laugh at people with silly names. In any case, names like Amy and Jack would have sounded pretty strange in those days . . .

Now where was I? Oh yes – about Balaam. Well, I was standing in my usual place outside the window one day when I saw some visitors coming. I knew who they were straight away. I can tell the king's servants a mile off – all posh clothes and no brains. They told Balaam that the king was frightened because the Israelite army were on the way and looked as though they were going to invade. He wanted Balaam to put a curse on the army because he thought it would stop them.

Balaam sent them away with a flea in their ear. 'I don't believe God wants me to do that,' he said. But they'd hardly disappeared over the horizon when some more arrived. I could tell they were even higher officials than the last lot – posher clothes and even less brains. They were really having a go at Balaam. 'Can't you just come along and say what the king wants?' they asked. 'You don't have to mean it, just keep the old so-and-so happy so that we can get a bit of peace.' Well, Balaam kept on saying no, but eventually they got to him and – for the sake of peace and quiet – he decided to go with them.

Now I could have told him that this wasn't a good idea, but he wouldn't have listened. You see, humans have small ears and big mouths – that's their problem. Now if you look at a donkey, you'll find that our ears are bigger than our mouths which is the right way round. We listen a lot, but we say very little. And I knew we were heading for trouble.

Sure enough, we hadn't got very far when we hit a roadblock. And I don't mean any old roadblock. None of your silly poles across the road; this was an angel – ten feet tall, shining like a hoarding in Piccadilly Circus. So of course I did the sensible thing – I turned off into a field. Balaam went mad at me.

• He *jerked on the reins*
• he used his *whip*
• he *waved his fists in the air*

Then it got worse: he kicked me, he shouted at me – and the language! Of course, I knew what the trouble was – Balaam's eyes are even smaller than his ears, and he couldn't see a ten-foot, digitally illuminated angel when it was right in front of him. I thought about telling him to open his silly eyes, but humans get so jealous of animals talking that I decided to keep mum. It didn't help, though, because we soon had the angel in front of us again, and this time there was nowhere to turn off. I tried to get through between the angel and the wall, but Balaam's foot got scraped against the stones and he yelled like mad. That's humans for you. They can drive nails into our feet, to fix shoes on, but if we so much as step on theirs they yell and shout fit to bust! By the next time I saw the angel, I'd had enough and I sat down. Balaam went mad! He started hitting me and kicking me, and I decided that was it. Like it or not, he was going to hear me talk.

'Are you potty?' I asked him. 'All these years I've been a good donkey to you – d'you think I'd do this for no reason?'

Of course, he looked more carefully then – and he saw it too. The angel wasn't very happy. 'What d'you mean by being cruel to a poor dumb animal?' he said. I wasn't sure that I liked the 'dumb' bit, but it's not often you get an angel on your side so I didn't complain. The angel went on, 'If it hadn't been for that donkey of yours you'd be dead by now.' Balaam was full of apologies, of course, and promised never to ill-treat me again. I'll believe that when I see it! Then he tried to turn me round and go home, but the angel stopped him.

'Carry on with your journey,' said the angel, 'but just be careful only to tell the king the truth – even if he doesn't like it.'

From what I gather, things got a bit silly after that, with Balaam refusing to say what the king wanted to hear, and the king trying to persuade him to do it. Eventually, the king realised it wasn't going to work and told Balaam to go home. Balaam was furious. 'All this way,' he said, 'and then he refused to listen to me just because I didn't say what he wanted me to. What do you think of that?'

Who? Me? Oh no! I know which side my bread's buttered. I kept quiet. And kept walking.

Our Story

Show the children the list of wishes and forecasts. Have any of the wishes come true? Almost certainly none of them will have, and the point can be made that merely wishing doesn't make things happen. How would the children have felt if they'd been promised those things and then let down? It's more important to be honest than to tell people what they want to hear.

Prayers

We're Sad

Loving God, please forgive us.
It's not always easy to be honest.
Then again, sometimes we're honest
in the wrong way, and we hurt people.
Help us to tell the truth,
and to be kind as well.

We're Glad

Thank you, God,
for people who are truthful to us
even when it's difficult.
It's good to have friends who care
enough to be honest with us.

Let's Pray for People

We pray for people
who have difficult jobs to do:
people who have to give advice
or take decisions
which others might not like.
Please God, help them to be honest,
to do and say what they know to be right.

Songs

Do what you know is right
Father I place into your hands
Jubilate, everybody
Out to the great wide world we go!

The Donkey's Tale

God's Story

Donkey   I'm going to tell you a story, but you mustn't let on that I told you because we donkeys aren't supposed to know things. It's great, being a donkey. Humans talk in front of us and think it doesn't matter. If you've got any secrets, don't mention them in front of donkeys, because we've got long ears.

Anyway, I used to work for a man called Balaam. I was standing outside the window one day when I saw some important visitors coming. I can tell the king's servants a mile off – all posh clothes and no brains.

1st Servant   The king needs your help, Balaam. The Israelite army look as though they're going to invade.

2nd Servant   You've got to put a curse on them and stop them.

Balaam   I don't believe God wants me to do that. Go away.

Donkey   Then some more arrived: even higher officials than the last lot – posher clothes and even less intelligence.

3rd Servant   Can't you just come and say what the king wants?

4th Servant   Just to keep the old so-and-so happy.

Donkey   Well, eventually – for the sake of peace and quiet – he decided to go with them. Now I could have told him that this was a bad idea, but he wouldn't have listened. Humans have small ears and big mouths, whereas our ears are bigger than our mouths which is the right way round. I knew we were heading for trouble, and sure enough, we hadn't got very far when we hit a road-block. And I don't mean any old roadblock. None of your silly poles across the road; this was a shining, ten foot angel. Of course, I did the sensible thing – I turned off into a field. Balaam went mad!

- He *jerked on the reins*
- he *used his whip*
- he *waved his fists in the air*

Balaam   You stupid donkey! Get back on the road!

Donkey   Now, Balaam's eyes are even smaller than his ears, and he couldn't see a ten-foot, digitally illuminated angel when it was right in front of him. I thought about telling him to look, but humans get jealous of animals talking. Then when I moved, so did the angel, and Balaam's foot got scraped against the wall.

Balaam   Ow! That hurt! You stupid animal!

Donkey   That's humans for you. They can drive nails into our feet, to fix shoes on, but if we so much as step on theirs they yell and shout fit to bust! Next time I saw the angel, I sat down. Balaam started hitting me and kicking me. Like it or not, he was going to hear me talk. 'Are you potty?' I said. 'All these years I've been a good donkey to you – d'you think I'd do this for no reason?' Then he got it from the angel as well.

Angel   What do you mean by hurting a poor dumb animal?

Donkey   Hey! who are you calling dumb?

Angel   But for your donkey, you'd be dead by now.

Balaam   I'm really sorry – honestly. I won't do it again.

Donkey   I'll believe that when I see it!

Angel   Carry on with your journey, but just be careful only to tell the king the truth – even if he doesn't like it.

Donkey   Things got a bit silly after that. The king refused to listen, and Balaam moaned all the way home.

Balaam   All this way, and he refused to listen to me just because I didn't say what he wanted. What do you think of that?

Donkey   Who? Me? Oh no. I know which side my bread's buttered. I kept quiet. And kept walking.

The Walls Came Tumbling Down

Based on Joshua 6

BEFORE THE DAY

Do the children like music? What kind? Or perhaps they just enjoy making a noise! Discuss with them the different kinds of noise. Do any of them play instruments? Would they play a short tune (or even just a few notes) in assembly? Do they have toys which make less pleasant noises? Perhaps one or two of them could be brought in for the assembly. (You might prefer to have the toys placed at the front, and not in the hands of the children!) What about unpleasant noises that are good, e.g. fire alarms?

• Think about the actions for all the children to join in during the story.

ON THE DAY

Introduction

We're going to think about noise in this assembly. Sometimes it's good, but sometimes it's bad. First, we say our 'Thank you' prayer.

'Thank you' Prayer

Thank you, God, for all you give us,
thank you for the earth and sea;
thank you, God, for special people,
thank you, God, for making me.

God's Story

Joshua wasn't happy. 'I wish,' he said, 'that Moses had never passed this job on to me! Being the leader of the Israelites is not easy!'

Joshua had taken over as leader when Moses died. Now he faced a real problem. Between his people and their new home stood a big city called Jericho. And around Jericho were some very high walls.

Meanwhile, the people in the city had seen the Israelites coming, and a soldier called Seth was giving orders. 'Hurry up and get those gates shut,' he shouted, 'or they'll be marching in here. That's better – now pile everything you can get up against them.'

Before long, the gate was completely hidden behind an enormous pile of tables, benches, boxes, rocks and all kinds of other things. Someone had even brought a baby's cradle! 'There!' said Seth, 'That should keep them out!'

What Seth didn't know was that Joshua wasn't going to attack the gates. God had better ideas. 'Don't worry about the gates,' he told Joshua, 'you're going to bring down the walls!'

Joshua could hardly believe his ears. 'Those walls must be ten feet thick!' he said.

'What's the matter,' asked God, 'haven't you ever heard of vibration? March the people round the walls every day for a week, and at the end of it you'll be able to shake the walls down by shouting.'

Well! Can you imagine the sight? Round and round they went, with soldiers in the front blowing their trumpets as loudly as they could. The enemy soldiers on top of the walls thought it was a great joke. Before long, they were selling tickets, and people were queuing up to buy them.

'Come and see the silly Israelites walking round the wall!' shouted Seth, and every day more people came to watch.

The Israelite people didn't like the job much – people shouted insults at them and dropped rubbish from the walls – but Joshua made them carry on going round. Then at last, after a week, he shouted, 'All right, let them have it!'

And what do you think they did?

• They *blew their trumpets*
• They *banged their drums*
• They *stamped their feet*
• They *shouted*

You never heard a noise like it (even just now!) The air shook with the noise, and the ground shook with the stamping of feet, and the people watching thought it was great fun – until the walls began to shake as well. Then, gradually, cracks started to appear in the walls. The cracks got bigger, and the walls began to sway, and then there was a great CRRRRRASH! The walls had fallen down. Poor old Seth was amazed, and just stood there scratching his head.

The Israelites could hardly believe what had happened. 'All we did was shout,' someone said, 'and the walls just came tumbling down!'

'Well, there you are,' smiled Joshua. 'It's amazing how much damage a bit of noise can do!'

Our Story

Demonstrate some of the 'instruments'. Some noises are nice – others aren't. But some 'bad' noises are necessary.

Prayers

We're Glad

Creator God,
thank you for music,
for singing;
thank you for making us able to talk,
and to hear.
But thank you for quietness, too,
and help us to know
when to sing and shout,
and when to be quiet.

We're Sad

Let's say 'sorry' to God
for the times we've upset people
by being too noisy.
We're sorry, God, for being thoughtless.
We don't mean to upset others,
but sometimes we're so busy enjoying ourselves
that we forget them.
Help us to remember other people.

Let's Pray for People

Loving God,
we pray for people who can't speak,
and for people who can't hear,
(*especially* . . .)
Help them to find other ways
of enjoying your world,
and having fun.
And please help us
to remember them,
and not to let them be left out.

Songs

He's got the whole world in his hand
Kum ba yah
Morning has broken
One more step

The Walls Came Tumbling Down

God's Story

Narrator Joshua had taken over as leader when Moses died. And he wasn't happy. Between his people and their new home stood a big city, called Jericho, and around Jericho were some very high walls. The people in the city had seen the Israelites coming, and a soldier called Seth was giving orders.

Seth Hurry up and get those gates shut or they'll be marching in here. That's better – now pile everything you can get up against them.

Narrator Before long, the gate was completely hidden behind an enormous pile of tables, benches, boxes, rocks and all kinds of other things. Someone had even brought a baby's cradle!

Seth There! That should keep them out! It'll take more than their little army to get through the gates now.

Narrator Now, Joshua was *really* fed up. And he thought it was time he told God so.

Joshua I wish Moses had never passed this job on to me! Being the leader of the Israelites is not easy! How are we ever going to break those gates down?

God Oh, don't worry about the gates; you're going to bring down the walls!

Joshua What?! Those walls must be ten feet thick!

God What's the matter? Haven't you ever heard of vibration? March the people round the walls every day for a week, and at the end of it you'll be able to shake the walls down by shouting.

Narrator Well! Can you imagine the sight? Round and round they went, with soldiers in the front blowing their trumpets as loudly as they could. The enemy soldiers on top of the walls thought it was a great joke. Before long, they were selling tickets, and people were queuing up to buy them.

Seth Roll up! Roll up! Come and see the silly Israelites walking round the wall!

Narrator Every day more people came to watch. The Israelite people didn't like the job much – people shouted insults at them and dropped rubbish from the walls – but Joshua made them carry on going round. Then at last, after a week, he gave the command.

Joshua All right, let them have it!

Narrator And what do you think they did?

- They *blew their trumpets*
- They *banged their drums*
- They *stamped their feet*
- They *shouted*

You never heard a noise like it (even just now!) The air shook with the noise, and the ground shook with the stamping of feet, and the people watching thought it was great fun – until the walls began to shake as well. Then, gradually, cracks started to appear in the walls. The cracks got bigger, and the walls began to sway, and then there was a great CRRRRRASH! The walls had fallen down. Poor old Seth was amazed, and just stood there scratching his head.

Seth I can't believe it! All you did was shout and the walls just came tumbling down!

Joshua Well, there you are. It's amazing how much damage a bit of noise can do!

All I Want Is a Baby

Based on 1 Samuel 1:1-20

BEFORE THE DAY

Some of the children must have baby brothers or sisters. What kinds of things do the parents have to do to care for them? Get the children to bring to school examples of baby care items (perhaps empty packets) to form a display.

• Think about the actions for all the children to join in during the story.

ON THE DAY

Introduction

We're going to hear the story of Hannah in a few minutes, but first we'll say our 'Thank you' prayer.

'Thank you' Prayer

Thank you, God, for all you give us,
thank you for the earth and sea;
thank you, God, for special people,
thank you, God, for making me.

God's Story

Once there lived a man called Elkanah, who had two wives. One of them was called Hannah, and the other was called Pennina, which is a very nice name but she wasn't a very nice person. She had lots of children, and in those days people thought that that made you very special. Hannah had no children, and that meant that everyone looked down on her. Hannah was very unhappy, because she really longed to have a child of her own.

What made things worse was that Pennina kept on sneering at Hannah.

• She used to *point at her*
• and *stick out her tongue*
• and *make nasty faces*

'You've got no children,' she would say. 'You're useless – can't even do a simple thing like that.'

Elkanah didn't help, either. Whenever the big festivals came round, he always gave lots more presents to Pennina than to Hannah. Of course, he would never admit that he loved Pennina more than Hannah. He would try to explain by saying, 'She needs more than you do, with all those children of hers.' And that just made Hannah feel even worse! What a silly thing to say!

One day, when Hannah was really upset and was crying, Elkanah tried to comfort her, but he wasn't very good at that kind of thing and whenever he opened his mouth he put his foot in it. 'Why are you crying?' he said. 'I know you've got no children, but that doesn't matter. After all, why do you want children when you've got me!'

That hadn't come out quite the way Elkanah meant it to, but Hannah didn't seem to notice. She was just angry. 'What d'you think's so special about you?' she said, through her tears. 'Just like a man to think you're all a woman could ever need!' Then she got up and ran out of the house. Elkanah started to run after her, but he was a bit out of condition and soon gave up.

Hannah ran to the place of worship. She was really upset and needed somewhere quiet to think. After she had been there a little while, she started praying. She didn't pray out loud, but just whispered the words so that no one else could hear. 'God,' she said, 'I really want to have a baby – I've always wanted one. If you let me have a child, I promise I'll nurse him well, and then as soon as he can eat ordinary food I'll give him to you. I won't mind – honestly – I'll be happy knowing I've got a child, even if I can't see him and play with him. I just want to be a mother. I promise I'll be a good one for as long as he's with me. Then I'll give him to you and he can serve you for the rest of his life.'

You may wonder why she assumed that the baby would be a boy. Well, that's just the way people thought and spoke in those days. It was a man's world even before he'd been born! Come to that, a lot of people still think that kind of way now!

Anyway, back to Hannah. What she didn't know was that Levi, a priest, was standing watching her. He could see her lips moving, but no words were coming out. 'Oh dear!' he thought. 'Another drunk. They think they can come in here to shelter from the rain, and they always end up embarrassing me.' So he went over to Hannah. 'I think you'd better leave,' he said.

Hannah didn't know he was talking to her, and just kept on praying.

'Did you hear what I said? Out!'

Hannah still carried on praying, until she felt her shoulder being shaken. 'Come on,' said the priest. 'I said out! It really is too much: you drunks come in here, getting in the way, annoying the paying – I mean praying public.'

'Oh no, sir,' said Hannah. 'I'm not drunk, just terribly unhappy.' And with that, she burst into tears.

Underneath all his priestly dignity, Eli actually had a fairly soft heart. He put his arm around Hannah and tried to comfort her. 'I'm sorry,' he said, 'but we have to be careful here, you know. Do you want to talk about it?'

Hannah told him the whole story. Eli was very angry and began to raise his voice. 'Someone ought to give that Pennina woman a good talking to!' he said. 'And where's your husband – I'll give him a lesson in sensitivity!'

'Oh, no, please don't do that,' said Hannah. 'They're not bad people, really – and I do have to live with them afterwards, you know. Don't worry – I've said my prayer, and now I'll have to leave it to God.'

Eli smiled. 'Well, you may be right,' he said. 'Off you go home, and try not to worry. I've been working for God for quite a long time, and he hasn't let me down yet.'

After that, Hannah seemed happier. Pennina couldn't annoy her with her snide remarks about children any more, so she changed her tactics.

'You're putting on weight,' she said one day. 'Elkanah won't like that. And it's not as if you've got any excuse, is it? I mean, I've still got my figure even after having *all those children*.'

Hannah just smiled mysteriously. She had a pretty good idea why she was putting on weight, and she was very happy about it.

Sure enough, a few months later Hannah had her baby. It was a beautiful little boy, and she called him Samuel. Elkanah was over the moon. He was so proud of Hannah he could hardly stand still. 'My son,' he said. 'He's going to be a really great man – perhaps a farmer, or a camel driver.'

'No, he's not,' said Hannah. 'I promised him to God. And just as soon as he can eat ordinary food I'm going to take him to the priest.'

And Hannah kept her word.

Our Story

Draw attention to the display and show that wishing for a baby isn't like wishing for a new bike – babies bring a lot more responsibility with them!

Prayers

We're Sad

Sometimes we're cruel to people
who are unhappy,
when we should be trying to help them.
Please forgive us, God;
help us to be kind to people,
even when we don't really understand.

We're Glad

Thank you, God, for people like Hannah,
who really love children.
And thank you for people like Eli
who know how to listen to people,
and who give us all faith.

Let's Pray for People

We pray for people who are sad,
because they can't have children
or because their children have died.
Please, God, help us all
to love one another,
and to keep faith and hope alive.

Songs

God's love is deeper
Hey, now, everybody sing!
Morning has broken
Out to the great wide world we go!
Sing hosanna!
Thank you, O God, for all our friends (SS)

All I Want Is a Baby

God's Story

Narrator   Once there lived a man called Elkanah, who had two wives. Men were allowed to do that, in those days; but no one had heard of women's liberation, so women could only have one husband – and often they had to share him. One of Elkanah's wives was called Hannah, and the other was called Pennina, which is a very nice name but she wasn't a very nice person. She was very cruel to Hannah.

- She used to *point at her*
- and *stick out her tongue*
- and *make nasty faces*

Pennina   You've got no children. You're useless – can't even do a simple thing like that.

Narrator   Elkanah didn't help, either. He always gave lots more presents to Pennina than to Hannah.

Elkanah   It's not that I love her more than you. She needs more than you do, with all those children of hers.

Narrator   Now wasn't that a clever thing to say! Whenever Elkanah opened his mouth he put his foot in it.

Elkanah   Why do you want children, when you've got me?

Narrator   That hadn't come out quite the way Elkanah meant it to, but Hannah was too angry to notice.

Hannah   Just like a man, to think you're all a woman needs!

Narrator   She got up and ran out of the house to the place of worship. She was really upset and needed somewhere quiet to think and pray. She didn't pray out loud, but just whispered the words.

Hannah   Please, God, if you let me have a child, I promise I'll nurse him well, and then as soon as he can eat ordinary food I'll give him to you.

Narrator	Hannah didn't notice Eli, an old priest, watching her.
Eli	*(Aside)* Oh dear! Another drunk. They think they can come in here to shelter from the rain, and they always end up embarrassing me. *(To Hannah)* I think you'd better leave. You're getting in the way, annoying the paying – I mean praying public.
Hannah	Oh no, sir, I'm not drunk, just terribly unhappy.
Narrator	With that, Hannah burst into tears. Underneath all his priestly dignity, Eli actually had a fairly soft heart. He put his arm around Hannah and tried to comfort her.
Eli	I'm sorry. Do you want to talk about it?
Narrator	Hannah told him the whole story. Eli was very angry.
Eli	Someone ought to give that Pennina woman a good talking to!
Hannah	Oh, no, please don't do that. She's not a bad person, really – and I do have to live with her afterwards, you know. Don't worry – I've said my prayer, and now I'll have to leave it to God.
Eli	Well, you may be right. Off you go home, and try not to worry. I've been working for God for quite a long time, and he hasn't let me down yet.
Narrator	Pennina carried on being nasty to Hannah.
Pennina	You're putting on weight. Elkanah won't like that. And it's not as if you've got any excuse, is it? I've still got my figure even after having *all those children.*
Narrator	Hannah just smiled mysteriously. A few months later she had her baby. It was a beautiful little boy, and she called him Samuel. Elkanah was over the moon.
Elkanah	He's going to be a really great camel driver.
Hannah	No, he's not. I promised him to God, and as soon as he can eat ordinary food, I'm going to take him to the priest.
Narrator	And Hannah kept her word.

Who Wants a Monarchy?

Based on 1 Samuel 8-10

BEFORE THE DAY

Ask the children to write down or draw things they wish their parents didn't ask them to do: 'I hate washing up'; 'Why should I tidy my room?' etc. Then ask them to draw or write the good things their parents give them: favourite foods, warm clothes, hugs, etc. Then jumble them all up on a display.

• Think about the actions for all the children to join in during the story.

ON THE DAY

Introduction

In a few moments, we'll be hearing about how the Israelites got their first king. Before that, we'll say our 'Thank you' prayer.

'Thank you' Prayer

Thank you, God, for all you give us,
thank you for the earth and sea;
thank you, God, for special people,
thank you, God, for making me.

God's Story

'It's all right for you,' Samuel grumbled. 'Ever since I've been a prophet, people have been moaning at me – they're just never satisfied. Now they've got it into their heads that a king would give them more than I can.'

'Tell me about it!' God replied. 'I've been in this business a lot longer than you have, and it's always been like that. Don't take it personally, though – it's me they're rejecting, not you.'

'I'll tell them you said no, then, shall I?' Samuel asked.

'If you do that, you'll never get any peace,' God replied. 'No, they're adults, so let them choose, but just make sure you tell them what a king will be like, that's all.'

Samuel really wasn't happy. 'Why do I get all the rotten jobs?' he mumbled as he went away to call a public meeting.

'Don't come crying to me,' he said to the people, 'when your sons have been drafted into the army, or into the armaments factories, and your daughters are working in sweatshops. Oh, and you needn't complain when the king steals your best land for his own use, either.'

'We don't care about that,' shouted Ben, a well-known troublemaker, 'we just want a king!'

'Yeah,' added his wife, Sarah, 'we want to be just like all the other nations. They've got kings, so we want one, too.'

'That's typical of you,' Samuel sighed, 'the greatest achievement you can imagine is just to be like everybody else!'

'A king would make everything OK,' said Ben. 'He'd fight all our battles for us, and tell us what to do, and we wouldn't have to think for ourselves any more.'

'Well that should suit you, anyway,' Samuel replied. 'If that's what you want, then you can have your king, but don't say I never warned you.'

Meanwhile, a long way away, a wealthy farmer called Kish was counting his donkeys. 'Oh, bother! Why won't they stand still when I'm trying to count them?' he groaned. 'I'm sure some have got out.'

'Having problems, Dad?' It was Saul, Kish's son; a tall, handsome young man. 'Perhaps I can help?'

'Only if you can find a way of keeping these donkeys still,' Kish grumbled.

Eventually, they managed to count them. 'I knew it!' said Kish. 'There are five donkeys missing. If I had a shekel for every time I've told the men to mend those fences . . . !'

'Don't worry, Dad,' said Saul, 'I'm sure they won't have gone far – why don't you let me go and look for them?'

'I suppose you'd better,' replied his father. 'Just don't you go getting lost as well, though.'

Saul set off, with a few servants, to find the donkeys, but after they had crossed five counties and still not found them, he began to think that they might have strayed a little further than he expected. 'It's no good,' he said to his servant. 'We'd better go home or Dad's going to forget about the donkeys and start worrying about me instead.'

'What about the holy man?' asked the servant.

'Oh, I don't think Dad'll be worrying about him,' Saul answered.

'I mean, why not ask the local prophet if he knows where the donkeys are?' the servant explained. So they set off to find Samuel.

Samuel was just on his way to worship when he saw Saul coming to meet him. 'Now, Samuel,' God said, 'remember what I told you yesterday. This is the man who's going to be king.'

Saul came up to Samuel and said, 'Can you tell me where I can find the local seer?' (That was a name they often used for prophets.)

'I'm a seer,' said Samuel. 'Actually, I'm a pretty good listener, too, but more of that later. Come and have something to eat, and later on I'll tell you what you want to know. Don't worry about those donkeys of yours – they're quite safe. You're going to be the main man around here before long.'

'What, me?' asked Saul. 'But I'm just an ordinary sort of chap, and I come from the least important tribe – why choose me?'

'Never mind that for now,' Samuel answered. 'Time to eat – we've saved the best food for you.'

It was a wonderful meal.

- There was soup to *slurp*
- bananas to *peel*
- and lots of juice to *drink*

After the meal was over, he told Saul, 'God has chosen you to be the first king. You're to look after his people, protect them and help them. Now go home and you'll find that the donkeys you lost are safe, and your father's started worrying about you instead.'

Saul was absolutely amazed at being chosen to be king, but not half so amazed as Ben and Sarah were when Samuel told them.

'What sort of a king is this?' Ben complained. 'We wanted a king that was better than everybody else's – one to put all our enemies in their place – this man's a nobody, from a tiny little tribe no one bothers about.'

Some people are just never satisfied, are they?

Our Story

Look at the display. None of us really likes having to do as we're told, but we all have to (even teachers, ministers and writers!) But being 'the boss' is about more than giving orders; it's about caring as well, and the two are jumbled up together, just like on this display. Sometimes, giving orders is a way of caring (even if it's not always the best one).

Prayers

We're Glad

Thank you, God, for leaders:
for parents, teachers,
and people who make important decisions.
Help us to trust and obey you
most of all.

We're Sad

Sometimes we're like Ben:
never satisfied.
We want other people to take charge,
and then we complain when they do.
Please God, help us always
to be fair to others.

Let's Pray for People

Loving God,
help all people in authority
to be kind and fair,
especially to those
who are in most need.

Songs

Brother, sister, let me serve you
From heaven you came
Jesus' love is very wonderful
Whether you're one

Who Wants a Monarchy?

God's Story

Narrator	Samuel wasn't happy.
Samuel	It's all right for you, God. Ever since I've been a prophet, people moaned at me. Now they're demanding a king.
God	Tell me about it! I've been in this business longer than you have, and it's always been like that. Don't take it personally, though – it's me they're rejecting, not you. All right, give them what they want, but just make sure you tell them what a king will be like, that's all.
Samuel	O great! Why do I get all the rotten jobs?
Narrator	Samuel went away to call a public meeting.
Samuel	Don't come crying to me when your sons have been drafted into the army, and your daughters are working in sweatshops, or when the king steals your best land.
Ben	We don't care about that; we just want a king!
Sarah	Ben's right. We want to be just like all the other nations. They've got kings, so we want one, too.
Samuel	That's typical of you, Sarah! The greatest achievement you can imagine is just to be like everybody else!
Ben	A king would make everything OK. He'd fight all our battles for us, and tell us what to do, and we wouldn't have to think for ourselves any more.
Samuel	Well that should suit you, anyway. All right, you can have your king. But don't say I never warned you.
Narrator	A few days later, on his way to worship, Samuel saw a young man coming to meet him.

God   Now, Samuel, this is the man I want to be king.

Saul   Hello, my name's Saul. Can you tell me where I can find the local prophet?

Samuel   That's me. Come and have something to eat. Don't worry about those lost donkeys your dad sent you to look for – they're quite safe.

Saul   How did you know about those?

Samuel   Trade secret, dear boy. Now to important matters. You'll be the main man around here before long.

Saul   What, me? But I'm just an ordinary sort of chap, and I come from the least important tribe – why choose me?

Samuel   Never mind that for now. Time to eat.

Narrator   It was a wonderful meal.

- There was soup to *slurp*
- bananas to *peel*
- and lots of juice to *drink*

Samuel   God has chosen you to be the first king. You're to look after his people, protect them and help them.

Narrator   Saul was absolutely amazed. So were the Israelites.

Ben   What sort of a king is this? We wanted a king that was better than everybody else's – one to put all our enemies in their place – this man's a nobody, from a tiny little tribe no one bothers about.

Narrator   Some people are just never satisfied, are they?

Appearances Can Be Deceptive

Based on 1 Samuel 16:1-13

BEFORE THE DAY

How about a spot of nature study? Have the children ever seen a hoverfly, which looks like a wasp but can't sting? Or what about some toadstools that look like mushrooms but are definitely not good to eat? Do the children know of any examples? Perhaps they could use their imaginations to create a few (along the lines of the police box that became a time machine, for instance!) Get them to draw pictures of real or imaginary examples.

• Think about the actions for all the children to join in during the story.

ON THE DAY

Introduction

Things are not always the way they look. We'll be thinking about that in a few minutes, but first we're going to say our 'Thank you' prayer.

'Thank you' Prayer

Thank you, God, for all you give us,
thank you for the earth and sea;
thank you, God, for special people,
thank you, God, for making me.

God's Story

God had a dangerous job for Samuel.

'I've had it with King Saul,' God said. 'I want you to anoint a new king.'

'What!' said Samuel. I might be religious, but I'm not potty.'

'Oh, do stop going on, Samuel,' said God. 'I'm not asking for your opinion. I make the decisions round here, remember?'

'Sorry, God,' said Samuel, 'I suppose you're right as usual.'

'I'm right, as *always*,' said God, indignantly.

'Yes, of course, God. Sorry God,' said Samuel in an embarrassed sort of voice. 'How do you want me to do it, then?'

'Go and see old Jesse, the sheep farmer at Bethlehem,' answered God.

'Since when did anything remotely important happen in Bethlehem?' said Samuel.

'My Word!' God answered. 'You ain't seen nothin' yet!'

'Pardon?' asked Samuel.

'Never mind,' replied God. 'That's my favourite quotation, but it's after your time.'

Samuel mopped his forehead with his sleeve. 'Can we just get back to this Bethlehem thing?' he asked.

'Just do as I say,' said God. 'I'll tell you which one of Jesse's sons you're to anoint as king.'

Well,' said Samuel, dolefully, 'I really hope you know what you're doing, because if Saul finds out what we've done one of us is going to get killed. And since you're immortal, I've got a pretty good idea who it will be.'

So Samuel went to Bethlehem.

'Hello, hello, hello,' called Jesse. 'It's good old Sam the prophet man! What message of doom is it this time?'

'I'm just the messenger,' Samuel sighed, 'so if you want to moan, moan at God.'

'Silly bloke – can't take a joke!' said Jesse, and Samuel cringed. Jesse fancied himself as a poet – why, no one could understand. Samuel had heard that he'd got a talented son, but the gift clearly didn't come from his father.

'Look, everything's all right. OK?' he assured Jesse. 'Now send for your family.'

Jesse answered, 'All right, Sammy, keep your wig on; how'd I know there's something big on?'

'Oh dear,' Samuel thought, 'I'd better get on and do it, or Jesse will put me through it. Good grief! He's got me at it, now.'

Jesse's sons got ready to meet Samuel.

• They *washed their faces*
• and they *cleaned their teeth*
• and they *combed their hair*

The first son, Eliab, looked every inch a king. Tall and strong, and with clear, sparkling eyes, he fitted the part perfectly.

'Don't go by what you see,' God said. 'Appearances can be deceptive. I don't look at people the way you do. I look at the heart.'

'Oh, I should think his heart's fine,' thought Samuel. 'Healthy looking chap like that.'

'Don't get clever with me,' said God.

Before Samuel could think of anything else to think, Abinadab arrived and Jesse introduced him. 'This is my son – another one.'

'I've got to get out of here,' thought Samuel, reaching for his oil.

'Not so fast, sonny!' said God. 'Not him.'

So Jesse brought the next son over. 'This one is Shammah – takes after his mamma.'

Altogether, Jesse presented seven sons to Samuel, but God didn't choose any of them.

'Have you got any more?' Samuel asked Jesse, knowing he'd probably wish he hadn't.

'Yes,' said Jesse. 'Yes, there's another – he's their baby brother.'

'Well, you'd better get him,' sighed Samuel, 'but let *him* tell me his name.'

'Well, I don't know what you want with him,' said Jesse. 'He's not like the rest – you've looked at the best. I let him earn his keep by caring for the sheep.'

The youngest son came when he was sent for. 'Hello,' he said, 'I'm David. I've heard all about you from my father.'

David was still quite young, and looked it. His hair probably hadn't seen a comb for days, and he seemed to be trying rather unsuccessfully to grow a beard.

'A nice lad,' thought Samuel, 'but . . .'

'That's the one!' God whispered, excitedly.

'I thought you said you knew what you were doing,' thought Samuel.

'No,' God corrected him. 'You said you hoped I did. I do, though – he's the one. Well, don't just sit there, get the oil out and do it. Then I'll let you get away from Jesse's silly rhymes.'

'It's a deal!' thought Samuel. And there and then, he poured some oil over David's head.

'That's it,' he said to Jesse. 'Now remember: don't tell Saul what I've done, or I'll be on the run. Oh, no! I've got to get out of here, before it gets me completely!'

As Samuel set of down the road he thought,

'David seems a strange choice. Still, there's one thing – he doesn't make up poetry. I wonder which one of them does.'

Our Story

Draw attention to the display; explain which examples are real and which imaginary and again see whether the other children can think of any more. Let them learn not to take things simply at face value.

Prayers

We're Sad

We're sorry, God,
for being unfair to people.
We jump to conclusions about them
just because of their appearance.
Please forgive us,
and help us to be fair.

We're Glad

Thank you, God, for wonderful surprises
when people turn out differently
from the way we expect.
Thank you for making the world
so unpredictable!

Let's Pray for People

Some people get badly treated
just because they look different.
Please, God, help them to know
that you love them all,
and help us to control our prejudice.

Songs

God our Father gave us life
I'm black, I'm white, I'm short, I'm tall
Stand up! Walk tall!

Appearances Can Be Deceptive

God's Story

Narrator	Long ago, God had a job for Samuel the prophet.
God	Samuel, I want you to go and see Jesse at Bethlehem and anoint one of his sons as king.
Samuel	Bethlehem? Nothing important happens in Bethlehem.
God	My Word! You ain't seen nothin' yet!
Samuel	Pardon?
God	That's my favourite quotation, but it's after your time.
Samuel	Can we just get back to this Bethlehem thing?
God	Just go – I'll tell you which one to anoint.
Narrator	So Samuel turned up at Jesse's house one afternoon.
Jesse	Hello, hello, hello! It's good old Sam the prophet man! Have you come with some message of doom?
Samuel	Look Jesse, I just say what God's given me to say, so if you want to moan at anybody, you'd better talk to him.
Jesse	Silly bloke – can't take a joke!
Narrator	The trouble was that Jesse fancied himself as a bit of a poet – why, no one could understand, although it was said that one of his sons was a bit of a songwriter.
Samuel	Just send for your family and we'll get started.
Jesse	All right, Sammy, keep your wig on; how'd I know there's something big on?
Narrator	Jesse's sons got ready for the celebration.

- They *washed their faces*
- and they *cleaned their teeth*
- and they *combed their hair*

Narrator	Samuel was really pleased when the first son arrived.
God	Don't go by his appearance. I look at the heart.
Samuel	Oh, his heart'll be fine – healthy looking chap.
God	Don't get clever with me. You know what I mean.
Narrator	The next one to arrive was Abinadab.
Jesse	This is my son – another one.
Samuel	*(Aside)* I've got to get out of here! Where's my oil?
God	Not so fast, sonny! This is not the one.
Jesse	This one is Shammah – takes after his mamma.
Narrator	How long was this going to go on for? Altogether, Jesse presented seven sons to Samuel.
Samuel	Have you got any more?
Jesse	Yes, there's another – he's their baby brother. He's not like the rest – you've looked at the best. I let him earn his keep by caring for the sheep. Here he is.
David	Hello, I'm David.
Samuel	Thank the Lord! He's not a jumped up amateur poet!
Narrator	David was young – and didn't look at all like a king.
God	That's the one! Don't just sit there, get the oil out.
Narrator	Samuel poured some oil over David's head.
Samuel	Well, that's it, Jesse. Don't tell Saul what I've done, or I'll be on the run. Oh, no! I've got to get out of here!
Narrator	With that, Samuel set off away from Jesse's farm.
Samuel	Well, there's one thing about David – he doesn't make up poetry. I wonder which one of them does.

David Becomes Famous

Based on 1 Samuel 18-19

BEFORE THE DAY

Who are the children's heroes? Get them to collect pictures, newspaper cuttings, etc., of their favourite singers, actors, sports personalities and so on. It's probably advisable not to use anything too valuable, just in case things get mislaid or damaged. Either the day before or the morning of the assembly, enlist the help of the children to put them up on the wall or a board.

• Think about the actions for all the children to join in during the story.

ON THE DAY

Introduction

We're going to hear a story about fame and jealousy in a minute, but first we'll say our 'Thank you' prayer.

'Thank you' Prayer

Thank you, God, for all you give us,
thank you for the earth and sea;
thank you, God, for special people,
thank you, God, for making me.

God's Story

After David had killed Goliath, King Saul was so pleased with him that he asked him to go and live at the palace. Everything seemed to be very good indeed, especially when Saul put David in charge of the army. Now what you have to remember is that there weren't any football clubs or record companies in those days, so if you wanted to be famous you had to do something pretty spectacular. And you hadn't got to be too fussy about what happened to other people, either. David soon made himself very popular by leading the army into battle with the Philistines. He always won, and every time he came back he was a little more famous than when he went away. Crowds of people would line the streets and cheer the army home.

One day, King Saul heard them shouting, 'King Saul has killed thousands, but David has killed tens of thousands!', which only goes to show that people could be as horrible and bloodthirsty then as they can now.

Anyway, Saul was upset. No, that's not true. He was absolutely madly, mind-blastingly furious! 'How can they say that David's a greater soldier than their king?' he thought. 'Just a minute, that's it! They'll be making him king, next. Well, that settles it: he's got to go.'

Next day, Saul wasn't feeling very well – and neither would you be if you'd spent the entire night thinking nasty jealous thoughts about someone else. So (and you can decide for yourself whether you think this was a good idea) David played the harp to him to try and cheer him up. The upshot of that was that Saul threw a spear at him (but since Saul was already in a bad mood it might not have been any reflection on David's playing). David dodged aside, and the spear made a terrible gash in the wall just behind where his head had been.

From then on, Saul kept on thinking of ways to get David killed. When he realised that his daughter Michal (no, not *that* Princess Michael) was in love with David, he thought he saw his chance. 'You can marry her if you like,' he said to David, 'just as soon as you've killed another hundred Philistines.' At the same time, he was thinking, 'With a bit of luck, they'll kill him before he gets to a hundred.'

That plan didn't work either. Saul had obviously forgotten David was even more lethal with a sword than he was with a harp, and before long not one but two hundred Philistines had bitten the dust and David was being fitted for his wedding suit. Michal was thrilled, because she loved David very much and didn't realise what had been in her father's mind. As far as she was concerned, they would marry, have ten-point-four children (people had bigger families in those days) and live happily ever after.

Meanwhile, David was winning more and more battles, and the people were shouting and screaming every time he appeared in public, while Saul could probably have walked down the street stark naked and not been noticed. So Saul decided it was time to get back to basics and use some good old-fashioned direct action. Yes, that's right: another spear, another gash in the wall, and David still alive to tell the tale – if a little breathlessly – to his wife.

'You're going to have to get away and hide,' said Michal, 'before that father of mine gets seriously businesslike. No, not that way, they're bound to be watching the door – anyone can tell you never went to the military academy.' She got a large laundry basket and a long rope. 'Get in, and I'll lower you down to the ground. They won't be expecting that. Now, have you got a clean hanky? And don't forget to wash your clothes regularly and clean your teeth three times a day.'

Michal had hardly finished lowering David out of the window when she heard a loud knocking, and a voice. 'Open the raid, this is a door. No, that's not right. Oh, you know what I mean.'

Michal looked around quickly and found a life-size statue of one of the family. Well, they didn't have cameras in those days, so it was the next best thing to a photograph. Meanwhile, the person outside the door was getting impatient.

- He *rattled the handle*
- he *peered through the keyhole*
- then he *hammered on the door violently*

'If you don't open this door, I'll – I'll – I'll get very cross.'

Michal covered up the statue with a blanket, and rubbed her eyes to make it look as though she had been crying.

'I'll huff, and I'll puff, and I'll – no, that won't work. I'll think of something, don't you worry,' the voice went on, outside the door.

'You could always turn the handle,' called Michal.

'Oh, yes. What a good idea!' The door opened and in came the captain of the guard. 'The King wants your husband. Pronto.'

'I'm sorry, but he's ill,' Michal sniffed. 'Look, there he is in bed. I'm ever so worried.'

Meanwhile, David went to see his old friend Samuel the prophet and told him the whole story.

'Don't you worry, Davey, boy,' exclaimed Samuel. 'My friends and I are more than a match for Saul. He might be a great warrior, but a crowd of charismatic prophets in full flow is too much even for him!'

And he was right. David was quite safe.

Our Story

Point out the display of famous people. Perhaps the larger group can name others, as well. Do they ever feel jealous? When they do, does it make them feel good, or bad like Saul? So what is the best response to other people's success?

Prayers

We're Glad

Thank you, God,
for all the good or clever
things we can do,
and all the special talents
other people have, too.

We're Sad

We're sorry, God,
for all the times we get jealous
and hurt other people,
just because they seem more clever
or more popular.
Teach us to work together
to improve your world.

Let's Pray for People

Loving God,
we pray for all people who feel threatened
by someone else's skills.
Help them to be confident
that what they can do
is just as important to you.

Songs

A new commandment
Do you ever wish you could fly
Goliath was big and Goliath was strong
  (Biggest isn't always best)
I'm black, I'm white, I'm short, I'm tall

David Becomes Famous

God's Story

Narrator   After David had killed Goliath, King Saul put him in charge of the army. Every time David won a battle, he was a little more famous than before. One day, King Saul heard the crowd shouting, 'King Saul has killed thousands, but David has killed tens of thousands!' Saul was upset. No, that's not true. He was absolutely furious!

Saul   How can they say that David's a greater soldier than their king? Just a minute, that's it! They'll be making him king, next. Well, that settles it: he's got to go.

Narrator   Next day, Saul wasn't feeling very well. So (and you can decide for yourself whether you think this was a good idea) David played the harp to try and cheer him up. Saul threw a spear at him, but since Saul was already in a bad mood it might not have been any reflection on David's playing. David dodged aside, and the spear made a terrible gash in the wall just behind him. From then on, Saul kept on thinking of ways to get David killed. When he realised that his daughter Michal was in love with David, he had an idea.

Saul   You can marry her if you like, David, just as soon as you've killed another hundred Philistines. (*Aside*) With a bit of luck, they'll kill him first.

Narrator   That plan didn't work either, and before long David was being fitted for his wedding suit. David kept on getting even more popular. So Saul decided it was time to get back to basics and use some good old-fashioned direct action. Yes, that's right: another spear, another gash in the wall, and David still alive to tell the tale.

Michal   You're going to have to get away, before that father of mine gets seriously businesslike. Get in the laundry

	basket, and I'll lower you down to the ground. Now, have you got a clean hanky? And don't forget to wash your clothes regularly and clean your teeth properly.
Narrator	Soon, the captain of the guard knocked on the door.
Captain	Open the raid, this is a door. No, that's not right. Oh, you know what I mean.
Narrator	Michal looked around quickly and found a life-size statue of one of the family, and put it in the bed. Meanwhile, the captain was getting impatient.

- He *rattled the handle*
- he *peered through the keyhole*
- then he *hammered on the door violently*

Captain	If you don't open this door, I'll – I'll – get very cross.
Narrator	Michal covered up the statue with a blanket, and rubbed her eyes to pretend she had been crying.
Captain	I'll huff, and I'll puff, and I'll – oh, it's not locked. Now: the King wants your husband. Pronto.
Michal	I'm sorry, but he's ill. Look, there he is in bed.
Narrator	Meanwhile, David went to see his old friend Samuel the prophet and told him the whole story.
Samuel	Don't you worry, Davey, boy, my friends and I are more than a match for Saul. He might be a great warrior, but a crowd of charismatic prophets in full flow is too much even for him!
Narrator	And he was right. David was quite safe.

Whose Baby?

Based on 1 Kings 3:16-28

BEFORE THE DAY

Play 'call my bluff!' Think of something the children have done together, such as a class outing, and get one or a group of them to describe it. Ask another individual or group to make up a different (but plausible) account of it. Have both versions written down and let each group choose someone to present it to the assembly.

• Think about the actions for all the children to join in during the story.

ON THE DAY

Introduction

In a little while, there'll be a game for us all to play, but first we're going to say our 'Thank you' prayer.

'Thank you' Prayer

Thank you, God, for all you give us,
thank you for the earth and sea;
thank you, God, for special people,
thank you, God, for making me.

God's Story

Becky and Sally were flatmates, but they didn't like one another. As it happened, they were both expecting babies.

'I bet mine will be better-looking than yours,' said Becky to Sally.

'Well, mine will be brainier because you've always been stupid,' answered Sally.

Becky's baby was born first. It was a beautiful little boy. Sally looked at him and said, 'Ugh! He's all red and wrinkled!'

'All children are like that to start with,' said Becky, crossly. 'But the wrinkles go after a few days. Why didn't yours?'

'Now, you two,' said the midwife, 'can't you stop quarrelling even at a time like this?'

'I don't care what you say,' Sally grumbled. 'My baby won't be red and wrinkled!' But he was. People used to come round and admire the babies, but Becky and Sally always tried to score points off one another. 'Of course, my baby has nicer eyes than hers,' Becky would say, and Sally would answer, 'Mine's ever so good you know – he hardly ever cries.'

One morning, Becky woke up and had a terrible shock. Her baby was dead. Becky screamed and cried.

But then she looked a little closer and realised it wasn't her baby. She rushed over to Sally's crib and there, sure enough, was her baby alive and well.

If she hadn't been so angry, Becky might have felt sorry for Sally – even though she didn't like her at all – but as it was she was just plain furious! 'You give me back my baby!' she yelled.

'You're mad!' said Sally. 'That's my baby.'

There was only one thing for it. They would have to get the law on it.

King Solomon was just finishing his breakfast when he heard the commotion at the palace gates. 'Really!' he said, in a fed up sort of voice. 'Can't a royal person even have his breakfast in peace?' He was a good king, though, so he put on his official clothes and went down to the palace gate. He always settled quarrels in public, so that everybody could see he was being fair and there were no more arguments about it.

When Solomon got to the gate, Becky and Sally were still hard at it.

'Give me my baby, you ugly little witch!' shouted Becky.

'Yours took one look at you and died of fright!' yelled Sally.

'Be quiet,' said Solomon, 'or I'll have you both locked up until you calm down. Now, what's all the fuss about?' Both women started to shout and argue again, and Solomon had to separate them. 'You first,' he said to Becky.

'It's like this,' said Becky, 'We both had babies and when I woke up this morning mine was dead. Then I realised that Prune-face here . . .'

'Don't you call me Prune-face, Banana-legs!' shouted Sally.

'One more word from you and I'll really lock you up!' said the king. 'Now, Becky, just tell me the story without any silly insults.'

'She swapped them,' said Becky. 'The live baby's mine and the dead one's hers.'

'She's lying,' screamed Sally. 'He's my baby.'

Of course, Solomon didn't know which he was, but he thought he might be able to find out. 'Get me a sword,' he said, and the whole crowd went deathly quiet. What was he going to do? 'We can't decide whose he is,' he said, 'so I'm going to cut him in two and you can have half each.'

'You can't do that!' Becky wailed.

Sally thought, 'At least then her baby will be dead a well as mine.' So she said, 'Sounds fair to me – give us half each.' Sally really was a nasty person, but Becky was no angel either even though she was right in this particular case.

The servant put the baby on a table, and another lifted the sword high above the baby. Becky couldn't stand it any more. 'Give him to her!' she shouted. 'I'd rather give him away than have him killed.'

Solomon gently handed the baby over to Becky. 'I can tell you're his mother,' he said. 'Take him home and look after him.'

Becky was thrilled.

- She *picked the baby up*
- she *rocked him in her arms*
- she *hugged him close*

One of Solomon's servants said to him, 'Your Majesty, you wouldn't really have cut that baby up, would you?'

'Of course not,' said Solomon, 'but it did the trick. You see, when you really love someone, you'd rather let them go than have them hurt. So I knew she was the real mother.'

Our Story

Get the two groups of children to present their stories, and then ask the whole assembly to vote for one or other as being correct. You could make it more fun, space permitting, by asking the children to move to one or other side of the hall. When the result has been announced, you can point out that we aren't all a clever as Solomon. Sometimes people get it wrong and unfair things happen. That's why honesty's so important.

Prayers

We're Sad

Sometimes we can be so selfish, or so angry
that we don't think straight.
Then innocent people get hurt,
and we end up unhappy as well.
Please God, help us to understand
that true happiness often means letting go.

We're Glad

Thank you, God, for wise people
who know how to get to the truth.
Thank you also for people who are so loving
that they would rather lose
than see innocents hurt.
Please teach us all to love unselfishly.

Let's Pray for People

We pray for people who make themselves
and other people unhappy
because they are selfish or angry.
Help us all to learn to let go
even of the most precious things
when it is the loving thing to do.

Songs

Friends, all gather here in a circle
He gave me eyes so I could see
He's got the whole world in his hand
Out to the great wide world we go!
Peace is flowing like a river

Whose Baby?

God's Story

Narrator	Becky and Sally were both expecting babies. They were flatmates, but they hated one another.
Becky	I bet mine will be better-looking than yours.
Sally	Mine will be brainier; you've always been stupid.
Narrator	See what I mean? They couldn't be nice to one another even if their lives depended on it. Becky's baby was born first. It was a beautiful little boy.
Sally	Ugh! He's all red and wrinkled – what an ugly child!
Becky	All children are like that to start with, but the wrinkles go after a few days. Why didn't yours?
Narrator	Sally's baby was born a few days later, and he was lovely – but Becky and Sally still couldn't be friends.
Becky	Of course, my baby has nicer eyes than yours.
Sally	Mine's ever so good you know – he hardly ever cries.
Narrator	One morning, Becky woke up and had a terrible shock. Her baby was very pale, and very cold, and he wasn't breathing. He was dead. Becky cried.
Sally	Hey, I'm trying to sleep. Beautiful women like me need their sleep – it makes no difference to you.
Narrator	Becky looked a little closer and realised it wasn't her baby. She rushed over to Sally's crib and there, sure enough, was her child alive and well.
Becky	You give me back my baby!
Sally	You're mad! Anyone can see that that's my baby.
Narrator	Then they started screaming and shouting at each other. There was only one thing for it. They would have to get the law on it. King Solomon was just finishing his breakfast when he heard the commotion outside.

Solomon Really! Can't a royal person even have his breakfast in peace? Be quiet, or I'll have you both locked up until you calm down. Now what's it all about? You first.

Becky We both had babies and when I woke up this morning mine was dead. Then I realised that Prune-face here . . .

Sally Don't you call me Prune-face, Banana-legs!

Solomon One more word from you and I'll lock you up. Now, Becky, just tell me the story without any silly insults.

Becky She swapped them. The live baby's mine.

Solomon Your turn, Sally.

Sally She's lying. He's my baby.

Solomon Give me the baby. I'm going to cut him in two and you can have half each.

Becky You can't cut my baby in half!

Sally Sounds fair to me – give us half each.

Narrator The servant put the baby on a table, and another took the sword. He lifted it up, high above the baby and waited for the king's command to cut the child in two.

Becky Give him to her! Give him to her. I'd rather give him away than have him killed.

- She *picked the baby up*
- she *rocked him in her arms*
- she *hugged him close*

Solomon I can tell you're his mother, Becky. When you really love someone, you'd rather let them go than have them hurt. I wouldn't really have hurt him, of course.

Narrator That was one reason why everybody said that Solomon was a very wise king indeed.

Elijah's Last Journeys

Based on 2 Kings 2:1-15

BEFORE THE DAY

Absent friends. Do the children have friends who have gone away? Have they themselves moved house/school and left friends behind? Write the friends' names up on a flipchart, leaving space to add others. If it is felt appropriate in the particular circumstances, this could also be an opportunity to talk sensitively about bereavement.

• Think about the actions for all the children to join in during the story.

ON THE DAY

Introduction

We'll hear a story soon about two friends who had to go separate ways. First, we're going to say our 'Thank you' prayer.

'Thank you' Prayer

Thank you, God, for all you give us,
thank you for the earth and sea;
thank you, God, for special people,
thank you, God, for making me.

God's Story

Elijah and Elisha were friends. Elijah was the chief prophet at the time, and Elisha was his pupil. Everyone guessed that God would probably ask Elisha to take over sometime.

One day, they both knew that it was going to happen. Elijah seemed restless.

'God wants me to go to Bethel,' said Elijah. 'You stay here and rest.'

'Not on your life!' answered Elisha. 'I want to be around when the action starts.'

'Well, all right, then,' grunted Elijah. 'Just make sure you keep up.' And he set off at a cracking pace toward Bethel. When they got there, they found a reception committee waiting for them. Some of them took Elisha aside and said, 'Did you know that God's going to take Elijah away, today?'

'Yes,' said Elisha, 'but don't tell him.'

Then Elisha sat down on a handy milestone and took his sandals off. 'My life!' he said. 'But can that man walk! I've got blisters where I didn't even know I'd got skin!'

Elijah came up to him and looked down at his feet for a moment. 'You young people!' he said. 'In my day we'd walk miles just to find a drink of water, and think nothing of it.' Then he smiled. 'Look, you stay here with these good people. I'm going to go to Jericho.'

'Whatever for?' exclaimed Elisha. Ever since Joshua's jam session, no one's dared throw a decent party in case something collapses. There's really nothing to go to in Jericho.'

Elijah was very patient. 'I've already said you can stay here,' he said.

'Not blooming likely!' said Elisha. 'I'm not leaving you today.'

So off they set, and Elijah didn't seem the least bit tired but went striding along ahead.

'What's the matter?' gasped Elisha. 'You're rushing around like there's no tomorrow.'

'Funny you should say that . . .' replied Elijah. And Elisha wished he hadn't.

At Jericho, there was another reception committee. One of them came up to Elisha. 'Sooth! Sooth!' he chanted.

'What d'you mean, "Sooth"?' snapped Elisha, impatiently.

'Sorry, Guv,' said the prophet, 'but I've got to say "Sooth" because I'm a "Sooth" sayer. D'you know your boss is leaving today?'

'Yes,' said Elisha, 'but don't tell to him. And don't go yelling "Sooth" in his ear, either – if you know what's good for you.'

• The man *raised his eyebrows*
• he *scratched his head*
• then he *rubbed his nose*

'Well!' he said. 'I've had my nose bitten off a few times, but that's what I call a mega bite!' And he went off, chuntering to himself.

Elisha sat down and looked mournfully at his feet. 'I've got blisters on my blisters, now!' he groaned.

'Oh, don't tell me about blisters, said Elijah. When I was a young prophet . . .'

'I know, I know!' Elisha interrupted. 'Up to your neck in muck and . . .'

'No need to be offensive!' Elijah sniffed. 'Anyway, you can have a rest now, because I'm going to Jordan. You wait here.'

'Not on your cotton-picking life!' said Elisha. 'After all this walking, you're going to a nice cool, fresh river, and you think I'm staying here?'

So off they went, and soon they got to Jordan. That's right – another reception committee.

'D'you know . . .' one of them began.

'Oh, don't you start as well!' said Elisha. 'I know he's leaving today, and I'm unhappy enough without you rubbing it in. And talking of rubbing – oh, my feet!'

'Sorry, I'm sure!' said the man, rather stiffly. Then Elijah came over and said, kindly, 'Sorry about all the walking, but we're about there now. Let's get across that water.'

Elijah took off his cloak and hit the water with it. There, before Elisha's astonished eyes, the water moved to each side and left a nice dry path to walk across. 'Come on,' said Elijah, 'or you'll miss the big moment.'

As they walked, Elijah said, 'Is there anything I can do for you before I go?'

Elisha was still amazed by what Elijah had just done. 'A double portion of whatever it is that you've got wouldn't go amiss!' he said.

'That's difficult,' said Elijah, 'but if you actually see me taken away, then you'll get your wish. So stick with me, kid – I'm going places.'

Elisha did exactly that, until suddenly he saw something bright and terrifying coming towards them. He did his best to stay close to Elijah, but the strange thing came rushing through between them and picked Elijah up. It was a horse and chariot which seemed to be made of fire! Up and up it went, carrying Elijah with it. As Elisha looked up in astonishment, he saw Elijah's cloak coming down from the chariot to land at his feet. He picked it up and put it on.

'That's it!' he thought. 'It's a sign!'

And it was. Elisha became a great prophet, just as Elijah had been.

Our Story

Explain about the names on the board, and invite the rest of the assembly to add others. Then offer a short prayer for the absent friends.

Prayers

We're Sad

Wonderful God,
we're not always like Elijah and Elisha.
Sometimes we let people down,
and we're not there when they need us.
We're sorry, God.
Help us to be better friends to each other.

We're Glad

God, our friend,
you're always here for us.
Even though we sometimes find it hard
to recognise you,
you never leave us on our own.
Thank you.

Let's Pray for People

Some people don't seem to have any real
    friends.
They have to get through the hard times
without the help they really need.
Make us alert to other people,
so that we recognise when they're lonely;
then we can be friends to them.

Songs

Friends, all gather here in a circle
I have a friend
One more step
Thank you, O God, for all our friends (SS)
When I needed a neighbour

Elijah's Last Journeys

God's Story

Narrator   Elijah, who was the chief prophet, was training Elisha. Elijah was often restless, but on this particular day he *really* seemed to have sand in his underwear!

Elijah   I'm going to Bethel. You stay here and have a rest.

Elisha   And miss the action? Not likely! I'm coming with you.

Narrator   When they arrived, they were met by a reception committee of priests and prophets.

1st Prophet   Do you know God's going to take Elijah away, today?

Elisha   Yes, but don't tell him. Gosh, can that man walk! I've got blisters where I didn't even know I'd got skin!

Elijah   Look, you rest here. I'm going to go to Jericho.

Elisha   Why? Nothing ever happens in Jericho. Ever since Joshua brought the walls down, no one's dared throw a party in case something collapses. Oh, all right – I'm coming.

Narrator   Elijah didn't seem at all tired but went striding ahead.

Narrator   In Jericho, they found another reception committee; this time from the Prophets' Commission, Department of Soothsaying.

2nd Prophet   Sooth! Sooth!

Elisha   *(Impatiently)* What d'you mean, 'Sooth'?

2nd Prophet   Sorry, Guv, but I've got to say 'Sooth' because I'm a 'Sooth' sayer. Your boss is going away today.

Elisha   Well, don't go yelling 'Sooth' in his ear – or else.

Narrator	The soothsayer looked hurt.

- He *raised his eyebrows*
- he *scratched his head*
- then he *rubbed his nose*

2nd Prophet	Well! I've had my nose bitten off a few times, but that's what I call a mega bite!
Elijah	I'm going to Jordan, Elisha. You wait here.
Elisha	Not on your life! I'm coming, so I can soak these feet!
Narrator	So they went. This time the reception committee was from the Prophets' Bureau.
3rd Prophet	Did you know . .
Elisha	Oh, don't you start as well! Oh, my feet!
3rd Prophet	Sorry, I'm sure!
Elijah	Sorry about all the walking, but we're about there now.
Narrator	Elijah hit the water with his cloak. There, to Elisha's amazement, the water moved aside and left a dry path.
Elijah	Come on, or you'll miss the big moment. Is there anything I can do for you before I go?
Elisha	Well, I'd like a double portion of whatever it is that you've got.
Elijah	I'll tell you what. If you see me taken away, then you'll get it. So stick with me, kid – I'm going places.
Narrator	Suddenly, a horse and chariot which seemed to be made of fire came rushing through between them and carried Elijah off. As Elisha watched he saw Elijah's cloak coming down to land at his feet. Elisha became a great prophet, and all the people said how like Elijah he was.

Elisha's Oil Well

Based on 2 Kings 4:1-7

BEFORE THE DAY

Get the children to think about the people they might turn to for help. Let them draw pictures of police, 'lollipop' men and women, doctors, shopkeepers, clergy – anyone identifiable, who might help them if they needed it. Put the pictures up before the assembly.

• Think about the actions for all the children to join in during the story.

ON THE DAY

Introduction

We're going to hear a story in a few minutes about how a community came together to solve a problem. First, we'll say our 'Thank you' prayer.

'Thank you' Prayer

Thank you, God, for all you give us,
thank you for the earth and sea;
thank you, God, for special people,
thank you, God, for making me.

God's Story

'I've got her now,' thought Joe. 'That Abbi woman's going to have to do whatever I want from now on.'

Joe was a loan shark, and as if he didn't make enough money from that he did a bit of slave-trading on the side. One of his loan clients was Abbi, the widow of a prophet who had recently been killed. Lots of people had been going round to say how sorry they were, and to offer whatever help they could. So when Abbi heard another knock on the door, she was very pleased to open it.

'Joe!' she smiled. 'How nice of you to call.'

'Never mind that,' snarled Joe. 'What about my money?'

'Surely you can wait a few days?' Abbi gasped. 'I'll pay you as soon as we've sorted out my husband's affairs.'

'Oh, don't you come the poor widow act with me,' Joe sneered. 'I know you've got something put by.'

'Honestly, I haven't,' Abbi assured him, 'but as soon as I can I'll find a way to pay you.'

'Not good enough,' said Joe, flatly. 'Either you pay me the money, or I find another way of getting it back. How are those sons of yours?'

Abbi's blood ran cold. 'You wouldn't take them?'

'Nice, fit young men they are – fetch a nice price at the slave market, they would. You have the money by the weekend or I'm taking them.'

What was Abbi to do? She knew she couldn't possibly pay Joe back so quickly.

Joe knew it, too. In fact, he was banking on it. Abbi's sons would fetch a lot more at the market than she owed him, and then he'd be able to keep on threatening her and make her do anything he wanted. He couldn't wait for the weekend to come, when he was sure she wouldn't have the money.

Abbi only knew one person who might be able to help her. So she put on her hat and scarf and went out to find Elisha, the chief prophet. She knew he would want to help.

'That dreadful leech!' exclaimed Elisha when he heard the story. 'Whatever it takes, I'll keep his hands off your family!'

'I knew you'd help,' said Abbi with relief. 'I'll pay you back as soon as I can.'

- She *dried her eyes*
- she *put on her best smile*
- and she *held out her hand* for the money

Elisha shook his head. 'I'm not going to lend you the money,' he said. 'That way, you'd still be in debt. No, we've got to sort this out once and for all. What have you got in your house?'

'Nothing of any value,' Abbi wept. 'All I've got is a jar of oil for cooking, and somehow the three of us have to live on that!'

Elisha's eyes lit up. Oil! 'Go home,' he said to her, 'and borrow all the pots and jugs you can, and pour the oil out of the jar into them.'

'I've got a *jar* of oil,' Abbi said. 'Not a well of it.'

'Just trust God,' Elisha replied.

Abbi went back and called her two sons. 'Josh, you go down this side of the street and borrow anything that'll hold liquid,' she said. 'Nick, you go the other way and do the same.' Nick returned first with two large vases. Even one of them on its own was much bigger than the jar of oil, and Abbi wondered what on earth Elisha was playing at. Still, she did as he said and began to pour the oil out of the jar into the first of the vases. How strange: the oil just kept on coming! Soon, the vase was completely full and she had to start on the second one. But the oil jar was still full, as well.

Just then, Josh came in. 'I've got these cooking pots,' he said, 'but old Eva down the road says you be sure to return hers.'

'Of course I will!' replied Abbi, and started to pour. Still the oil jar was full, and the oil just went pouring out into the two pots. Josh and Nick got very fit that day; they couldn't borrow the containers fast enough. And all the time, Abbi just stood there pouring oil from the tiny jar and filling the enormous vessels. Eventually, they had to stop. The neighbours had run out of pots! Then Abbi made a big sign to put outside the house: 'Oil for heating and cooking. Best prices in town.' The word spread that Abbi's oil was cheaper and better than anyone else's, and she even had to send for Elisha to help serve the customers!

Come the weekend, Joe was knocking on the door with handcuffs and leg-irons at the ready.

'Bring out your sons!' he shouted, with a mean grin on his face.

Abbi went to the door. 'Never mind my boys,' she said. 'Here's your money, with interest. Now get out, and don't go peddling your loans around here any more. From now on, my neighbours and I are helping each other. We don't need your sort.'

Joe was very unhappy. What was he going to do? If he lost his business, he might even end up having to go to a loan shark himself!

Our Story

Ask the assembly to look at the pictures. Can they add any more ideas? They've probably been so busy trying to think of 'official' people, they've not thought of themselves or each other. But it was the whole community that sorted Joe out, wasn't it?

Prayers

We're Glad

Thank you, God,
for people who trust you
and help one another.

We're Sad

Sometimes we could do more than we do
to help people in trouble.
Please forgive us, God,
and show us the best way
to be helpful.

Let's Pray for People

Some people are so poor
that others can easily take advantage.
Please God, help all people
to be good neighbours
and help each other out of love,
not out of greed.

Songs

A new commandment
Brother, sister, let me serve you
Give me joy in my heart
I'm black, I'm white, I'm short, I'm tall
When I needed a neighbour

Elisha's Oil Well

God's Story

Narrator   Joe was a loan shark, and as if he didn't make enough money from that he did a bit of slave-trading on the side. One of his loan clients was Abbi, the widow of a prophet who had recently been killed. Lots of people had been going round to say how sorry they were, and to offer whatever help they could. So when Abbi heard another knock on the door, she was very pleased to open it.

Abbi   Joe! How nice of you to call.

Joe   Never mind that. What about my money?

Abbi   Surely you can wait a few days? I'll pay you as soon as we've sorted out my husband's affairs.

Joe   Oh, don't you come the poor widow act with me. I know you've got something put by.

Abbi   Honestly, I haven't, but as soon as I can I'll find a way to pay you.

Joe   Not good enough. Either you pay me the money, or I'll sell your sons at the slave market.

Narrator   Abbi knew she couldn't possibly pay Joe back so quickly. Joe was banking on it: her sons would fetch a lot more at the market than she owed him. He couldn't wait for the weekend to come, when he was sure she wouldn't have the money. Desperately, Abbi told her story to Elisha, the chief prophet.

Elisha   That dreadful leech! Whatever it takes, I'll keep Joe's hands off your family!

Narrator   Abbi was thrilled.

- She *dried her eyes*
- she *put on her best smile*
- and she *held out her hand* for the money

Elisha	I'm not going to lend you the money. We've got to sort this out once and for all. What have you got at home?
Abbi	Nothing I can sell – just a jar of oil for cooking, and somehow the three of us have to live on that!
Elisha	Oil! Go home, and borrow all the pots and jugs you can, and pour the oil out of the jar into them.
Abbi	I've got a *jar* of oil, not a well of it.
Elisha	Just trust God.
Abbi	My sons can help. Josh, you go down this side of the street and borrow anything that'll hold liquid. Nick, you go the other way and do the same.
Narrator	Soon, Abbi had dozens of pots. And no matter how many she filled, the oil jar was still full. It was a miracle! Abbi made a big sign to put outside the house: 'Oil for heating and cooking. Best prices in town'. Come the weekend, Joe was knocking on the door with handcuffs and leg-irons at the ready.
Joe	Bring out your sons!
Abbi	Never mind my boys. Here's your money, with interest. Now get out of here, and don't go peddling your loans around here any more. From now on, my neighbours and I are helping each other. We don't need your sort.
Narrator	Joe was very unhappy. What was he going to do? If he lost his business, he might even end up having to go to a loan shark himself!

Room at the Top

Based on 2 Kings 4:8-17

BEFORE THE DAY

How many different ways can the children think of by which to show friendship? Would they share their chocolate, let their friends join in their games, or write to them when they're ill? Get them to design a motorway-style 'services' sign with symbols for the different ideas.

• Think about the actions for all the children to join in during the story.

ON THE DAY

Introduction

In a little while, we'll be thinking about friendship. First, we're going to say our 'Thank you' prayer.

'Thank you' Prayer

Thank you, God, for all you give us,
thank you for the earth and sea;
thank you, God, for special people,
thank you, God, for making me.

God's Story

This story is about a woman whose name no one knows. She's usually called 'the Shunemite woman', because she lived in Shunem, but we're going to call her Deborah.

Deborah was a very important woman. Now some people who seem as important as that aren't very nice, but Deborah was a lovely person. One day she saw a man walking past who looked as though he could do with a rest and a good meal. So Deborah went over and said, 'Hello, you're a stranger round here, aren't you?'

'That's right,' the man answered. 'My name's Elisha. I travel around quite a bit, but this is my first visit to Shunem.'

'Well, you're very welcome,' Deborah told him. 'Would you like to come in?'

'Oh, no, thank you very much all the same,' answered Elisha. 'I've travelled a long way, and I'm afraid my coat isn't very clean. I wouldn't want to mess up your nice furniture.'

'That doesn't matter in the slightest,' Deborah assured him. 'I have someone who comes in three times a week to clean, and he may as well earn his wages.'

'Well, it really is very kind of you,' said Elisha, 'but I'm sure you've got important things to do.'

'Nonsense!' exclaimed Deborah. 'What could be more important than sharing a meal with a nice person like you. You must have some wonderful tales to tell if you travel about as much as you say.'

'I must admit, I've seen a thing or two,' mused Elisha, 'like that time my best friend got carried away in a flying chariot.'

'Now that I really must hear!' exclaimed Deborah, and she took Elisha by the arm and led him into her house.

'This is beautiful,' said Elisha. 'I really can't sit on those lovely cushions with these clothes on.'

'Well, I don't think you'd better take them off,' laughed Deborah. 'Go on – sit down!'

While Elisha was there, Deborah's husband came in. We don't know his name, either, so we'll call him Bart. He and Elisha got on like a house on fire, and soon it was as though they had all known each other for years. Elisha often visited Shunem after that, and he always called on Bart and Deborah.

One day, Deborah said to Bart, 'I think there's more to Elisha than meets the eye. I think he's some sort of prophet or holy man.'

'You could be right,' Bart replied. 'He seems very wise as well as kind.'

'I think we ought to build a spare room,' said Deborah. 'Then Elisha can stay here in comfort.'

'Well, I don't know where we're going to build an extra room,' said Bart. 'The garden's not very big, and we've already taken up part of it with that little garage for the chariot.'

Deborah couldn't think at first, either. She really wanted to do it, but she knew Bart was right. There wasn't any room. Then one day she had a bit of time to herself and decided to do a spot of sunbathing. She could have a nice snooze while she was at it. So she settled down in the garden, sat back and closed her eyes.

It was no good; every time Deborah began to doze off, someone would pass by and call out 'Hello!'

Then she had an idea. 'If I were up on the flat roof, she thought, 'no one would be able to see me.' So she went and got a ladder and propped it against the side of the house. It was very nice on the roof, but a little uncomfortable, so after a while Deborah went down for a deckchair which she hauled up to the roof using a rope. Before long, she'd got a footstool, a little table with a cool drink on it, two or three cushions and a sunshade, and she was really comfortable. She lay back in her deckchair and started to doze off.

Then just as she was falling asleep, she heard a voice! But this time it was her own thoughts she was hearing. 'Why not build a room for Elisha up here?' the thought said. Deborah was so excited she forgot about sunbathing and went rushing out to find Bart, who had gone to market.

'You'll never believe it,' she told him. 'I was just lying on the roof . . .'

'You were what?' said Bart, astonished.

'Lying on the roof,' answered Deborah. 'Doesn't everybody?'

When Bart got over his amazement, he thought Deborah's idea was a very good one. So they called in a builder.

- The builder *drew some plans*
- and *built some walls*
- and *hammered in some nails*

Soon there was a lovely little guest room on the roof.

Next time Elisha came, they showed him that he had his own special room.

'I don't know how to thank you,' he said.

'No need,' said Deborah. We just love having you to stay.'

'There must be something I can do,' Elisha insisted. 'Perhaps I'll put a good word in for you with the king.'

'Don't be silly,' laughed Deborah. 'I know him like my own brother. The only thing we want, nobody can give us. Unless you've got a spare child hidden in your luggage, just forget it. We love having you here and you don't have to repay us.'

'Ah!' exclaimed Elisha. 'So that's what you want. Well, by this time next year, you will have a lovely little baby boy in your arms. You've got God's word for that.'

And Elisha was absolutely right. But that's another story.

Our Story

Explain to the assembly what the sign is generally about, and then see whether they can interpret the specific symbols. Would they want to add anything else?

Prayers

We're Sad

Sometimes we're so wrapped up in our own problems
that we don't notice what other people need.
It's not that we mean to be unkind;
we just don't notice them.
Please forgive us, God,
and make us more aware of others.

We're Glad

Thank you, God, for all the different people
you send our way.
Thank you for the different things
we can learn from each of them,
and the friendships we can have with them.

Let's Pray for People

We pray for people who help others.
Help them to know that what they do
is noticed and appreciated.
Show us what we can do to support them.

Songs

Friends, all gather here in a circle
One more step
Out to the great wide world we go!
Thank you, O God, for all our friends (SS)
When I needed a neighbour

Room at the Top

God's Story

Narrator   Deborah was an important woman who lived in Shunem. One day she saw a man walking past who looked as though he could do with a rest and a good meal.

Deborah   Hello, you're a stranger round here, aren't you?

Elisha   Yes; my name's Elisha. This is my first visit here.

Deborah   Would you like to come in and have some food?

Elisha   Well, it's very kind of you, but I wouldn't want to be any trouble, and you must have important things to do.

Deborah   Nonsense! You must have some wonderful tales to tell from your travels.

Elisha   I've certainly seen a thing or two. There was that time my best friend got carried away by some flying horses.

Deborah   Now that I really must hear! Come on in.

Narrator   While Elisha was there, Deborah's husband, Bart, came in. He and Elisha got on like a house on fire, and Elisha often visited them after that.

Deborah   You know, Bart, I think Elisha might be a prophet.

Bart   You could be right.

Deborah   I think we ought to build a spare room for him.

Bart   Well, I don't know. We haven't much space.

Narrator   Deborah went and sat outside to think quietly. It *should* have been very peaceful in the garden.

Neighbour   Hello, Deborah, having a nice rest?

Deborah   (*Patiently*) No, but I'd like to.

Narrator	It was no good, though. Every time anyone walked past, they called out and disturbed her. So to get a bit of peace, she went and got a ladder and climbed up onto the roof. Peace at last – then she had an idea!
Deborah	That's it! Why not build a room for Elisha up here?
Narrator	Deborah was so excited she forgot about sunbathing and rushed off to find Bart, who had gone to market.
Deborah	You'll never believe it – I was just lying on the roof . . .
Bart	You were what?
Deborah	Lying on the roof. Doesn't everybody?
Narrator	Bart liked Deborah's idea and called in a builder.

- The builders *drew some plans*
- and *built some walls*
- and *hammered in some nails*

And soon Elisha had a lovely little room on the roof.

Elisha	I don't know how to thank you.
Deborah	No need. We love having you to stay.
Elisha	There must be something I can do. Perhaps I'll put a good word in for you with the king.
Deborah	Don't be silly! I know him like my own brother. The only thing we want, nobody can give us. Unless you're hiding a spare child in your luggage, just forget it. We love having you here and you don't have to repay us.
Elisha	Ah! So that's what you want. Well, by this time next year, you will have a lovely little baby boy in your arms. You've got God's word for that.
Narrator	And Elisha was absolutely right. But that's another story.

Life's Like That!

Based on 2 Kings 4:18-37

BEFORE THE DAY

This story is an opportunity to explore the fact that we don't always get what we deserve, but it works both ways – we get good things as well as bad. Let the children draw some examples of both, e.g. people suffering the effects of floods or gales, lottery winners receiving their (unearned) cheques, sports matches being rained off, beautiful weather at the seaside, etc. Put the pictures up in a display, not in separate categories but randomly mixed.

• Think about the actions for all the children to join in during the story.

ON THE DAY

Introduction

The world doesn't seem to be a very fair place, and we're going to think about that in a few minutes. First, we're going to say our 'Thank you' prayer.

'Thank you' Prayer

Thank you, God, for all you give us,
thank you for the earth and sea;
thank you, God, for special people,
thank you, God, for making me.

God's Story

Deborah, the Shunemite woman who was a friend of Elisha, was really worried. Her husband, Bart, seemed bad-tempered and unreasonable. He made some very unkind remarks about her cooking – just because she was trying out a few new recipes of her own.

Bart, of course, had his own version of the story to tell, and he told it to his next-door neighbour, Luke. 'I don't know what's got into her!' he said one day. 'Last week, the only food she would cook was figs and onions. We had them on toast for breakfast, and then in an omelette for lunch, followed by figs and onions in chocolate sauce for dessert.'

'Well, there's one thing,' Luke laughed. 'It can't get any worse!'

'Oh can't it!' answered Bart. 'That's what you know. This week it was stewed oranges in camel-meat stock. I'm not kidding you, my stomach's not been right for weeks!'

Luke thought he had the answer.

• He *scratched his head*
• and he *stroked his beard*
• and he *frowned very wisely*

'She needs help,' he said, looking very wise. 'She's obviously having a breakdown. You wouldn't understand the details, but take it from me – that's what she's having.'

Bart didn't like to ask any more questions, since Luke was now looking very knowledgeable and superior, and Bart was sure he really ought to understand all this – but just then they heard a very worrying sound.

It was the sound of laughter. Shrieking, uncontrollable, hysterical laughter. 'Terribly sorry, old man,' said Luke. 'Sounds like a really serious case to me.'

'That's not Deborah,' Bart said. 'That's coming from your house.'

Sure enough, just inside Luke's kitchen window was his wife, Sandy, with tears streaming down her face, and laughing fit to bust! 'You pair of silly, pompous men!' she gasped in between peals of laughter. 'Deborah's not ill – she's pregnant!'

'Don't be silly!' answered Luke. 'What would you know about it?'

'Well, I've been there myself five times,' giggled Sandy, 'which is five times more than both of you put together. You should know that women often fancy strange food when they're pregnant.'

Sandy was absolutely right. Elisha had promised Deborah and Bart a child, and it was actually happening!

And what a baby it was! A lovely little boy whom they named Tom. He grew up into a strong, sturdy child who liked striding around the fields with his dad. He very quickly learned all about caring for the land and growing crops. Everybody loved Tom very much, and especially Elisha who always played with him on his visits.

One day, out in the fields, Tom started feeling ill. Soon, he had a raging headache and the whole world seemed to be spinning round. 'I'm not feeling very well,' he said.

Bart asked one of the farmhands to take him back to the house. Poor Deborah did all she could, but it was no use. Tom was a lot more sick than anyone had realised, and he just got worse and worse until he died.

Deborah was beside herself with grief and anger. She took Tom upstairs into the special room she'd had built and laid him on Elisha's bed, and then she got on a donkey and went out to find the prophet. He went to meet her and gave her a hug.

'Why did you do this? Deborah asked. 'Why did your God give us a child, just to make us unhappy by taking him away?'

Elisha was horrified! 'Let's go to your house!' he said. They hurried off, and when they arrived Elisha went up to his room and found Tom's body on his bed. After he had prayed he picked Tom up and hugged him. Tom's body started to get warm again. Elisha put him down on the bed and prayed again, and then he picked him up and hugged him again, and this time he could just feel a little heart beating away against him. Then Tom's eyes opened and he said, 'Oh, hello! When did you get here?'

Elisha went to the door and opened it. When Deborah saw Tom alive, she started crying all over again, but this time it was with happiness!

Deborah and Bart hugged Tom and thanked Elisha.

'Don't thank me,' said Elisha. 'It's God that's done this. He doesn't break his word. And he doesn't play around with people's feelings, either.'

Our Story

Look at the pictures and point out that none of those people have deserved what has happened – to some extent, life's a lottery! Explain that the pictures are randomly placed, because happy and sad things often seem to be mixed up together in life, as well. How does this affect our attitudes to people who have had a raw deal from life?

Prayers

We're Sad

Sometimes, we don't understand
why other people are angry,
and we get angry in return
when we should be listening.
Please forgive us, God,
and help us to be better friends.

We're Glad

Thank you, God, for people like Elisha,
who really care about other people.
Thank you for patient people, who understand
when others say things they don't mean.
Thank you, God, for wonderful friends.

Let's Pray for People

Sometimes dreadful, unfair things happen.
Sometimes people who don't deserve it get hurt.
Please, God, give them friends who
    understand,
who will listen to what they need to say
even when it's hurtful.

Songs

Our God is so great
Thank you, O God, for all our friends (SS)
When I needed a neighbour

Life's Like That!

God's Story

Narrator   Deborah, the Shunemite woman who was a friend of Elisha, was really worried about her husband, Bart. He seemed to be very bad-tempered and unreasonable, and was most unkind about her cooking. But Bart saw things differently, and said so to their neighbour.

Bart   I don't know what's got into her, Luke! Last week, the only food she would cook was figs and onions.

Luke   Figs and onions! You're having me on!

Bart   Would I joke about something as serious as my dinner? Before that, it was stewed oranges in camel-meat stock. My stomach's not been right for weeks!

Narrator   Luke thought he had the answer.

- He *scratched his head*
- and he *stroked his beard*
- and he *frowned very wisely*

Luke   She's having some sort of breakdown.

Bart   Some sort of what?

Luke   Oh, it's very technical. You wouldn't understand – I don't think we'll really understand it for thousands of years yet, but that's what she's having all right.

Narrator   Bart didn't like to ask any more questions, since Luke was now looking very knowledgeable and superior. Just then, though, they heard the sound of shrieking, uncontrollable, hysterical laughter.

Luke   Terribly sorry, old man. Sounds like a serious case.

Bart   That's coming from *your* house. It's *your* wife.

Narrator   Bart was right. Just inside the kitchen window was Luke's wife, Sandy, doubled up, with tears streaming down her face, and laughing fit to bust!

Sandy   You silly, pompous men! Deborah's pregnant!

Luke   Don't be silly, Sandy! What would you know about it?

Sandy   Well, I've been there myself five times, which is five times more than both of you put together. You should know that women often fancy strange foods when they're pregnant.

Narrator   Poor Luke felt nearly as silly as he looked – but it would have been impossible to have felt *that* silly!

Bart   What a relief! So we aren't falling out of love, after all! Elisha promised us a child, and we're having one!

Narrator   Soon, they had a lovely little boy whom they named Tom. He grew very strong and healthy for a few years, but then for no apparent reason he died. Deborah was beside herself with grief and anger, and went to find Elisha.

Deborah   Why did you do this? We'd got used to not having a child. Why did your God give us one, just to make us unhappy by taking him away?

Elisha   Let's go to your house!

Narrator   They hurried off, and when they arrived Elisha went up to his room and found Tom's body on his bed. As he prayed, and hugged Tom, a wonderful thing happened. Tom's body started to get warm again, and soon his eyes opened. He really was alive!

Elisha   Deborah, Bart, you can come in now – he's fine.

Deborah   This is wonderful! How can we ever thank you?

Elisha   Don't thank me. It's God that's done this. He doesn't break his word. And he doesn't play around with people's feelings, either.

Keep It Simple

Based on 2 Kings 5:1-14

BEFORE THE DAY

Get the children to use their imaginations and design outlandish, complicated versions of simply everyday objects: a tooth cleaning machine with lots of rotary brushes and toothpaste dispensers attached to robotic arms around a chair; a tin-opener made from a hacksaw mounted on a stand, with jigs for holding the tins still and magnets for removing the severed lids; an alarm clock operated by water dripping steadily into a container – when the water level is just right, a series of rubber balls run down a tube to land on the skin of a drum. The more outlandish and complicated the devices are, the better!

• Think about the actions for all the children to join in during the story.

ON THE DAY

Introduction

We've got some interesting new inventions to look at shortly, but first we're going to say our 'Thank you' prayer.

'Thank you' Prayer

Thank you, God, for all you give us,
thank you for the earth and sea;
thank you, God, for special people,
thank you, God, for making me.

God's Story

Naaman lived in the country of Aram, and was a commander in the king's army. He was a great soldier who had been involved in lots of battles and had the scars to prove it, but when he wasn't soldiering he lived quietly with his wife, Jessica, in their house near the barracks.

Naaman and his army were often sent by the king of Aram to raid Israel and bring back treasure. The king wasn't really such a bad man; kings just thought they could do that kind of thing in those days, and a lot of rulers and politicians still haven't learnt any better, now.

Anyway, on one of the raids Naaman brought back a young girl called Anna and gave her to his wife as a slave. Now you might have thought that Anna would hate Naaman and Jessica for that, but she always tried not to. 'After all,' she used to say, 'we've all got to live together and hating them would just make me feel even more unhappy.' So although she missed her home very much, and longed to go back, she always tried to think kindly of Naaman and Jessica and to be helpful.

- She *dusted their furniture*
- she *cooked their food (stirring action)*
- she *chopped wood for the fire*

One day, Anna said to Jessica, 'I hope you won't mind my saying this, my Lady, but the commander doesn't seem very well. That nasty rash is getting worse.'

It was true. Naaman had a really uncomfortable skin disease, and it seemed to be spreading, but none of the doctors in Aram could do anything about it. 'I know someone who can, though,' said Anna. 'Send him to Israel to meet the prophet who lives there, and he'll make the commander well again.'

When the king of Aram heard about it he thought it was certainly worth a try, so he sent Naaman to the king of Israel with a letter, saying, 'Please make my army commander better.'

'Oh dear,' groaned the king of Israel. 'He's trying to pick a quarrel with me – how on earth can I make this soldier better?' And he got really frightened.

Well, you know how rumours about royal families spread – before long the whole country was talking about how frightened the king was, and wondering if it meant the end of the monarchy.

'It's true, you know,' someone said in the market place. 'He's so frightened he never goes to sleep any more. What sort of a king is he?'

Standing nearby was a man called Elisha. He was the prophet Anna had meant, but that's the trouble with some people: they think only kings and queens have the answers to anything – so Naaman had been sent to the wrong person! Still, it wasn't too late. Elisha sent a message to the king of Israel, saying, 'Send Naaman to me – I'll help him, and then you can get a good night's sleep.'

So it was that Naaman turned up at Elisha's door. When Elisha opened it, Naaman stood and waited for something spectacular to happen; you know, a flashing light, or something, or perhaps God would zap him and make him fall over. He liked a bit of theatre, did Naaman. But all Elisha said was, 'Oh, it's you. Right. Go and take a dip in the river Jordan. In fact, while you're at it, take seven – you've had a long journey. Then you'll get rid of your rash.'

Well! What a let down! Naaman got back on his horse, and set off for home. He was furious! 'I'm not being made a fool of by any Israelite!' he said, but his servant was actually a lot wiser than him – which is often the case.

'Why not do it?' the servant asked. 'After all, if he'd asked you to do something difficult you'd have done it, just to get a bit of glory – so why not do something simple?'

It seemed like a good point. Anyway, Naaman was hot and sticky, and covered in dust, so he thought he might just give it a try. He stopped on the river bank and took off his clothes while his servant kept watch. Then he went into the river and ducked under. 'Ugh!' he thought, 'what do they empty into the river around here?' But he didn't want to look like a coward, so he went under seven times, just as he'd been told. Then he got out of the water and started to dry himself. 'There!' he said to his servant. 'Satisfied now? Let's go home before I have to do anything else that's stupid …What on earth's the matter with you now?'

His servant was staring at him as though he'd seen a ghost. 'Sir! Sir!' he shouted. 'Your rash has gone!' Naaman looked down, and sure enough, it had! His skin looked fresh and healthy again – almost like a baby's skin.

Naaman went rushing back to see Elisha and say thank you to him. He offered Elisha presents – beautiful clothes, gold and silver – but Elisha wouldn't accept any of them. That wasn't why he had helped Naaman. So Naaman set out for home, and thought what a lot he had learned during his visit to Israel.

When Naaman got home, everybody celebrated. Jessica was overjoyed to see Naaman looking so healthy, and not scratching himself all the time, and Anna was really pleased to see how happy they both were.

Naaman thanked Anna, and he thanked his servant, too. 'I'll never be too proud to do something simple again,' he said. 'Very often, the simplest ideas are really the best ones.'

Our Story

Show the whole group the designs, and let them have a bit of fun working out how they function, or even what they are. Then show them the everyday versions of them. Be careful to keep the atmosphere light-hearted so the children who did the designs can enjoy the fun and not feel ridiculed. Congratulate them on the ingenuity of their ideas.

Prayers

We're Sad

Loving God,
sometimes we're so proud!
Forgive us for being snobbish,
and show us how you work
in simple ways.

We're Glad

Thank you, God,
for the simple things in life:
for smiles, and hugs,
and for friendship.

Let's Pray for People

Let's pray for busy people;
people whose lives are so complicated
that they don't have time for simple beauty,
or for little joys.
Please help us make space in our own lives,
so that we can show how much those things
     matter.

Songs

He's got the whole world in his hand
Morning has broken
Out to the great wide world we go!
Water of life

Keep It Simple

God's Story

Narrator Naaman lived in the country of Aram, and was a commander in the king's army. Naaman and his army were often sent by the king of Aram to raid Israel and bring back treasure. On one of the raids Naaman brought back a young girl called Anna as a slave for his wife, Jessica.

Anna Now you might have thought that I would hate Naaman and Jessica for that, but I always tried not to. After all, we've all got to live together and hating them would just make me feel even more unhappy. So I tried to be a good servant to them.

- I *dusted their furniture*
- I *cooked their food (stirring action)*
- and I *chopped wood for the fire*

Narrator One day, Anna noticed something very worrying about Naaman, and spoke to Jessica about it.

Anna I hope you won't mind me saying this, my Lady, but the commander doesn't seem very well. That nasty rash is getting worse. I think you should send him to the prophet who lives in Israel, and he'll cure him.

Narrator The king of Aram thought it was certainly worth a try, so he sent Naaman to the king of Israel with a letter saying, 'Please make my army commander better'. The king of Israel thought Naaman's king was trying to pick a quarrel with him. How could he make anyone better? He got really frightened. And then – well, you know how rumours about royal families spread – before long the whole country was talking about it, and wondering if it meant the end of the monarchy. But Naaman should have gone to Elisha.

Elisha	Why do people think only kings and queens have the answers to anything? Send him to me.
Narrator	A bit later, Naaman knocked on Elisha's door.
Elisha	Oh, it's you. Go and take seven dips in the river.
Naaman	Is that it? I didn't come here to be made a fool of.
Narrator	Fortunately, as is often the case, Naaman's servant was actually a lot wiser than he was.
Servant	If he'd asked you to do something difficult you'd have done it, just to show off – so why not do this?
Naaman	I suppose so. Anyway, it's hot and I fancy a swim.
Narrator	So Naaman took off his clothes and jumped in.
Naaman	Ugh! What do they empty into the river around here?
Narrator	But Naaman didn't want to look like a wimp – so he went under seven times, just as he'd been told. Then he got out of the water and started to dry himself.
Naaman	There! Satisfied now?
Servant	Sir! Sir! Your rash has gone!
Naaman	Well, well! So it has. How amazing!
Servant	Very often, the simplest ideas are really the best ones.
Naaman	That's funny – Anna's always saying that, and I've only just realised how true it is. I should listen to my servants more. You know, you're quite a philosopher.
Servant	I've been called some names in my time, but really!

Live Connections

Based on Ezekiel 37:1-14

BEFORE THE DAY

Let the children help gather together a collection of simple musical instruments – tambourines, recorders etc., and recruit some volunteers to demonstrate them. They do not need to perform, but simply blow or hit the instruments to produce a noise; however, if you can do something more ambitious, why not?

• Think about the actions for all the children to join in during the story.

ON THE DAY

Introduction

This morning, we're going to celebrate being alive! But first, let's say our 'Thank you' prayer.

'Thank you' Prayer

Thank you, God, for all you give us,
thank you for the earth and sea;
thank you, God, for special people,
thank you, God, for making me.

God's Story

Hello, there! My name's Ezekiel, but you can call me Zeek if you like. I'm going to tell you about a really amazing dream that I had. Well, I say it was a dream – more of a vision, really, because God taught me something very important through it.

It was at the time when everybody in Israel had given up hope. I don't know why, but for some strange reason the whole world seemed to be against Israel. Every tuppenny-ha'penny dictator within a thousand miles seemed to want to have a go at us. It had got to the stage where a lot of people had left and gone to live elsewhere, and others had been taken away to be slaves. Some of the beautiful towns looked absolutely horrible – all derelict buildings and people crying in the streets. Really depressing it was, I don't mind telling you. Now I'm not a prophet of doom – not really – but I must admit I was beginning to think that the Department of Moans and Groans had got it right. People were going around complaining – even more than your lot do about the weather – and it was really an uphill struggle for a poor prophet trying to talk about hope.

After a while, I got a bit fed up, too. And it was then that God gave me this dream – sorry, vision. I seemed to be in a deep valley. There must have been a terrible battle there, sometime, I thought, because the whole valley was covered in skeletons. Honestly! And they weren't just lying there neatly the way they do in the movies. No, they were scattered all over the place. There were skulls lying next to shin bones, and jawbones next to toe bones – and they were brilliant white. No one had invented biological washing powders then, so I guessed it must have been the sun that had done it. They were bleached and – well, I can't find any other way of saying it – bone dry.

I was wondering how I could get out, fast – before my bones got added to all of those. I tell you everything was so dry that there weren't even any vultures around. They like their food dead – but not *that* dead. Anyway, while I was wondering, I heard this voice. 'Strange,' I thought, 'I wonder who that is. What sort of person would come to a place like this? You'd either have to be mad or be God!'

When I listened carefully, I heard what the voice was saying. 'Hey, you! Human being! Homo Sapiens, or whatever your name is.'

'Who, me?' I asked.

'I don't see anyone else here, do you?' the voice answered.

'Er – what can I do for you?'

'Not a lot,' said the voice. 'It's really what I can do for you. Tell me, do you think that these dry bones can live?'

Now what sort of a question was that? 'God knows!' I said.

'Yes, that's right, I do,' said the voice and I nearly jumped out of my skin – and that would have been particularly uncomfortable in the heat.

'Oh, I'm very sorry,' I said, 'I didn't recognise your voice.'

'No, a lot of people don't,' said God. 'Now

I'm going to show you something really special. All you have to do is say the words I dictate to you.'

Then God told me what to say. I tried to remember it as best I could but it was awfully long.* 'Now listen here, you dry bones,' I said. 'God's going to join you all together again. Now all you toe bones have got to join up with foot bones, and you ankle-bones look snappy and get hooked onto the other side. That's good! Now where are all you shin bones? All right – tibs and fibs if you want to be technical – you've got to join on to the ankle-bones, and pick up a kneecap along the way. Right on! Now, I want thigh bones, and hip bones, and I want lots of itsy bitsy back bones, and you all join together in just the right order. Now, give me some rib bones, some shoulder bones, some rib-ticklin' funny bones and where have those arm bones got to? Now some finger bones and, what've I forgotten? Well, would you believe it – what about some skull bones, then? And if you promise not to chatter you can have your jawbones too.'

Well, that about did it. When all the rattling died down the valley was a lot tidier, but they were still just lying there. 'Come on, now,' I said. 'Let's have some muscles and some tendons, and for goodness' sake put some skin on – you look revolting.' And it all happened! I could hardly believe it! But they were just as dead as when I'd started. Not a breath of life in a single one of them.

'Well, don't just stand there,' said God. 'Talk to the wind – get a bit of breath into them.'

So I called out to the four winds, and d'you know I'd hardly opened my mouth when there was such a whoosh you've never heard before and suddenly all the bodies began to move.

- They *wiggled their fingers*
- they *shook their hands*
- they *turned their heads*

They looked around and started to stand up. There were thousands of living bodies there. I couldn't help thinking that there was still something missing, but that was the end of the vision.

'That's how it's going to be,' God said to me. 'Where you think there's no hope, I'm going to bring new life. People will be happy again, and they'll know that I love them, and they'll all live together and really enjoy life.'

I was just about to say something when God interrupted me.

'By the way,' he said. 'You forgot their clothes. Must I think of everything?'

Our Story

Show the assembly the musical instruments, simply lying on a table top. You could suggest sitting and waiting until the instruments 'come to life' on their own! Let the children demonstrate the instruments simply or, if it's practicable, play a short piece of music together. The point is, of course, that the instruments can only 'come to life' with a bit of help from outside. Just like us!

Prayers

We're Sad

Sometimes, God, we're like dead bones,
just lying around waiting
for someone else to do something!
Please help us to be full of life,
ready to do things for you.

We're Glad

Thank you, God, for life!
Thank you for making this wonderful world
and for giving us something to do in it.
Help us to work with you
to make the whole world more lively.

Let's Pray for People

We pray for people who think there is no hope:
people who are ill, or sad;
people who always seem to see
the worst in everything.
Please, God, teach us all
that however bad things seem
there is always hope.

Songs

Give thanks to the Lord
God's love is deeper
He's got the whole world in his hands
Morning has broken

* If preferred, in place of the paragraph, a group of children could sing the 'Dry bones' song (see page 210)

Live Connections

God's Story

Ezekiel Hello, there! My name's Ezekiel, but you can call me Zeek if you like. I'm going to tell you about a really amazing vision that I had. I was in a deep valley with bones scattered all over the place. I tell you everything was so dry that there weren't even any vultures around. They like their food dead – but not *that* dead. Anyway, while I was wondering, I heard this voice.

God Hey! Zeek!

Ezekiel Strange, I wonder who that is. What sort of person would come to a place like this? You'd either have to be mad or be God!

God Hey, you! Human being! Homo Sapiens, or whatever your name is.

Ezekiel Who, me?

God I don't see anyone else here, do you?

Ezekiel Er – what can I do for you?

God Not a lot. It's really what I can do for you. Tell me, do you think that these dry bones can live?

Ezekiel God knows!

God Yes, that's right, I do.

Ezekiel Oh, I'm very sorry. I didn't recognise your voice.

God No, a lot of people don't. Now I'm going to show you something really special. All you have to do is say the words I dictate to you.

Ezekiel OK. *(Listens)* Yes . . . Mmmm . . . Sorry, I missed that bit. Look, are you sure that's what you want? OK, OK, you're the boss.*

* If preferred, in place of the next paragraph, a group of children could sing the 'Dry bones' song (see page 210)

Ezekiel Now listen here, you dry bones, God's going to join you all together again. Now all you toe bones have got to join up with foot bones, and you ankle-bones look snappy and get hooked onto the other side. That's good! Now where are all you shin bones? All right – tibs and fibs if you want to be technical – you've got to join on to the ankle-bones, and pick up a kneecap along the way. Right on! Now, I want thigh bones, and hip bones, and I want lots of itsy bitsy backbones, and you all join together in just the right order. Now, give me some rib bones, some shoulder bones, some rib-ticklin' funny bones and where have those arm bones got to? Now some finger bones and, what've I forgotten? Well, would you believe it – what about some skull bones, then? And if you promise not to chatter you can have your jawbones too.

Now, what was the next bit again? *(Listens)*

Oh, yes – that's it. Let's have some muscles and some tendons, and for goodness' sake put some skin on – you look revolting.

Well, that's better – but they're not very lively are they?

God Well, don't just stand there! Talk to the wind.

Ezekiel So I called out to the four winds, and d'you know I'd hardly opened my mouth when there was such a whoosh you've never heard before and suddenly all the bodies started to move.

- They *wiggled their fingers*
- they *shook their hands*
- they *turned their heads*

I couldn't help thinking that there was still something missing, but that was the end of the vision.

God That's how it's going to be. Where you think there's no hope, I'm going to bring new life. People will be happy again, and they'll know that I love them, and they'll all live together and really enjoy life. By the way, you forgot their clothes. Must I think of everything?

Ride That Camel! Chase That Star!

Based on Matthew 2:1-12

BEFORE THE DAY

Curiosity is a wonderful thing! Looking carefully at ordinary things, we can see aspects not noticed before. Get the children to look at flowers, leaves and anything else you can think of through magnifying glasses, and to draw what they see.

• Think about the actions for all the children to join in during the story.

ON THE DAY

Introduction

This morning, we're going to hear about some people who were very curious and who saw things that other people didn't notice. That's how they came to go on a very exciting journey. But first we'll say our 'Thank you' prayer.

'Thank you' Prayer

Thank you, God, for all you give us,
thank you for the earth and sea;
thank you, God, for special people,
thank you, God, for making me.

God's Story

Melchior, Caspar and Balthazar were wise men. They met together often to look at the stars and try to work out what they were about. They would sit around late at night (long after well-behaved children were asleep!) discussing whatever new star they had most recently seen.

One evening, Melchior got very excited. 'Look over there!' he shouted. 'There's a big new star.'

'Yes,' said Caspar, 'I wonder what it means.'

So Balthazar got the special books and looked it up. 'Let me see,' he said, ' "Star – extra bright . . ." ' then he got really excited.

'It says here,' he told the others, 'that it means an important king has been born.'

'Right!' said Melchior. 'Let's go and find him.'

Everybody suddenly got very busy. Melchior called his servants, and said, 'Load up the camels. We'll need plenty of food, lots of water, changes of clothes, tents – and don't forget the first aid kit.' So everyone worked hard and, next night, they started off to follow the star – the wise men first and the servants behind with the luggage. How do you think they travelled?

• Would they *ride* on donkey's?
• Would they *drive* in a car?
• Would they *ride* on bicycles?

Of course, they rode on camels, didn't they? Sometimes it got very scary; they could hear wild animals howling, and some of the servants began to get nervous. But eventually, they saw a big city ahead.

'That should be Jerusalem!' said Balthazar. 'That's a capital city. So if we find the palace, we'll find the king.'

Now the king in Jerusalem was the wicked king Herod – and he got worried when he heard the wise men's story. 'A new born king?' he thought. 'I'm the king! There's not room for another one.'

Then one of his courtiers whispered to him, 'That sounds like the king the Bible speaks of – the great leader promised by God. He must be in Bethlehem'

'Well, then,' Herod whispered back, 'we'd better find him and get rid of him. Let's leave it to these people to find him for us.' He turned back to the wise men, and pretended to smile. 'I think the king you're looking for is in Bethlehem,' he said. 'When you've found him, would you tell me where he is, so that I can visit him, as well?'

Off went the wise men, and Herod turned to his courtiers and said, 'Right! When those silly men tell us where this so-called king is, we'll go and get him. King indeed!'

The wise men went to Bethlehem, and when they got there the star showed them exactly where the new king was. So they went in and found Mary and Joseph with Jesus.

'Hello,' said Melchior, 'I hope we're not disturbing you; my name is Melchior, and these are my friends, Caspar and Balthazar. We've come all the way across the desert to find your son.'

'Well,' said Mary, 'this is Jesus. He does seem to be causing a lot of excitement. We've had all kinds of visitors.'

Melchior went over to Jesus. 'We've brought you some presents,' he said. 'Look: gold, for a king.'

'But not just any king,' said Caspar, 'God's very special king. So I've brought some incense.'

'And I've brought you some myrrh,' Balthazar said. 'Being a king is hard, and you will have to suffer.'

Later, the wise men went away to their tents to sleep. 'We mustn't forget,' said Melchior, 'to call on that nice king Herod tomorrow, and tell him where Jesus is.'

But that night Melchior had a strange dream. An angel came to him and said, 'That "nice king Herod" as you call him is bad news. Whatever you do, don't tell him where the new king is, or there'll really be trouble.'

So the next day Melchior told the others, 'We're taking the pretty route home.'

'What about Herod?' said Balthazar.

'Shifty character,' said Melchior. 'Don't trust him a millimetre! I vote we give him a miss.'

'Good idea!' said Caspar. 'Let's go home.'

Our Story

Draw attention to the pictures which the class drew in preparation. See how much more they noticed when they really looked. Curiosity's 'in' and can lead the way to great discoveries!

Prayers

We're Glad

Dear God,
sometimes we have to make an effort:
search for what we want,
think about things, work things out.
That's why you gave us eyes, and brains.
Help us to use them,
and make us thankful that we've got them.

We're Sad

We're sorry about being lazy.
We're sorry about the things we miss,
that you're trying to show us, or tell us.
We're sorry for the times
when we couldn't be bothered to think,
to try to understand
what you were saying.
Forgive us,
make us more curious, more interested.

Let's Pray for People

Loving God,
we pray for people who are sick,
and can't go out,
people who can't walk very well,
people who can't see and hear
the wonderful things in the world.
Show us if there are ways
we can help them,
so that they will know
what a good world this is.

Songs

I'm black, I'm white, I'm short, I'm tall
Morning has broken
Ride that camel! Chase that star! (SS)
Tick tock
When I needed a neighbour

Ride That Camel! Chase That Star!
God's Story

Narrator   Melchior, Caspar and Balthazar were three wise men. They used to meet together often to talk about important things, and to look at the stars. They would sit around, very late at night (long after well-behaved children were asleep!) discussing whatever new star they had most recently seen. One evening, Melchior got very excited.

Melchior   Look over there! There's a great big star that I've never seen before. I wonder what it means.

Balthazar   I'll look it up. Let me see, 'Star – extra bright . . .' Hey, it says here that it means a special king has been born, and the star will lead us to him.

Melchior   Then what are we waiting for? Let's go and follow it.

Narrator   Everybody suddenly got very busy, packing the things they would need, and by the next night, when the star appeared again, they were ready to go.
How do you think they travelled?

- Would they *ride* on donkeys?
- Would they *drive* in a car?
- Would they *ride* on bicycles?

Of course, they would ride on camels, wouldn't they?

Balthazar   Come on everyone, let's get moving! The three of us will ride ahead and the servants follow behind with all the food and water and camping kit – and I hope you've remembered to pack the kettle.

Narrator   They travelled through the desert for many weeks, moving at night when they could see the star, and sleeping in their tents during the day. Eventually, they saw a big city ahead.

Melchior   Where are we?

Caspar	According to my reckoning that should be Jerusalem.
Balthazar	Good, that's a capital city. Let's find the palace.
Narrator	Now this was definitely a bad idea. The king in Jerusalem was the wicked king Herod – and he got a bit worried when he heard what the wise men wanted.
Herod	*(Aside, to audience)* I'm the king! There's not room for another one. I'd better find him and get rid of him.
Narrator	So Herod did a bit of checking up, and then went back to the wise men.
Herod	I think the king you're looking for is in Bethlehem. When you've found him, would you let me know, so that I can go to see him, as well?
Narrator	So off went the wise men, and Herod turned to his courtiers and started making plans.
Herod	Right! When those silly men come back and tell me where this so-called king is, I'll have him killed. King indeed!
Narrator	The wise men went to Bethlehem, and found Mary and Joseph with Jesus. They had some presents for the baby.

- *Gold*, for a king.
- *Frankincense*, for God's special king.
- *Myrrh*, for his suffering.

Then they went to their tents to sleep. And next morning they got ready to leave for home.

Balthazar	We mustn't forget to stop and tell that nice king Herod where Jesus is.
Melchior	I don't think so. I've found out that 'that nice king Herod' as you call him is bad news.
Caspar	I knew it! Shifty character! Don't trust him a millimetre! I vote we give him a miss.
Melchior	Good idea! Let's go home the pretty way.

Trials and Temptations

Based on Matthew 4:1-11

BEFORE THE DAY

Get the children to collect (or draw their own) pictures of sports stars, circus performers, stunt men and women, etc. Then ask them to draw pictures or bring in photographs of people who care for them – parents, grandparents, brothers and sisters, neighbours etc. Pin or stick them on boards for display.

• Think about the actions for all the children to join in during the story.

ON THE DAY

Introduction

This morning, we'll be hearing about how Jesus was tempted to misuse his power. First, we're going to say our 'Thank you' prayer.

'Thank you' Prayer

Thank you, God, for all you give us,
thank you for the earth and sea;
thank you, God, for special people,
thank you, God, for making me.

God's Story

Jesus was sure God had a very special job for him; he'd always believed that, right from being a child, but it wasn't clear exactly what he should do.

'I think I'll get away for a bit and think,' he said to his mother. 'I really need to do a lot of praying, and work things out.'

'How long will you be?' asked Mary.

'Can't say,' said Jesus. 'God always seems to do things at his own speed, so don't wait up for me.'

I hope she didn't – because Jesus was away for well over a month. He found a really quiet place where he knew people didn't often go, and he spent the time praying and thinking, trying to hear what God was asking him to do.

One day, he heard a voice. Jesus knew it wasn't God; it had a cunning, deceitful sort of sound to it. You know the sort of voice – the kind people sometimes use when they're trying to get you to do something wrong. 'I bet you're hungry,' it said. 'Why don't you have something to eat?'

'Because I'm trying to concentrate,' answered Jesus. 'Anyway, there isn't anything.'

'Oh, come on! You know better than that!' said the voice. 'You know you're special to God. You could do anything you liked. So why not make some bread out of these stones? Might I recommend a nice granary wholemeal? What about a tasty fig and honey sandwich?'

'Oh no,' said Jesus, 'I'm not falling for that. Whatever power I have isn't for my benefit. It's got to be used to help others.'

'Oh, don't be so prissy!' said the voice. What's wrong with indulging yourself a little?'

'That's not what I'm here for,' said Jesus. 'Anyway, there are more important things than bread. The Bible says that we don't only live by bread, but by the word of God.'

'Oh, well,' said the voice, 'if you're going to start quoting the Bible . . .' Then it went on. 'Look, if you've got a special mission, you've got to get people to listen to you. How are you going to do that?'

'That,' said Jesus, 'is exactly what I'm trying to work out. So why don't you just run away and play, and let me get on with it?'

'All right, then,' the voice continued, 'since you're good at quoting the Bible, let me quote it to you. Doesn't it say somewhere that God won't let you come to harm? Why don't you go to the temple and jump off the tower? The Bible says that God will send angels to catch you, and stop you hurting yourself. Now that would be a gimmick! You start walking back, and I'll go ahead and drum up the crowds.'

'I'm not here to do stunts,' said Jesus.

'Not stunts,' said the voice, 'miracles.'

'Stunts,' said Jesus. 'Miracles are only done to help people. Stunts are to show off and get attention. And since you want to throw Bible texts around, you probably know that it says we shouldn't try to test God.'

'Oh, that!' said the voice. 'It all depends what you mean by "test", doesn't it? Anyway, you should listen to me. I can be good for you. Why not take a look around?'

Jesus looked around and could hardly believe his eyes!

- He *looked to the left*
- he *looked to the right*
- and he *blinked in amazement!*

Was it a dream, or a vision, or was he imagining it? He seemed to be able to see all the wonderful things in the world: tall buildings and towers, with roofs shaped like onions but brightly coloured; huge triangular buildings that looked like synthetic mountains; wonderful forests and jungles with beautiful wild animals and birds; great mountain ranges covered in snow. It was like being up in a space shuttle with a telescope – except no one had thought of telescopes in those days.

'There!' said the voice. 'I can give it all to you. You could control everything. All you have to do is just do things my way. And while you're about it, you could put in a good word for us devils – we're having a hard time at present. So – do we have a deal?'

'What?' said Jesus. 'All that doesn't belong to you. You didn't make it. I'm sticking with God. He's the one who made all of that, and it belongs to him. So why don't you just go and find a quiet hole to crawl into?'

There was a long silence, and then a very shocked, faltering voice said, 'Are you sure you wouldn't like a sandwich? Call it a free sample. No obligation.'

'No!' said Jesus. 'Go on, push off!'

'Oh, all right,' said the voice, sulkily. 'But I didn't say I wouldn't come back. See you around.'

As Jesus set off for home, he knew things weren't going to be easy. The easy way would have been to do the things the voice had suggested. He'd chosen the harder way. He knew it would be difficult. He also knew that that horrible little voice would be back, but he wasn't too worried about it. After all, he'd turned down its best offer once, and he could do it again.

Our Story

Look at the two groups of pictures. Which, on the face of it, are the most spectacular – the most likely to pull a crowd? Then explain who the 'caring' group of pictures are, and what they do – or let the children themselves explain. So who's important now? Who would the children go to if they had hurt themselves, or were upset? Jesus never indulged in stunts or tricks: he cared.

Prayers

We're Sad

Please forgive us, God,
for worrying about ourselves
when we should be listening to you;
for showing off to get attention;
for trying to find the easy way
instead of the right way.
Please help us to trust you more.

We're Glad

Thank you, God, for always being with us,
even when life seems like a desert.
Thank you for helping us to do what's right,
even when other things seem more tempting.
Thank you, God, for just being you.

Let's Pray for People

We pray for people who have hard decisions
    to make;
politicians, torn between doing what is right
and trying to make themselves more popular;
people in business who want to be fair
to their customers and their workers;
teachers and others who have to be kind
but also have to be strict, sometimes.
Please God, help us all to make good decisions.

Songs

A still small voice
It's me, O Lord
Jesus went away to the desert
Kum ba yah
Out to the great wide world we go!

Trials and Temptations

God's Story

Narrator Jesus was sure God had a very special job for him, but wasn't clear exactly what he should do.

Jesus I think I'll get away somewhere quiet for a bit, Mother.

Mary How long will you be gone?

Jesus You never know with God – don't wait up.

Narrator Jesus stayed away for well over a month. One day, he heard a cunning, deceitful little voice.

Devil I bet you're hungry. Why not have something to eat?

Jesus I'm trying to concentrate. Anyway, there isn't anything.

Devil Oh, come on! You know better than that! Why not make bread out of these stones? Might I recommend a nice fig sandwich?

Jesus That's not what I'm here for. The Bible says that we don't only live by bread, but by the word of God.

Devil Oh, if you're going to quote the Bible . . .Look, you've got to get people's attention. How will you do that?

Jesus That is exactly what I'm trying to work out. So why not just run away and play, and let me get on with it?

Devil Well, since you're good at quoting the Bible, doesn't it say that God won't let you get hurt? Why not jump off the temple tower? Now there's a gimmick!

Jesus I'm not here to do stunts.

Devil (*Persuasively*) Not stunts: miracles!

Jesus Stunts. Miracles are to help people. Stunts are to show off. And Scripture says we shouldn't test God.

Devil Oh, that! It all depends what you mean by 'test', doesn't it? Anyway, you should listen to me. I can be good for you. Why don't you take a look around?

Jesus I don't need to. The answer's not out there; it's in me.

Devil Oh, don't be such a stuffed toga! Live a little! Dream a little!

Narrator Jesus looked around and could hardly believe his eyes!

- He *looked to the left*
- he *looked to the right*
- and he *blinked in amazement*

He could see all the wonderful things in the world: tall buildings, and towers with onion-shaped roofs; huge triangular buildings like synthetic mountains; wonderful jungles with beautiful wild animals and birds; it was like being up in a space shuttle with a telescope – except no one had invented telescopes in those days.

Devil I can give it all to you if you just do things my way. And while you're about it, you could put in a good word for us devils; we're having a hard time at present. Do we have a deal?

Jesus All that isn't yours to give. I'm sticking with God, so why don't you just find a quiet hole to crawl into?

Narrator There was a long silence, and when the voice came again, it sounded different.

Devil *(Weakly)* Are you sure you wouldn't like a sandwich? Call it a free sample. No obligation.

Jesus I've already said no! So go on, push off!

Devil *(Sulkily)* All right, but I'll be back. See you around.

Narrator As Jesus set off for home, he knew he'd chosen the harder way. He also knew that that horrible little voice would be back, but he wasn't too worried about it. After all, he'd turned down its best offer once, and he could do it again.

Jesus Makes Matthew Rich

Based on Matthew 9:9-13

BEFORE THE DAY

Get the children to collect containers and place the 'wrong' things inside them: a hat in a shoebox, for example, or sugar in a coffee jar. You could put a different dust jacket on a book. Just for a surprising twist, you might like to put the right things in one or two of them.

• Think about the actions for all the children to join in during the story.

ON THE DAY

Introduction

Our story this morning is about someone who was changed by meeting Jesus. First, we're going to say our 'Thank you' prayer.

'Thank you' Prayer

Thank you, God, for all you give us,
thank you for the earth and sea;
thank you, God, for special people,
thank you, God, for making me.

God's Story

When the Romans invaded Israel, most of the Israelites were very angry about it, but not everyone. Matthew knew that wherever there are soldiers there are money. One day the local Roman governor sent for him and said, 'How would you like to collect taxes for me?'

'That depends,' Matthew answered. 'What's in it for me?'

'Whatever you like,' answered the governor. 'I don't care how much you cheat these people, just as long as you get the taxes in.'

'I'm not sure,' said Matthew.

'Well, let me help you make up your mind,' said the governor – with a smile that was just a little too nice. 'If you work for me, I'll let you keep your head.'

'Yes, yes, of course, Your Excellency!' Matthew babbled in panic. 'It would be an honour to work for the glorious Roman Empire.'

So, next morning, Matthew was in a new office with a big desk and chair, and with a notice on the outside saying *All Taxes Collected. No credit – No IOUs – No Forged Fivers, Dubious Dollars or Duff Denarii.*

Matthew quickly became very rich, but he found that there was a price to his wealth. When he met his old friend Adam in the street, Adam didn't say hello. 'Hey,' shouted Matthew, 'You blind or something?'

'Not so blind I can't recognise a traitor when I see one!' answered Adam, and kept on walking. When Matthew went home after work he found dreadful words written on his front door: like 'Traitor' and 'Filthy Scum'. He had to have armed guards with him the whole time – he couldn't even pop down the road to buy a pomegranate without three big men to keep him company. He began to wonder whether being so rich was worth it.

One day, he was sitting at his desk having an argument with a taxpayer. 'You're charging too much,' the man was saying.

'Look, Smartie-pants,' said Matthew sarcastically, 'If you had to do this rotten job you'd charge a lot, too.'

'Oh, hearts and flowers!' replied the other man. 'Some people would be glad to have a job at all, with the way things are going. Ever since this lot took over, *decent* people haven't been able to make an honest living.'

Then a new voice joined in. 'You having a spot of bother, Matthew?'

Matthew looked up and saw Jesus standing there. Jesus always said there were more important things than money, and Matthew used to think that was silly, but not any more – and only partly because he hadn't got any friends to say it to. If the truth be told, he was beginning to think the chap had a point. Suddenly, he sat up bolt upright in his chair.

'Tell you what,' he said to his client, 'Why don't we just forget the whole thing?'

What?' said the man, in amazement.

'Go away,' said Matthew. 'Keep your money. I don't know what you see in the lousy stuff anyway! Here you are, everybody.'

- He *handed out money*
- then he started *throwing it around*
- then he *washed his hands*

Matthew turned to Jesus. 'That's it!' he said. 'I've had it with money.'

'Don't blame the money,' said Jesus. 'We all need a bit of that. Your problem is that you're addicted to it – and that's what's wrong. Now if you were with me, you'd never have the chance to get addicted to anything – there's never enough of it around!'

Matthew looked at Jesus, and the friends he had around him, with their creased clothes and untidy hair. 'If you don't mind my saying so,' he said, 'you're not exactly an advert for simple living, are you?'

'Oh, I don't know,' said Jesus. 'No one writes nasty things on my front door, because I haven't got one – and I don't have trouble with my tailor, either. I'll tell you what I have got, though. I've got friends. If I fancy a nice comfortable bed for the night, there's always somewhere I can go. And when it comes to money . . .'

'All right! said Matthew. 'You can start by coming for lunch with me. I've had it with this lousy job!'

When the religious leaders saw where Jesus was going, they were horrified. 'Jesus mixes with the wrong people!' they said.

'Well, if you're as good as you think you are,' Jesus answered, 'you don't need me anyway. Doctors don't do house calls for people who are fit.'

As soon as the meal was over, Matthew told his bodyguard: 'I'm resigning. Tell the governor to find someone else.'

'He'll have your head for that!' grumbled the bodyguard.

'Ah,' said Matthew. 'He'll have to find me first, and as of right now I haven't got an address.'

Our Story

Ask the children to try to guess what's in the containers. You could make it more fun by dividing them into teams and giving them options from which to choose the correct answer. You can make the point that things – and people – cannot always be judged by outward appearances.

Prayers

We're Sad

We're sorry, God,
for times when we hurt people
because we think they're bad and we're good.
Teach us never to judge people,
always to remember that things may be
less simple, or obvious, than we think.

We're Glad

Thank you, God,
for forgiving us when we're not as good
as you would like us to be.
Thank you for those wonderful people
who always seem able to be nice to us
even when we don't deserve it.
Help us to be more like them.

Let's Pray for People

We pray for people who think they are good,
and people who think they are bad;
people who judge others,
and people who don't like themselves.
Help them to know your love,
which makes us all truly rich.

Songs

It's me, O Lord
Jesus can make us truly rich (SS)
Jesus had all kinds of friends
Out to the great wide world we go!

Jesus Makes Matthew Rich

God's Story

Narrator When the Romans invaded Israel, most of the Israelites were very angry about it – but not Matthew. He could make a profit out of anything – including an invasion. One day the Roman governor sent for him.

Governor How would you like to collect taxes for me?'

Matthew That depends. What's in it for me?

Governor Whatever you like. I don't care how much you cheat these people, just as long as you get the taxes in.

Matthew Sounds good, but I'm not sure. Everyone will hate me.

Governor Yes, but if you refuse me I might hate you.

Matthew Yes, yes, of course, Your Excellency! It would be an honour to work for the glorious Roman Empire.

Narrator So, next morning, Matthew was in a new office with a big desk and chair, and with a notice on the outside saying *All Taxes Collected. No credit – No IOUs – No Forged Fivers or Duff Denarii.* Matthew quickly became very rich – but unhappy.

Matthew It's awful! I haven't any friends any more. People call me names, and write things on my front door, and I can't even pop down the road to buy a pomegranate without a bodyguard.

Narrator One day, he was having an argument with a taxpayer.

Taxpayer You're charging too much.

Matthew Look, Smartie-pants, if you had to do this rotten job . . .

Taxpayer Oh, hearts and flowers! Some people would be glad to have a job at all.

Jesus You having a spot of bother, Matthew?

Narrator	Matthew looked up and saw Jesus. He'd always thought Jesus was a useless, woolly minded romantic – saying silly things like there were more important things than money. Suddenly, he sat bolt upright.
Matthew	Tell you what, let's just forget the whole thing. Go away. Keep your money. I don't know what you see in the lousy stuff any way! Nothing but trouble, if you ask me. Here you are, everybody.

  * He *handed out money*
  * then he started *throwing it around*
  * then he *washed his hands*

That's it, Jesus! I've had it with money. Filthy stuff.

Jesus	Don't blame the money – we all need a bit of that. Your problem is that you're addicted to it. Now if you were with me, you'd never have the chance to get addicted to anything – there's never enough of it around!
Matthew	If you don't mind my saying so, your appearance isn't exactly an advert for simple living, is it?
Jesus	Oh, I don't know. No one writes nasty things on my front door, because I haven't got one – and I don't have trouble with my tailor, either. I'll tell you what I have got, though. I've got friends – I'm never short of a place to stay – and when it comes to money . . .
Matthew	All right! You can start by coming for lunch with me.
Narrator	The religious leaders were horrified – and said so.
Pharisee	That Jesus fellow mixes with all the wrong people!
Jesus	Well, if you're as good as you think you are, you don't need me. Doctors don't do house calls for people who are fit. By the way, Matthew, you do realise that if you resign the Governor will have your head for it?
Matthew	He'll have to find me first, and as of right now I haven't got an address.

Don't Be Stingy

Based on Matthew 13:1-9

BEFORE THE DAY

Collect some empty packets from seeds which use different kinds of soil – acid, alkaline, sheltered, sunny, etc. Put the packets onto a board and label each one, e.g: 'I like rich soil'.

• Think about the actions for all the children to join in during the story.

ON THE DAY

Introduction

We're having a bit of a gardening session today! First, we're going to say our 'Thank you' prayer.

'Thank you' Prayer

Thank you, God, for all you give us,
thank you for the earth and sea;
thank you, God, for special people,
thank you, God, for making me.

God's Story

Jesus wanted to show how generous God is with his love. So he told a story a bit like this one:

Sally was a farmer. She grew quite a lot of different crops, and she always had enough to feed her family and plenty to sell so that they could have some money to buy the things they couldn't grow. Everyone knew what a good farmer Sally was; everyone that is except her next door neighbour, Jake.

Jake didn't like waste. He hated seeing anything, no matter how small, not being used as well as possible. Now that's not such a bad thing, up to a point – sensible people don't waste valuable things – but Jake took it to ridiculous extremes. He would lean over the fence, while Sally was working hard in her garden, and say things like, 'You've got to make as much profit as you can, you know,' or, 'You ought to target your resources where they will be most effective.' Sally didn't really understand what all that meant, but she enjoyed her work and it always seemed to provide for her. She liked Jake, as well, even though he was a pain in the posterior most of the time; so she didn't say hurtful things back, but just smiled and nodded – and ignored him!

Sally's crops were doing very well, and one day she said to her husband, Tom, 'I think we should grow our own wheat. It's silly to go and buy flour when we could produce our own.'

So Sally found a nice little plot of land, and got it ready for sowing. Jake looked over the fence. 'Growing some wheat, are we?' he said. 'No money in wheat, these days, the big boys have got all that buttoned up. You'll never grow enough to make it pay. What d'you pay for your seeds? More than you should, I'll bet. You've got to keep your unit costs in mind, you know.'

Sally smiled. After she had got the ground ready she went into the potting shed and got her precious bag of seeds. She went out and started scattering them around. Poor Jake nearly had a heart attack!

- He *leaned on the fence*
- and he *shook his head*
- and he *stroked his beard*

'You can't just go scattering seeds around like that,' he said. 'Target your resources – how often must I tell you! Look, you've gone and spilt some among those thistles. You'd better get them out – they'll never grow there.'

'Thank you,' said Sally, and carried on sowing her seed. Then Jake got really agitated, and said, 'Hey! Mind the path! Nothing will grow there, you know.'

'No, said Sally, calmly, 'I don't suppose it will.'

'Mind the rockery!' roared Jake. 'Really, Sally, I don't know how you expect ever to make a living as a farmer! Just like a woman!'

Sally decided to ignore that. She finished off her work, wished Jake a good afternoon and went inside. Jake just stood there, leaning on the fence, and shaking his head in despair.

Sally looked and saw a flock of birds on the path, eating the seeds she had dropped there. 'Well,' she thought, 'They've got to eat as well. And if they eat the seed on the path, they're leaving the rest alone.'

A few days later, Tom got really excited. 'Your seeds are growing,' he said to Sally. Sure enough, the rockery was sprouting wheat. 'I wouldn't get too excited,' she said to Tom. 'There's not enough soil there, so it won't last.' When the sun got really hot, the wheat was scorched and it died. 'Not to worry,' said Sally, 'I expected that.'

Next time Sally was outside, Jake was leaning on the fence as usual. 'I told you not to do it,' he said. 'It won't grow, you know.' Then he looked over to the thistle patch. 'There's a bit sprouting there,' he said, 'but it won't last. You mark my words.'

He was right. The thistles were very strong weeds, and they'd had a lot of time to get well set in. So they just choked the new wheat shoots, and never gave them a chance.

'See,' said Jake. 'You women should really listen to us men. I don't know why your husband doesn't keep you straight.'

Sally laughed, 'Tom wouldn't know a cauliflower from a buttercup! He's a fisherman!' And she chuckled as she went inside. Tom laughed when she told him, too.

Over the next few months, the plot of land started to change. Little green shoots appeared first, and Sally and Tom started to get excited. Then the shoots grew tall, and very soon they were dense and high enough for rabbits and field mice to hide in them without being seen. Sally and Tom watched as the colour changed gradually, and eventually they had a wonderful plot of land filled with golden wheat waving gently in the wind.

As soon as it was ripe, Sally got Tom to act as labourer for her and they harvested the wheat. Jake looked over the fence and gave them occasional advice. 'Don't miss any,' he said. 'You've got to exploit the potential of your investment to the full.'

When the wheat was gathered in, they weighed it and Sally was overjoyed. 'According to what I've worked out,' she said to Tom, 'those seeds we bought have given us thousands more in return. Some of them must have produced thirty, or sixty or even a hundred times as much!'

'Hmmph!' snorted Jake over the fence. 'If you'd been more careful, you'd have had even more.'

'If I'd followed your advice,' retorted Sally, 'I'd never have sown any seeds at all.'

Our Story

Draw attention to the board. Whatever kind of soil we find, God has provided something that will grow in it. It really is true that God loves *everything* that he has made!

Prayers

We're Sad

Please forgive us, God, for being so careful –
with our money, with our things,
and most of all with our love.
Teach us how much joy we can get
from throwing love around!

We're Glad

Thank you, God!
You don't take advice from 'wise' people;
you scatter love around
as though it's going out of fashion!
Thank you for giving us so much.

Let's Pray for People

Let's pray especially for lonely people.
Some people are lonely because
other people are too 'careful' with their love.
Others are lonely because they themselves
are too selfish, afraid of losing out.
Please, God, help us all to understand
that you never run out of love,
and however much we 'waste'
you will always give us more.

Songs

Out to the great wide world we go!
Sing a song of weather (SS)
Think of a world without any flowers
We can plough and dig the land
When I needed a neighbour

Don't Be Stingy!

God's Story

Narrator   Jesus wanted to show how generous God is with his love. So he told a story a bit like this one:

It's about Sally, who was a very good farmer – but her neighbour, Jake, didn't approve of her. He would lean on the fence while Sally worked, and make comments.

Jake   You've got to make as much profit as you can, you know. You ought to target your resources.

Narrator   One day, Sally decided to start growing her own wheat, to make bread. She started getting the land ready for sowing, while Jake looked over the fence.

Jake   Growing some wheat? No money in it these days; the big boys have got it buttoned up. You'll never make it pay. What d'you pay for your seeds? Too much, I'll bet. You've got to keep unit costs in mind, you know.

Narrator   When Sally sowed her seeds, Jake was shocked.

- He *leaned on the fence*
- and he *shook his head*
- and he *stroked his beard*

Jake   You can't just go scattering seeds around like that! Target your resources – how often must I tell you! Look, you've gone and spilt some among those thistles. Hey! Mind the path! Nothing will grow there.

Sally   No, I don't suppose it will.

Jake   Mind the rockery! Really, Sally, you'll never make a proper living as a farmer! Just like a woman!

Narrator   Sally decided to ignore that. She finished off her work and went inside. Jake just stood there, leaning on the fence, and shaking his head in despair. Sally looked out of the window and saw a flock of birds on the path, eating the seeds she had dropped there.

Sally	Well, they've got to eat as well. And if they eat the seed on the path, they're leaving the rest alone.
Narrator	Very soon, wheat started to sprout – in the rockery.
Sally	I won't get too excited. There's not enough soil there, so it won't last. Still, I expected that.
Narrator	Sure enough, when the sun got really hot, the wheat was scorched and it died.
Jake	I said it wouldn't grow. There's a bit sprouting there, in the thistles, but it won't last. You mark my words.
Narrator	He was right. The thistles were very strong and they just choked the new wheat shoots.
Jake	See? You women should really listen to us men. I don't know why your husband doesn't sort you out.
Sally	What, Tom? Tom wouldn't know a cauliflower from a buttercup! He's a fisherman. Oh, what a joke – Tom will love that one!
Narrator	Over the next few months, little green shoots appeared and grew tall. Very soon they were dense and high enough for rabbits and field mice to hide in them. Sally and Tom watched as the colour changed gradually, and eventually they had a wonderful crop of golden wheat waving gently in the wind. As soon as it was ripe, Sally and Tom harvested the corn, while Jake looked over the fence and gave them advice.
Jake	Don't miss any. Make the most of your investment.
Narrator	When the wheat was gathered in, Sally was overjoyed.
Sally	Some of those seeds must have produced thirty, or sixty or even a hundred times as much!
Jake	If you'd been more careful, you'd have had even more.
Sally	If I'd followed your advice, I'd never have sown any seeds at all.

The Barley and the Bindweed

Based on Matthew 13:24-30

BEFORE THE DAY

Get the children to paint pictures of flowers, shrubs, vegetables, etc., on pieces of paper, and write 'You are a . . .' on each one. When they are dry, fold them and put them all in a container ready for the assembly.

• Think about the actions for all the children to join in during the story.

ON THE DAY
Introduction

We're going to play a kind of gardening game in a little while, but first, we'll say our 'Thank you' prayer.

'Thank you' Prayer

Thank you, God, for all you give us,
thank you for the earth and sea;
thank you, God, for special people,
thank you, God, for making me.

God's Story

Sally and Jake were both farmers, but they farmed in very different ways. Jake was greedy. He always farmed every bit of his land, and never left anything behind when he harvested.

Sally was a lot more relaxed about things. She used to leave a bit of one of her fields wild to encourage butterflies and other beautiful wildlife. Jake thought she was mad.

'You'll never make any money out of butterflies,' he used to say. 'You have to get everything you can out of your land – that's what good farming's about.'

Sally told her workers to vary the crops so that the fields had a change, and to leave one field each year without anything growing in it. 'We've got to take care of the land,' she used to say. 'Then it will take care of us.'

Jake thought this was just a load of sentimental nonsense. 'It's a matter of good stewardship,' he used to say. 'You've got to get all you can from the land.'

'No,' said Sally. 'Good stewardship is about caring for the land – and it'll give you more in the long run.'

'Bah! Humbug!' Exclaimed Jake, and waited for Sally to get really poor. 'When she is, I can buy her fields cheaply,' he thought.

Well, Jake watched and waited, and every harvest he thought he'd see Sally packing it in because it wasn't paying. But what he actually saw was Sally's farm doing better and better.

• She *dug*
• she *hoed*
• and she *watered the crops*

After a little while, Jake's farm started to produce smaller crops. 'I can't understand it,' his foreman said one day. 'The cabbages always used to do well in that field, but they're just not growing now.'

'Well,' said Jake, 'we'll just have to put more seed in to compensate.'

Sally overheard the conversation. 'If you don't mind my saying so,' she said, 'that'll just make it worse. You're taking all the goodness out of the land. Why not give it a rest for a year, and grow something different?'

'I do mind you saying so, actually,' he snapped. 'Mind your own business!'

Jake was really jealous of Sally. 'She doesn't work half as hard as I do,' he complained to his labourer. 'And just look at her crops!'

Well, the years went by and Jake just could not understand what was happening. Sally's farm was thriving, with lovely rich soil producing good crops while Jake's crops got smaller and smaller. Then his soil began to go all powdery and dry, and every time there was a strong wind some of it blew away and landed on Sally's farm.

'That's the problem!' thought Jake. 'She's got better soil than mine. Now if I had her soil I could grow ten times as much as she does, but I can't afford to buy her land from her even if she would sell. If only I could find some way of reducing the value of her farm.' Then he had a terrible idea.

Although he couldn't grow good food crops any more, Jake had plenty of thistles and dandelions, and enormous quantities of bindweed. So he dug up some of them, and put them into his greenhouse where he tended them very carefully.

Jake saved all the seeds the weeds produced, and then late at night, while Sally was fast asleep in bed, he went out and headed for Sally's best fields. And there, among the crops, he scattered the thistle, dandelion and bindweed seeds. Then he sneaked home and waited.

One morning, Sally's foreman came running up and said, 'Quick! Come and look at the fields!' Sally hurried off to see what all the fuss was about, and there, all mixed in among the crops were thousands of nasty looking weeds.

'I can't think what went wrong,' stammered the foreman apologetically.

'Don't worry, it's not your fault,' Sally assured him. 'Someone's been up to mischief, and I think I know who.'

'Well, I'd better get them out,' said the foreman.

'Oh no! Don't do that!' exclaimed Sally. 'You'll probably pull up some good plants as well. No, just let them grow together. My crops are good enough to stand a bit of competition from a few weeds. We can separate them at harvest.'

Sally was quite right: her crop stood up to the weeds very well, and when the harvest time came they had a grand sort out.

Jake's little plan hadn't worked at all. In fact, it was he who went out of business, because he'd destroyed the very land upon which he depended. Then Sally bought his farm at a bargain price and set about correcting the harm that Jake had done.

Our Story

Hand out the different pieces of folded paper to children at random, around the group. Then ask them to open them and say what they've got. If the children really were flowers or vegetables, of course, you probably wouldn't have all those things growing in the same field, but that's the nice thing about being a human being – we can all grow up together, whatever we are!

Prayers

We're Sad

Dear God, we're sorry for our jealousy.
Help us to be truly happy
when other people succeed,
and to be ready to learn from them.

We're Glad

Thank you, God, for talented people.
Thank you for people who succeed
at discovering new things,
at healing people who are sick,
at creating beautiful art.
Thank you for the pleasure they give us.

Let's Pray for People

Some people are unhappy
because they don't feel 'successful'.
But it's not compulsory to be brilliant, is it?
Please God, help them to enjoy being truly
    human,
and to be proud of that.
Teach us to value people for what they are,
not for what they do,
and give us grace to show it.

Songs

All things bright and beautiful
God knows me
Sing a song of weather! (SS)
Thank you, O God, for all our friends (SS)
We can plough and dig the land

The Barley and the Bindweed

God's Story

Narrator	Sally and Jake were both farmers, and they had been friends once, although they farmed in very different ways. Jake was greedy. He grew as much as he possibly could and sold it for the very highest possible price. Every single square inch of Jake's farm was always growing something. Sally used to leave a bit of her land wild to encourage butterflies and other wildlife.
Jake	You'll never make any money out of butterflies.
Sally	We've got to take care of the land, and not ask too much of it. Then it will take care of us.
Jake	Sentimental nonsense! It's a matter of good stewardship. You've got to get all you can from the land.
Sally	No, good stewardship is about caring for the land – and it'll give you more in the long run.
Jake	Bah! Humbug! *(Aside to audience)* when she gets really poor I'll buy her fields at a knockdown price. Then I'll show her how a *real* farmer works the land!
Narrator	Sally worked very hard on her farm.

- She *dug*
- she *hoed*
- and she *watered the crops*

Narrator	Sally's farm did better and better, while Jake's crops got smaller. His foreman was worried.
Foreman 1	I can't understand it. The cabbages always used to do well in that field, but for the last year or two they've definitely been smaller.
Jake	All the crops get smaller every year. Well, we'll just have to put more seed in to compensate.

Narrator   Sally overheard the conversation.

Sally   If you don't mind my saying so, that'll just make it worse. You're taking all the goodness out of the land. Why not give it a rest for a year, and grow something different?

Jake   I do mind you saying so, actually. You go and mind your own business, Mrs Know-it-all!

Narrator   Jake was really jealous of Sally, and started to hatch a very nasty plan. Although he couldn't grow good food crops any more, Jake had plenty of weeds because they will grow anywhere, as any gardener will tell you. So he collected the seeds from them, and one night, while Sally was fast asleep in bed, he scattered the seeds among her crops. Very soon, Sally's foreman came running up to her, very upset.

Foreman 2   Quick! Come and look at the fields!

Narrator   Sally hurried off to see what all the fuss was about, and there, all mixed in among the crops, were thousands of nasty-looking weeds.

Foreman 2   I can't think what went wrong.

Sally   Don't worry, it's not your fault. I think I know who's done this.

Foreman 2   Well, I'd better get them out.

Sally   Oh no! Don't do that! You'll probably pull up some good plants as well. No, just let them grow together. My crops are good enough to stand a bit of competition from a few weeds. When we harvest it, that will be the time to separate them out.

Narrator   Sally was quite right: her crop stood up to the weeds very well, and at harvest time they had a grand sort out. Jake soon went out of business, because he'd destroyed the very land upon which he depended. Then Sally bought his farm at a bargain price and set about correcting the harm that Jake had done.

The Sale of the Century

Based on Matthew 13:45-46

BEFORE THE DAY

Get the children to think about the things that are most important to them. You may need to steer them away from computers and roller skates, perhaps by specifying 'people', 'sounds', 'smells' and so on. Let them write them down, or perhaps paint pictures. Finally, put them in a box and label it 'Class X's Treasure Box' in large letters.

• Think about the actions for all the children to join in during the story.

ON THE DAY

Introduction

In a little while, we shall be thinking about the things that are important to us. First, we're going to say our 'Thank you' prayer.

'Thank you' Prayer

Thank you, God, for all you give us,
thank you for the earth and sea;
thank you, God, for special people,
thank you, God, for making me.

God's Story

Abe was a very wealthy man. He had a big house, with lots of rooms, and each room was full of beautiful furniture. He was never cold at night, because he had lovely warm rugs on his bed, and thick carpets on his floors. At every window hung colourful, heavy curtains which kept out the draughts and looked impressive as well.

Every day, Abe fed on the best food money could buy, and drank excellent wines. He really knew how to enjoy life, and he could afford to do it. His friends used to say that even if the whole world went bankrupt, Abe would be all right. He was incredibly rich.

How had he got rich? Well, Abe was a merchant. That meant that he bought and sold things – but not just any old things. Abe was a pearl trader. He used to make long journeys to visit the pearl fishers. They would spend all day diving in the sea looking for oysters which had pearls in them, and then they would sell the pearls they found to people like Abe who would take them to the markets and sell them to people like you and me. It was a lovely business to be in, and Abe really enjoyed it.

And yet, Abe was not really happy. Even with his fine house, his large stables full of beautiful horses and camels, his wonderful gardens stretching as far as the eye could see – even with all that, he was not really happy. He was sure there was a beautiful pearl out there somewhere, which he had not yet seen. Abe didn't just trade pearls for money – he actually enjoyed pearls for themselves. And he had a lifelong ambition to find his perfect pearl, but he knew that he would probably never be lucky enough to fulfil it.

Then one day, it happened.

He was walking along the beach where the pearl fishers worked when he felt a nudge and heard a voice say, 'Hey, Guv, want to see something really special?'

There was something familiar about the voice, which made Abe turn and look. It was Josh, one of the pearl fishers. 'It's a pearl!' Josh said. 'That pearl you've always been after.'

'Look, Josh, I don't mind a joke,' said Abe, 'but it's been a really hard day, so just drop it will you?'

'No wind-up, Guv – honest!' said Josh. 'Go on – won't hurt to look. What've you got to lose?'

'All right, Josh,' said Abe, wearily, 'but it'd better not be a wind-up. Let's have a look, then.'

Josh looked horrified. 'What, here? D'you want the whole world to know about it? Lord love me, Guv, I couldn't sleep safe in me bed if I thought anyone knew.' With that, Josh led Abe to a deserted corner of the beach, and then, looking furtively around him, drew back some branches from the mouth of a cave. 'No one knows about this, Guv,' he said. 'Get in, quick.'

Once inside, Josh lit a candle and rummaged under a pile of moss. Then, before Abe's amazed eyes, he brought out the most wonderful pearl Abe had ever seen. More than that, it was beyond anything he could ever have imagined. It was perfectly round, with a silky smooth surface, and seemed to absorb the light of the candle. In return, it gave off all the colours of the rainbow. Abe was absolutely entranced by it.

- He *held it up to the light*
- and *polished it on his sleeve*
- then he *held it up to the light* again

And in that moment he knew that this was the chance to fulfil his life's ambition.

As Abe turned to face Josh, he did his best to look casual. 'It's, er, quite a nice one,' he said. 'How much d'you want for it.'

Josh was now full of confidence. He'd known that all he had to do was to get Abe to look at it and it would be sold. 'Come off it, Guvnor,' he said. 'It's not "quite nice" – it's absolutely stupendous. You've never seen anything like it before and I doubt you will again. Now if you want it it's yours but if you don't I can soon find another punter.'

'Oh, no! Don't do that!' gasped Abe. 'How much d'you want for it?'

'Well,' said Josh. 'I'm not a greedy man. All I want is a big house, a stable full of fine horses, and enough money to keep me in luxury the rest of my life. Shall we say a million?'

Abe nearly died of heart failure. That would take everything he'd got. His beautiful house, his stables, his fine clothes and furniture – everything he'd worked for all his life would have to be sold to buy this one pearl.

'I don't know,' he said. 'That's an awful lot of money.'

'It's an awful lot of pearl,' said Josh. 'Still, if you don't want it . . .'

'Hold on – I never said that!' said Abe, hastily. 'All right. I'll get the money.'

Abe sold his house, with all its furniture and equipment, and went to live in a tent. He sold his horses and camels, and all the other things he had. Then he went to the bank and drew out all his money, and eventually he just managed to scrape together the million that Josh wanted. Then he went back to see Josh. 'There you are,' he said. 'You can count it if you like.'

'I will,' said Josh, and when he had he

handed over the pearl to Abe. 'Tell me, Abe,' he said, 'what makes you want this so badly that you've sold everything you worked for just to buy this one pearl?'

'Well,' said Abe. 'Some things are worth much more than money, or comfort. You have to be prepared to give up the less important things if you want to have what's really valuable.'

Our Story

Open the treasure box and take out the contents one by one. Either ask the children to describe their 'treasures' or, if they are a bit timid, explain for them. Then ask the rest of the assembly which they would treasure most.

Prayers

We're Sad

Please forgive us, God,
for clinging to things
which can't make us happy,
and ignoring the things that can.
Help us to treasure love and goodness,
and each other.

We're Glad

Thank you, God, for giving us your love.
Thank you for showing us
just how important we are
by sacrificing everything for us.
Teach us to love and value one another
the way you love and value us.

Let's Pray for People

We pray for people who miss out
on the really wonderful things of life,
because they're trying to cling on
to things that aren't as good.
Please, God, help all people
to share your sense of values.

Songs

Be still and know
God our Father gave us life
God's love is deeper
Out to the great wide world we go!

The Sale of the Century

God's Story

Narrator   Abe was a very wealthy man. He had a big house, and fed on the best food money could buy. He was incredibly rich. How had he got rich? Well, he was a pearl trader. He used to make long journeys to visit the pearl fishers. They would sell him the pearls they found and he would take them to the markets and sell them to people like you and me. It was a lovely business, and Abe enjoyed it – but he wasn't really happy.

Abe   I'm sure there's a really beautiful pearl out there somewhere, and I want it.

Narrator   Then one day, it happened.

Josh   Hey, Guv, want to see a the pearl of your dreams?

Abe   I don't mind a joke, Josh, but it's been a really hard day.

Josh   No wind up Guv, honest! Go on – won't hurt to look.

Abe   All right, but it'd better be good. Let's have a look.

Josh   What, here? D'you want the whole world to know about it? Lord love me, Guv, I couldn't sleep safe in me bed if I thought anyone knew.

Narrator   Josh led Abe to a deserted cove, and furtively drew back some branches from the mouth of a cave.

Josh   No one knows about this, Guv,' he said. 'Get in, quick.'

Narrator   Once inside, Josh lit a candle and rummaged under a pile of moss. Then, before Abe's amazed eyes, he brought out the most wonderful pearl Abe had ever seen. More than that, it was beyond anything he could ever have imagined. It was perfectly round, silky smooth, and seemed to turn the light of the candle into all the colours of the rainbow. Abe was entranced.

- He *held it up to the light*
- and *polished it on his sleeve*
- then he *held it up to the light* again

Abe   It's, er, quite a nice one. How much d'you want for it.

Josh   Come off it, Guv'nor. It's not 'quite nice' – it's absolutely stupendous. You've never seen anything like it before and I doubt you will again. Now if you want it, it's yours, but if you don't I can soon find another punter.

Abe   Oh, no! Don't do that! How much d'you want for it?

Josh   Well, I'm not a greedy man. All I want is a big house, some fine horses, and enough money to keep me in luxury the rest of my life. Shall we say a million?

Narrator   Abe nearly died of heart failure. That would take everything he'd got. His beautiful house, his stables, his fine clothes and furniture – everything he'd worked for all his life would have to be sold to buy this one pearl.

Abe   I don't know – that's an awful lot of money.

Josh   It's an awful lot of pearl. Still, if you don't want it . . .

Abe   Hold on – I never said that! OK, I'll get the money.

Narrator   Abe sold his house, with all its furniture and equipment, and went to live in a tent. He sold his horses and camels, and all the other things he had. Then he went to the bank and drew out all his money, and eventually he just managed to scrape together the million that Josh wanted.

Abe   There you are – a million – just what you asked for.

Josh   Tell me, Guv, how come you've sold everything you worked for just to buy this one pearl?

Abe   Well, some things are worth much more than money, or comfort. You have to be prepared to give up the less important things if you want to have what's really valuable.

Come On, Cough Up!

Based on Matthew 18:21-34

BEFORE THE DAY

What are the children's favourite toys? Ask them to draw pictures of them. (Bringing them into school might be a little risky!)

• Think about the actions for all the children to join in during the story.

ON THE DAY

Introduction

We're going to hear about someone who was very kind, and someone else who was not at all kind! But first we'll say our 'Thank you' prayer.

'Thank you' Prayer

Thank you, God, for all you give us,
thank you for the earth and sea;
thank you, God, for special people,
thank you, God, for making me.

God's Story

Bart was a very rich man, who often helped out people who were poor. One day, he realised that one man – called Joel – owed him a million pounds. He didn't really mind, but he thought he should remind Joel. 'I just wonder whether you realise,' he asked, 'that you owe me a million pounds?'

Joel got very frightened. 'I'm sorry,' he pleaded, 'but one of my children is getting married, and my wife's ill. Please don't ask for it back yet.' Bart felt sorry for Joel.

'Look,' he said, 'why not just forget about it?'

'For how long?' asked Joel.

'Just forget about it,' said Bart kindly. 'Don't worry about paying me back, ever.'

Joel was amazed! 'Thank you ever so much,' he said. 'I'm really grateful to you.' And Joel went off, walking on air! 'I must find some way of showing how grateful I am,'

he thought. 'Perhaps I could buy him a present, if I had some money.'

Just then he saw his neighbour, Nick. Nick owed Joel fifty pounds.

'Er, Nick,' said Joel, 'you know that fifty pounds you owe me – I'm afraid I need it back.'

'I'm sorry,' said Nick, 'but I haven't got it. My father died, and I've got the funeral to pay for. I'll pay you as soon as I can.'

'Give me my money!' shouted Joel grabbing Nick by the throat. 'Come on, cough up!'

Nick was certainly coughing! 'All right,' he spluttered. 'I'll have to borrow it.'

'Just get it,' said Joel roughly. Then he went on his way, thinking, 'Won't Bart be pleased when he gets his present?'

Meanwhile Nick was very worried. He couldn't find anyone to help, until someone said, 'Why don't you ask Bart? He'll lend it to you.' So Nick went off to Bart's house.

'Of course, I'll lend you the money,' said Bart. 'Might I ask what it's for?' Nick told him the whole story, not realising that Bart knew Joel. 'What!' shouted Bart. 'Do you mean he attacked you over a fifty pound debt?' Then he sent for Joel.

Now a few days earlier, Joel would have knocked politely on Bart's door and waited to be invited in. But now, he thought it was different. He breezed in and said, 'Wotcha, Bart!'

'Get out and knock!' Bart bellowed. 'And don't come in until I tell you.' Joel ran outside and closed the door. He was scared stiff!

• His *hands* were *trembling*
• His *teeth* were *chattering*
• His *hair* was *standing on end*

It took him quite a few moments to pluck up the courage to knock.

Inside the room, Bart heard the knock and recited a little rhyme to himself:

'One, two, three, four,
let him sweat a little more.
Five, six, seven, eight,
bet he's getting in a state!'

Then he shouted, 'Come in – I'm waiting!'

Joel went in. 'What's this I hear about you being unkind to Nick?' asked Bart.

'I only asked for what he owes me,' said Joel.

'Asked him? Jolly near throttled him, from what I hear!' Bart corrected him.

'I only did it because I wanted to buy you a present to show my gratitude,' said Joel.

'So you show me you're grateful by bullying my friends, do you?' roared Bart. 'And to think I let you off a million pounds! Well, I want it back by next week.'

'What, all of it?' gulped Joel.

'Every single penny!' said Bart. 'And if you fail I've got a nice damp dungeon waiting for you.'

'I'll get it, I'll get it!' babbled Joel.

'Well don't get it by threatening any more people,' said Bart, 'or it will be worse for you!'

Poor old Joel. If only he'd been as kind to Nick as Bart was to him, he'd never have got into all that trouble, would he?

Our Story

Draw attention to the display. Would the children let others play with their favourite toys? What if they broke them? Emphasise that forgiveness doesn't absolve the other person of responsibility – as Joel found out!

Prayers

We're Glad

Thank you, God,
for being so good to us
even though we don't deserve it.
Thank you for people who are kind,
and who don't ask us
to repay their kindness.
But help us to do it, anyway,
by being kind to other people.

We're Sad

We're not always kind.
Sometimes we're quite cruel,
even though other people are kind to us.
We're sorry, Jesus,
help us to remember
how much you've forgiven us,
and that we should forgive others, too.

Let's Pray for People

Some people are very unhappy
because they can't forgive others.
They bear grudges,
and they keep reminding themselves
of how they've been hurt.
Help them to learn
that by forgiving people
they help make themselves happier, too.

Songs

God knows me
Jesus had all kinds of friends
Out to the great wide world we go!
When I needed a neighbour

Come On, Cough Up!

God's Story

Narrator	Bart was a very rich man, who often helped out people who were poor. One day, he realised that one man – called Joel – owed him a million pounds. He didn't really mind, but he thought he should remind Joel.
Bart	I just wonder whether you realise that you owe me a million pounds?
Joel	I'm sorry, but one of my children is getting married, and my wife's ill. Please don't ask for it back yet.
Bart	Look, why not just forget about it? Don't worry about paying me back, ever.
Joel	Wow! Thank you ever so much. I'm really grateful.
Narrator	Joel went off, walking on air!
Joel	I must find some way of showing how grateful I am. I could buy him a present, if I had some money.
Narrator	Just then Joel saw his neighbour, Nick. Nick owed Joel fifty pounds.
Joel	Er, Nick, you know that fifty pounds you owe me – I'm afraid I need it back.
Nick	I'm sorry, but I haven't got it. My father died, and I've got the funeral to pay for. I'll pay you as soon as I can.
Joel	(Grabbing hold of Nick) Give me my money! Come on, cough up!
Nick	All right, I'll have to borrow it.
Narrator	Nick was really worried, and decided to ask Bart for help.
Bart	Of course I'll lend you the money. Might I ask what it's for?

Narrator Nick told Bart the whole story, not realising that Bart knew Joel!

Bart What! Do you mean he attacked you over fifty pounds?

Narrator Then Bart sent for Joel, who walked into the office without even knocking!

Joel Wotcha, Bart!

Bart *(Shouts)* Get out and knock! And don't come in until I tell you.

Narrator Joel ran outside and closed the door. He was scared stiff!

- His *hands* were *trembling*
- His *teeth* were *chattering*
- His *hair* was *standing on end*

When he knocked, Bart recited a little rhyme to himself:

Bart One, two, three, four, let him sweat a little more.
Five, six, seven, eight, bet he's getting in a state!
(louder) Come in – I'm waiting!

Bart What's this I hear about you being unkind to Nick?

Joel I only asked for what he owes me.

Bart Asked him? Jolly near throttled him, from what I hear!

Joel I only wanted to buy you a 'thank you' present.

Bart What, by bullying my friends? And to think I let you off a million pounds! Well, I want it back by next week. And if you fail I've got a nice damp dungeon waiting for you.

Joel I'll get it, I'll get it!

Narrator Poor old Joel! If only he'd been as kind to Nick as Bart was to him, he'd never have got into all that trouble, would he?

Jesus Gets Angry

Based on Matthew 21:12-14

BEFORE THE DAY

Perhaps it isn't always wrong to be angry. Some people get angry about unfairness; others when they see people being bullied, and so on. Discuss with the children the things that make them angry, and make a list on a flipchart.

• Think about the actions for all the children to join in during the story.

ON THE DAY

Introduction

Soon, we're going to hear a story about some people who made Jesus very angry. First, we're going to say our 'Thank you' prayer.

'Thank you' Prayer

Thank you, God, for all you give us,
thank you for the earth and sea;
thank you, God, for special people,
thank you, God, for making me.

God's Story

Dan, the money changer, was setting up his stall as usual in the temple. Next to him, in his accustomed place, was Joe, a dove merchant. People who went to the temple needed doves because they were used in the worship, so it made sense for them to be sold there. And they needed special money to put in the offering, so Dan was there to change their ordinary money into special temple money. That all seems perfectly reasonable. But you know the old saying, 'It ain't what you do, it's the way that you do it'.

'I like it here,' Dan was saying. 'Better than standing outside in the rain.'

'Yes,' said Joe. 'Mind you, I sometimes get a bit embarrassed about the space we take up. It makes it difficult for less able people to get in when these stalls are all over the place.'

'Who cares about them?' scoffed Dan.

'They've never got any money anyway.'

'That's true,' said Joe, 'and of course there's another advantage to being in here.'

'What's that?' asked Dan.

'Simple,' said Joe. 'It's harder for the customers to compare our prices with the ordinary shops. And once they're in they don't feel like going back out anyway, so we can charge extra.'

'You're right,' said Dan. 'It's a pretty good swindle – and it's legal!'

'Just a minute,' said Joe. 'What's all that noise outside?'

They listened carefully. There seemed to be some kind of celebration going on. They could just about make out words like 'Hosanna!' but they couldn't understand what it was about. Then a man they thought they recognised strode into the temple and stood looking around in a disapproving way.

'Isn't that that Jesus character?' asked Joe. 'He doesn't look very happy – d'you think he's going to cause trouble?'

'What! Him?' laughed Dan. 'He's a wimp! Talks about "love" and "forgiveness" all the time. He actually tells people that if someone hits them they should let them do it again!'

'You're kidding!' exclaimed Joe, and they roared with laughter.

The traders ignored Jesus.

• Dan *counted his money*
• Joe *stroked one of his doves*
• while Jesus *looked from side to side*

Jesus turned to Andrew. 'Look at this!' he said. 'We had to climb over sick and disabled people to get in here, and all the space is taken up by these money-grabbing swindlers!'

Andrew was worried. 'Why don't we just go and find a quiet drink somewhere?' he asked. 'It's been a big day for you.'

Jesus didn't hear him. He was too concerned with what was happening.

'What do you people think you're doing?' he asked, just a little too quietly.

'Just a bit of honest trade, sir,' grinned Joe. 'Can I interest you in a pair of doves? Best prices in town.'

'Best for you, you mean,' said Jesus. And

then, without warning, he grabbed the front of Joe's stall and turned it over. The cages burst open and doves started flying everywhere. Then Jesus went over to Dan.

'Now look here,' Dan said hastily, 'I've got a licence to trade here; I paid a high bribe – I mean tax – for it.' But Jesus wasn't listening. He grabbed Dan's tray of money and threw it on the floor, and then picked up his table and turned it upside down. Well, there was pandemonium. Worshippers were scrabbling around in the dust and fighting over the most valuable coins. Then Jesus went over to the animal pens and drove the animals out of the temple. The owners went after them to try to catch them, and Joe and Dan also decided to cut their losses and leave at the same time. The scramble for money died down as the best coins were snapped up, and by the time the temple police arrived it was all over. Well, nothing changes, does it!

Then a wonderful thing happened. Into the temple came a procession of people who had never been in there before. Some of them had to be carried or helped by others; some were blind and had to have someone to guide them. They came over to where Jesus was standing, still a little out of breath, and the first one, who was leaning on a stick spoke to him.

'Thank you,' she said. 'We haven't been able to get in before. The traders took up so much room, and all the people bustling about doing their shopping meant that only the really fit people could cope with it.'

'I know,' said Jesus, 'and it makes me angry! But while you're here why don't we do something about that leg of yours?'

Jesus took hold of her hand and suddenly her leg grew strong again. Jesus moved on to the next person. Soon the temple was full of people laughing, singing and praising God while they jumped and ran around celebrating their new-found health and strength.

From then on, a lot of new people joined in things at the temple, who had never been able to get in before. They were very happy about it, although Dan and Joe and their friends weren't. But then, you can't please everybody, can you – so why try?

Our Story

Use the flipchart list to talk about what makes the children angry, *and what can be done about it*, e.g., if someone is being bullied, tell a teacher, etc.

Prayers

We're Sad

We say patience is a virtue,
but sometimes that's an excuse.
We're sorry, God, for being too tolerant
when other people are getting hurt.
Help us to know when it's right to be patient,
and when we should protest.

We're Glad

Thank you, loving God,
for people who protest against evil.
Thank you for using them
to make the world a better place for us all.

Let's Pray for People

We pray for people who are kept out,
who aren't able to protest for themselves
and get brushed aside.
Especially we pray for disabled people
in a world run by the able-bodied.
Please God, help us to be angry for them,
and give us the courage to protest.

Songs

I'm black, I'm white, I'm short, I'm tall
Jesus had all kinds of friends
Thank you, O God, for all our friends (SS)
There are people who live in mansions
When I needed a neighbour

Jesus Gets Angry

God's Story

Narrator	Dan, the money changer was setting up his stall as usual in the temple, next to Joe, a dove merchant.
Dan	I like it here, Joe – better than being out in the rain.
Joe	Yes. Mind you, our stalls make it difficult for less able people to get in.
Dan	Who cares about them? They've never got any money.
Joe	That's true, and of course in here it's harder for the customers to compare our prices with the ordinary shops.
Dan	That's right. It's a pretty good swindle – and it's legal!
Joe	Just a minute – what's all that noise outside?
Narrator	They listened carefully. It seemed to be some kind of celebration. They could just about make out words like 'Hosanna!'. Then Jesus strode into the temple with his friends, and stood looking around.
Joe	He doesn't look very happy – he might cause trouble.
Dan	What! Him? He's a wimp! Talks about 'love' and 'forgiveness' all the time. He's a nobody – ignore him.
Narrator	So they did.

- Dan *counted his money*
- Joe *stroked one of his doves*
- while Jesus *looked from side to side*

Jesus	There are sick and disabled people outside who can't get in, and all the space is taken up by these money-grabbing swindlers!
Narrator	Jesus went over to Joe.
Jesus	What do you people think you're doing?

Joe	Just a bit of honest trade, sir. Best prices in town.
Jesus	Best prices for you, you mean.
Narrator	And then, without warning, Jesus grabbed Joe's stall and turned it over. The cages burst open and doves flew everywhere. Then Jesus went over to Dan.
Dan	Now look here, I've got a licence to trade here; I paid a high bribe – I mean tax – for it.
Narrator	Jesus wasn't listening. He threw Dan's tray of money on the floor and overturned his table. After that, he drove the animals and all the traders out of the temple. By the time the temple police arrived it was all over. Well, nothing changes, does it! Then a wonderful thing happened. Into the temple came a procession of people who had never been in there before. Some couldn't walk and had to be helped by friends; others were blind and had to be guided. They came over to where Jesus was standing, still a little out of breath, and Esther, a woman with a stick, spoke to him.
Esther	Thank you. We haven't been able to get in before. The traders took up so much room, and all the people bustling about doing their shopping meant that only the really fit people could cope with it.
Jesus	I know, and it makes me angry! Now you're here, why don't we do something about that leg of yours?
Esther	I've tried every doctor in the area, but it's incurable.
Narrator	Jesus took hold of her hand, and suddenly the woman's leg grew strong again. Jesus moved on to the next person, and soon the temple was full of people laughing, singing and praising God while they jumped and ran around celebrating their new-found health and strength. From then on, a lot of new people joined in things at the temple, who had never been able to get in before. They were very happy about it, although Dan and Joe and their friends weren't. But then, you can't please everybody, can you – so why try?

What Have You Done With My Money?

Based on Matthew 25:14-30

BEFORE THE DAY

What are the children good at? Why not produce a display of their work?

• Think about the actions for all the children to join in during the story.

ON THE DAY

Introduction

We'll be thinking about talents in a few moments. But first we'll say our 'Thank you' prayer.

'Thank you' Prayer

Thank you, God, for all you give us,
thank you for the earth and sea;
thank you, God, for special people,
thank you, God, for making me.

God's Story

David was very rich. One day, when he was going away, he called three of his workers, and said, 'I want you to increase my business while I'm away. Let's start with you, Chloe. What are you good at?'

'I can grow things,' said Chloe.

'Then why not open a garden centre?' said David. 'Here's ten thousand pounds to start you off.' Chloe went away, very excited, and David turned to Barney. 'Well,' he said, 'what would you do with five thousand pounds?'

'I could start a catering business,' Barney replied. 'There's a real need for that.'

'Good!' said David, and Barney went off to get started. Then David turned to the third worker. 'Phil,' he said. 'Here's two thousand pounds. What will you do?' Phil was scared to death. He thought that if he failed David would be really angry. So he just mumbled

something about having to think about it. 'You make sure you do,' said David, and went away.

Chloe bought some land and ordered the things she would need. Phil watched her, and thought, 'She'll have lost all that money before David comes home.'

Barney bought a shop, and had it fitted out as a bakery. Then he ordered cooking pots and dishes.

Phil watched Barney, and thought, 'He'll soon have wasted all that money, and then he'll be in real trouble.'

Phil couldn't think what to do. 'Whatever I do will fail,' he thought, gloomily. Eventually, he decided to dig a hole and bury it all! 'I won't make any profit,' he thought. 'But at least I won't have wasted it, like those other two.'

So that's what he did:

• He *dug* a deep hole
• He *lowered* the money in
• He *patted* the earth over

Meanwhile, signs were appearing all over the town, saying 'Come to Chloe's for Cucumbers.' There were other signs, too, that said 'Barney's Better Caterers', (don't confuse this with the other BBC, though, will you?) Soon, people came from miles away to buy flowers from Chloe, or wedding cakes from Barney. They had to make the High Street one way to prevent camel jams!

When David came back, Chloe and Barney closed up and went to meet him. Phil dug up the money he'd buried. Somehow, he knew he was in trouble!

'Well,' said David. 'What have you done while I've been away?'

Chloe stepped forward. 'The garden centre's done really well,' she said, 'I've got your ten thousand pounds here, and another ten thousand as well.'

'Well done, Chloe,' said David. 'I'll make you a partner in my business. Well, Barney, how's the catering business?'

'Excellent, thank you,' said Barney. 'I've got your five thousand pounds, and I've made another five thousand as well.'

'Wonderful!' exclaimed David. 'I'm making you a partner in my business, too.' Then he turned to Phil and said, 'What did you finally decide on?' Phil was very frightened, and ashamed.

'Er . . . um . . . ah . . . that is, well, you see you're such a good businessman – and I knew you'd be angry if I lost your money, so I decided to play safe.'

'Out with it!' David roared. 'What have you done with my money?'

'N-n-nothing, sir,' stammered Phil. 'I kept it safe for you. Here it is.'

'Is that all you've done?' asked David. 'At the very least you could have put it in the bank and got some interest. You know I wouldn't have minded if you'd tried, and failed. But not even to try at all – there's no excuse for that.' Then he turned to Chloe. 'Could you use another couple of thousand?' he asked.

'You bet,' said Chloe. 'I could open a refreshment room.'

'Yes,' said Barney, 'and I could do the catering.'

So everyone was happy – except poor old Phil, that is. If only he'd realised that there's no shame in failing – only in not even trying!

Our Story

Talk about the things the children have achieved, and about the work and commitment which it involved. Do they sometimes feel afraid of failure? Phil wasn't criticised for failing, but for not trying! In any case, is not the greatest talent of all the ability to make others happy?

Prayers

We're Glad

Thank you, God,
for trusting us.
We can all do something
to make the world a better place.
Help us to trust you,
and to use whatever you've given us
to make other people happy.

We're Sad

There are lots of things we can do
to help other people:
We can smile,
we can listen,
we can cheer them up if they're sad,
all sorts of things.
But sometimes we don't do them,
because we're afraid of getting things wrong.
But even if we did,
at least they'd know we'd tried!
We're sorry, Jesus,
help us to trust you more.

Let's Pray for People

Some people are always nervous,
afraid of getting things wrong.
So they never really enjoy life,
they miss so much!
We pray for them, Jesus,
give them confidence,
and help us to show them
how important they are to us.

Songs

All that I am
Out to the great wide world we go!
We can plough and dig the land
Who put the colours in the rainbow?

What Have You Done With My Money?

God's Story

Narrator	David was very rich. One day, when he was going away, he called three of his workers to a meeting.
David	I want you to increase my business while I'm away. Let's start with you, Chloe. What are you good at?
Chloe	I can grow things.
David	Then why not open a garden centre? Here's ten thousand pounds to start you off.
Narrator	Chloe went away, and David turned to Barney.
David	What would you do with five thousand pounds?
Barney	I could start a catering business.
David	Good!
Narrator	Barney left, and David turned to the third worker.
David	Phil, here's two thousand pounds. What will you do?
Narrator	Phil was scared to death.
Phil	Er . . . I'll have to think about it.
David	You make sure you do. Well, good-bye everybody.
Narrator	Chloe bought some land and Barney bought a shop. Phil watched thinking that they were going to waste all David's money. But he couldn't think what to do with his.
Phil	Whatever I do will fail and I'll be in trouble. I know – I'll bury the money safely in the ground.

Narrator   So that's what he did:

- He *dug* a deep hole
- He *lowered* the money in
- He *patted* the earth over

Meanwhile, signs were appearing all over the town, saying 'Come to Chloe's for Cucumbers' and 'Barney's Better Caterers'. (Don't confuse this with the other BBC, though, will you?) Business boomed and they had to make the High Street one way to prevent camel jams! Eventually David came back.

David   Well, how have you done while I've been away?

Chloe   Really well. I've made ten thousand pounds profit.

David   Well done, Chloe! I'll make you a partner in my business. Well, Barney.

Barney   I've made another five thousand pounds profit.

David   Wonderful! I'm making you a partner in my business, too. Now, Phil, what about you?

Phil   Er . . . um . . . ah . . . that is, well, you see . . .

David   Out with it! What have you done with my money?

Phil   N-n-nothing, sir. I kept it safe for you. Here it is.

David   Is that all you've done? I wouldn't have minded if you'd tried and failed. But not even to try at all – there's no excuse for that. Chloe, could you use another couple of thousand?

Chloe   You bet! I could open a refreshment room.

Barney   Yes, and I could do the catering.

Narrator   Poor old Phil! If only he'd realised that there's no shame in failing – only in not even trying!

Nancy's Nightmare

Based on Matthew 25:31-end

BEFORE THE DAY

Discuss with the children ways in which they can respond to people's needs: carrying shopping, visiting a lonely neighbour, sending a card, giving to charity, etc. Let them use their imaginations and draw pictures of these examples, which can then be fixed to a board ready for the assembly, with the heading 'You Did It For Me' over the top.

Important note:

This version has been carefully adapted to avoid encouraging children to open the door to strangers. Teachers may wish to reinforce the point that this story is about a grown up, and children can live it out by being kind to people they *know*.

• Think about the actions for all the children to join in during the story.

ON THE DAY

Introduction

In a little while, we'll be thinking about ways we can show that we love God by being kind to people. First, though, we're going to say our 'Thank you' prayer.

'Thank you' Prayer

Thank you, God, for all you give us,
thank you for the earth and sea;
thank you, God, for special people,
thank you, God, for making me.

God's Story

It was just a night like any other when Nancy went to bed, but what she didn't know was that everything was going to change.

The first inkling of that came when she found herself in a strange place without knowing how she'd got there. Gradually it began to dawn on her. 'I've died,' she thought. 'So this must be heaven.' Nancy had always known she'd go to heaven, because she knew what a good person she was. She always went to church, never used a naughty word, and always kept her home beautifully clean and saved her money carefully. So you can see why Nancy was very confident that she'd go to heaven. And here she was! Then she heard a voice. 'Hi, Nance! What you doing here?'

Nancy was horrified; it was Sheila, her neighbour. Now Sheila hadn't been near a church in forty years, except to get married – and the less said about that the better! Apart from that, she used to use words Nancy wouldn't dream of saying, and her house was always untidy. Well it would be: she was never there to clean it – always gallivanting off to cook at the night shelter, or visit people in prison. Nancy didn't hold with that. 'People shouldn't get themselves in trouble in the first place,' was how she saw it. Well, Sheila wouldn't get into heaven!

Before long, they found themselves standing in front of God's throne. Nancy put on her best smile, and waited for a big welcome. God spoke to Sheila first. 'Welcome!' he said. 'Come in. After all, when I was hungry you gave me food, and when I was thirsty you gave me a drink. Then when I was homeless you found me somewhere to live – and d'you remember when I turned up without any clothes and you gave me some?' Nancy was horrified. God actually seemed to think *that* idea was amusing! 'Oh, yes,' he said, 'and of course when I was sick you came to see me – and even when I was in prison.'

Sheila's face was a picture. 'Me?' she said. 'I never even knew you existed. When could I possibly have done all those things for you?'

'You did them for other people,' said God. 'And whatever you did for them, you did for me.' Then a big door opened and an angel came and took Sheila through. Nancy couldn't see much but she could hear some amazing singing and it sounded as if a party was going on. How strange – having *that* kind of music in heaven – and parties!

Then God turned to Nancy. 'I hope you don't think you're coming in here,' he said.

'What?' she gasped. 'I've been at church

every Sunday since I can remember, I've always been clean living and responsible – not like some people!'

'But where were you when I needed you?' asked God. 'Where were you when I was hungry, or thirsty? Why wouldn't you help me when I was homeless – instead of just shouting names at me? And what about that time when I was naked?'

Nancy didn't know what to say. The whole idea of God going around without any clothes on was beyond her! Then God went on, 'And the number of times I've been in hospital, or in prison, and I might as well not have existed for all the notice you took.'

Poor Nancy! 'I – I don't remember any of this,' she stammered. 'I've never seen you before – certainly not in *that* condition!'

'No,' said God, 'but you've seen my people like that, which is just the same, and you've done nothing.'

Nancy started to argue, but God stopped her. 'No arguments!' he said. 'No appeal – no strings you can pull.' And he was gone. Everything was dark and cold. Then Nancy could feel herself falling, and she closed her eyes tightly until she landed with a bump. 'This must be it,' she thought. Slowly she opened her eyes. Everything was dark, and there were strange shapes and grotesque shadows. Ugh! Then she heard a click and a voice said, 'This is the early morning news from the BBC.' It was Nancy's radio alarm clock! It had all been a horrible nightmare – so horrible that poor Nancy had fallen out of bed!

What a relief! Nancy got up and made herself a cup of tea. She didn't think she was half such a nice person as she had the night before. 'Perhaps there are more important things than being respectable,' she thought. She got dressed in some very practical clothes – the 'old' ones she wore for cleaning the house, which anybody else would have thought were lovely! 'Let me see,' she thought. 'Hungry, thirsty, strangers . . .' and then she swallowed very hard, '*Naked* . . . sick, in prison . . . Where on earth do I start! I need some advice.'

- Nancy *looked in the phone book*
- she *picked up the telephone*
- and she *dialled the number*

'Hello, Sheila – it's Nancy. Could I possibly come round to see you sometime?'

And quite a lot of people lived happily ever after.

Our Story

Draw attention to the display and explain – or let the children explain – what the different pictures represent. What other ideas do the wider group have?

Prayers

We're Sad

Please forgive us, God,
when we're too concerned with being good
to notice what other people need.
Forgive us for being unkind to people
just because they are poor, or merely different.
Help us to recognise you in other people.

We're Glad

Thank you, God, for not just staying in heaven
but living among us in this world.
Thank you for showing yourself to us
in the people we meet,
and in ways we never expect.
Thank you, God, for being a God of surprises.

Let's Pray for People

We pray for people who get pushed aside,
because they are poor, or sick,
or because other people don't approve of them.
And we pray for people like Nancy,
who miss out on the real joys of life.
Please God, help them all
to find you in one another.

Songs

It's me, O Lord
Make me a channel of your peace
Out to the great wide world we go!
Thank you, O God, for all our friends (SS)
When I needed a neighbour

Nancy's Nightmare

God's Story

Narrator   It was an ordinary night when Nancy went to bed, but next thing she knew she was in a very strange place.

Nancy   I've died. That's what it is. So this must be heaven.

Narrator   Nancy had always known she was a good person. She always went to church, never used a naughty word, always kept her home clean and saved her money. So she was not surprised to find herself in heaven.

Sheila   Hi, Nance! What're you doing here?

Narrator   Nancy was horrified; it was Sheila, her neighbour, who hadn't been near a church in forty years – and her house was always untidy. Well it would be: she was never there to clean it – always off helping at the night shelter, or prison visiting. Well, *she* wouldn't be getting into heaven! Nancy put on her best smile, and waited for a big welcome. God spoke to Sheila first.

God   Welcome! Thank you for feeding me when I was hungry and thirsty – and for helping me when I was homeless – and d'you remember when I hadn't any clothes and you gave me some? Oh, yes, and of course when I was sick you came to see me – and even when I was in prison.

Sheila   Me? I never did those things for you!

God   You did them for other people – people who seemed unimportant. And that means you did them for me.

Narrator   A door opened and an angel took Sheila through. It sounded as if a party was going on through there. Fancy having *that* kind of music in heaven!

God   Well, Nancy, I hope you don't think you're coming in.

Nancy   What? I've been at church every Sunday! I've always been clean and responsible – not like some people!

God	Maybe, but where were you when I was hungry, or thirsty? Why wouldn't you answer the door when I was a stranger – instead of calling the police and shouting at me? And what about that time when I was naked?
Narrator	Nancy didn't know what to say. The whole idea of God going around without any clothes on was beyond her! Nice people didn't do that kind of thing!
God	And whenever I've been in hospital, or in prison, I might as well not have existed for all you cared.
Nancy	I – I don't remember any of this. I've never seen you anywhere before – and certainly not in *that* condition!
God	No, but you've seen my people like that, which is just the same, and you've done nothing. No arguments, now! There are no strings you can pull here.
Narrator	Suddenly, he was gone. Everything was dark and cold. Nancy could feel herself falling, and landed with a bump. Slowly she opened her eyes. She could see grotesque shadows. Ugh! Then she heard a click.
Announcer	This is the early morning news from the BBC.
Narrator	It had all been a horrible nightmare – and poor Nancy had fallen out of bed! What a relief! Nancy got up and made a cup of tea, and began to think about herself. She didn't seem half such a nice person any more.
Nancy	Perhaps there are more important things than being respectable, and I'm going to start doing them. Let me see: hungry, thirsty, strangers, naked, sick, in prison . . . Where on earth do I start! I need some advice.
Narrator	• Nancy *looked in the phone book* • she *picked up the telephone* • and she *dialled the number*
Nancy	Hello, Sheila. Could I come to see you sometime?
Narrator	And quite a lot of people lived happily ever after.

The Voice in the Wilderness

Based on Mark 1:1-11

BEFORE THE DAY

You can have some fun with this one! Make up a few large pieces of paper – as tall as one of the children. Cut a hole in each one to pass over the child's head, and on the front draw different types of clothes to represent very different 'images'.

• Think about the actions for all the children to join in during the story.

ON THE DAY

Introduction

We're going to have a fashion show in a few minutes, but first, we'll say our 'Thank you' prayer.

'Thank you' Prayer

Thank you, God, for all you give us,
thank you for the earth and sea;
thank you, God, for special people,
thank you, God, for making me.

God's Story

There was once a priest called Zechariah, who was married to Elizabeth. They had a son, John, who they thought was a real blessing from God – but there were times when they could find other names for him! John never combed his hair and he always went around in old, scruffy clothes.

One day, Elizabeth shouted at John, 'I'm fed up with you looking as though you don't belong to anybody!'

'There are more important things than looking good, Mother,' answered John – and found his pocket money stopped for a week for being cheeky. 'There are more important things than money, as well,' he said, and got sent to bed without his supper.

'What will the neighbours say?' moaned Elizabeth.

'Never mind the neighbours!' answered Zechariah. 'What will the *congregation* say?'

When John grew up, he didn't get any better. He seemed to be developing some very strange ideas. Worse still, he'd got some friends who thought the same. Then John started preaching. 'Repent your sins!' he shouted. 'Prepare to meet your God!'

The trouble was, lots of people seemed to believe John, and he spent days at a time at the river Jordan baptising people. One day, some of Zechariah's friends who were also priests, offered to help. 'We'll talk to him,' they said. 'He'll listen to us.' So they put on their best robes and went to see John.

When he saw them coming, John pointed at them and shouted at the top of his voice, 'Ooh, you wicked people! You snakes! Don't come to me for easy forgiveness! You just wait until you see what God is going to do to you. You think you're so special, but you're not. God could make better priests than you out of stones!'

One of the priests, whose name was Levi, went up to John. 'Just who do you think you are? Elijah or somebody?' he asked. 'Perhaps you think you're a great prophet come back to life.'

'All I am,' said John, 'is a voice – a voice in the wilderness warning you of someone greater who is following me. Someone so great that I'm not good enough even to help him take off his shoes.'

Levi didn't get the chance to answer, because John was suddenly surrounded by people wanting to know what to do to stop God being angry with them. 'Share everything you have,' he said, 'and treat poor people fairly.'

'What about me?' asked Matthew, the tax collector.

'Charge people a fair tax,' said John, 'and don't fiddle the books.' Everybody laughed at that, because they hated tax collectors.

'What about us?' said some soldiers.

'Don't abuse your power,' John answered, 'and be satisfied with your pay.'

'And what about me?' asked a quiet voice. 'Will you baptise me?'

John stopped and stared in amazement. It was Jesus, the local carpenter. 'I can't baptise you,' John protested. 'You're good – it's you who should baptise me.'

Levi and his friends were horrified! How could John call this common carpenter good, after all he'd said about them? But while they were watching, Jesus went into the water with John to be baptised.

- When he came out, he *wiped his eyes*
- he *brushed back his hair*
- and *dried himself on a towel*

Then an amazing thing happened. It looked as though a dove was hovering over Jesus – but everyone knows that doves can't hover. That was the first strange thing, but it got stranger. There was a voice – a rather strange kind of voice, not quite like anything the people had heard before. Was it a man? Was it a woman? Was it a child? It wasn't shouting, and yet it could be clearly heard.

'This is my son, whom I love very much,' said the voice. So of course Levi thought it must be Joseph, but he couldn't see him anywhere. When Levi looked back, he was surprised because the dove had gone and everything seemed normal. Jesus was drying himself off on a towel, and John was talking to him.

Levi was puzzled. Had he imagined it all? He'd have liked to think that, but his friends seemed to have seen it as well. 'It must have been real,' said one of them. 'We heard it with out own ears.'

'Oh, that doesn't mean anything,' said Levi, 'I'm sure there's a natural explanation. After all, we're educated men, and we know better than to trust our experience.'

Even so, Levi couldn't help being a little worried as he and his friends went away to see Zechariah and Elizabeth.

'Well,' said Zechariah, 'what happened? Did he listen to you?'

'Had he combed his hair recently?' asked Elizabeth.

'I'm afraid it's bad news,' said Levi. 'He's obviously not going to listen to us, and he's got some really strange friends. I don't think we've heard the last of them by a long way.'

Our Story

Ask the model to stand at the front and 'dress' him or her in the various outfits, asking the children questions about the different impressions they create. You might ask whether they would trust the person, believe what they said etc., on the basis of the different clothes, and then make the point that the person wearing them is what matters. When a similar device was used in assembly, the staff were rightly horrified to hear a number of children say they would accept a lift in a car from someone dressed as a priest, even if they did not know him. The speaker carefully pointed out that clothes alone are not a reliable guide.

Prayers

We're Sad

Sometimes we make fun of people
or refuse to take them seriously,
just because they are different.
Please God, forgive us if we've been hurtful,
or if we've missed something important
that you were trying to tell us.

We're Glad

It's good that we're not all the same;
what a dull world it would be!
Thank you, God, for people
who challenge us, and make us think.
Thank you for speaking to us
even when we're too proud to listen!

Let's Pray for People

Please God, help us to listen to you
when you speak through people
who seem to us to be strange.
Help both us and them
to realise how important they are.

Songs

He's got the whole world in his hand
I'm black, I'm white, I'm short, I'm tall
It's me, O Lord
Jesus had all kinds of friends
Out to the great wide world we go!
Thank you, O God, for all our friends (SS)
Water of life
When I needed a neighbour

The Voice in the Wilderness

God's Story

Narrator	There was once a priest called Zechariah, who was married to Elizabeth. They had a son, John, who was turning out to be a real embarrassment to them.
Elizabeth	I'm fed up with you looking scruffy. Tidy yourself up!
John	There are more important things than looks, Mother.
Zechariah	Right! No pocket money for a week, for being cheeky.
John	There are more important things than money, as well.
Elizabeth	That does it! Off to bed with you – and no supper! What will the neighbours say?
Zechariah	What will the *congregation* say?
Narrator	As John grew up, he didn't get any better. He picked up some very strange ideas, and when he preached his father cringed in embarrassment.
John	Repent your sins! Prepare to meet your God!
Narrator	The trouble was, lots of people seemed to believe John, and he spent days at a time at the river Jordan baptising people. One day, some of Zechariah's friends, who were also priests, offered to help.
Levi	We'll talk to him. He'll listen to us.
Zechariah	Thank you, Levi. That's good of you.
Narrator	So they put on their best robes and went to see John.
John	Ooh, you snakes! You think you're so special, but God could make better priests out of stones!
Levi	Just who do you think you are? Elijah or somebody? I bet you think you're a great prophet come back to life.

John All I am is a voice in the wilderness warning you of someone greater who is on his way. I'm not good enough even to help him take off his shoes.

Narrator Levi didn't get the chance to answer, because John was suddenly surrounded by people wanting to know what to do to be better people.

John Share everything, and treat poor people fairly. You tax collectors should charge people a fair tax, and don't cheat. And soldiers, don't abuse your power.

Jesus And what about me? Will you baptise me?

John *(Amazed)* I can't baptise you, Jesus – you're good – it's you who should baptise me.

Narrator Levi and his friends were horrified! How could John call this common carpenter good, after all he'd said about them? But while they were watching, Jesus went into the water with John to be baptised.

- When he came out, he *wiped his eyes*
- he *brushed his hair*
- and *dried himself on a towel*

Then an amazing thing happened. A dove seemed to be hovering over Jesus – but everyone knows that doves can't hover. Then there was a voice – not quite like anything they had heard before. Was it a man? Was it a woman? Was it a child? It was very mysterious.

God This is my son, whom I love very much.

Narrator Levi couldn't help being puzzled and a little worried as he and his friends went away to see John's parents.

Zechariah Well, what happened? Did he listen to you?

Elizabeth Had he combed his hair recently?

Levi I'm afraid it's bad news. He's obviously not going to listen to us, and he's got some really strange friends. I don't think we've heard the last of them by a long way.

Wake Up, Little Girl

Based on Mark 5:22-43

BEFORE THE DAY

Think about having fun! What kind of things do the children enjoy doing? Perhaps they can draw some pictures, or maybe they have some photographs of themselves at fairgrounds or theme parks.

• Think about the actions for all the children to join in during the story.

ON THE DAY

Introduction

We're going to hear shortly about a little girl who really enjoyed life. But first we'll say our 'Thank you' prayer.

'Thank you' Prayer

Thank you, God, for all you give us,
thank you for the earth and sea;
thank you, God, for special people,
thank you, God, for making me.

God's Story

Jairus was a very important man in the synagogue, but he wasn't bossy. He was always kind to everybody, and so he had lots of friends in the town.

Jairus was married to Susie, and they had a daughter called Hannah aged about twelve. Just like other children, Hannah loved to play and explore with her friends. If there was a tree in sight Hannah would climb it, and if not she'd find something else. She was very energetic. She was also very caring. She would never hurt anyone, and was most upset if anyone was unhappy. Hannah had lots of friends as well.

One day Hannah didn't seem very well. She just sat indoors, and when her friends asked her out, she said, 'Not today, thank you; I think I'll just have a quiet day at home.'

'You never have quiet days at home,' said Susie. 'Are you ill?'

'I'm all right!' snapped Hannah. 'Why can't you leave me alone?' And what do you think she did next?

- She *clenched her fists*
- She *screwed up her face*
- She *waved her fists in the air*

And she stamped off to her room, leaving Susie standing with her mouth open in amazement.

When Jairus came in, Susie said, 'I'm terribly worried about Hannah. She's been really unwell all day. And this afternoon she actually shouted at me.'

'You're joking!' said Jairus. 'Hannah never shouts at anybody.'

'I'm *not* joking,' replied Susie. 'Hannah shouted at me, stamped her foot, and went off to her room, and she hasn't come out since.'

Jairus knocked on the door of Hannah's room and went in. Straight away, he knew she was ill. So Susie hurried out to the doctor's surgery and soon came back with the doctor. He went into Hannah's room. After a few moments, he came out. 'I'm afraid Hannah's very ill,' the doctor explained, 'and there's nothing I can do. What she needs is a miracle.'

After the doctor had left, Jairus and Susie sat beside Hannah's bed, and racked their brains trying to think of anyone else who could help them. 'Of course!' Susie said. 'We know someone who can work miracles.'

'Yes,' said Jairus, 'Jesus works miracles. But some people at the synagogue have been very unkind to him.'

'Jesus is too good a person to say 'no' just because of that,' said Susie. So Jairus went to look for him.

Jairus hunted everywhere, until he found Jesus. 'Please help me,' he gasped. 'My daughter's very ill.'

Jesus smiled at him. 'You'd better show me,' he said, 'and don't worry – she'll be all right.'

But then one of Jairus's neighbours arrived. 'I'm terribly sorry, Jairus,' she said, 'but it's too late. Don't bother Jesus now – I'll take you home.'

'What do you mean, "Too late"?' asked Jesus. 'With God, it's *never* too late! Don't worry Jairus, I said she'd be all right, and I don't break my promises.'

When they got to the house, it was full of people crying because Hannah was dead. Jesus asked them to leave. 'I don't know what he thinks he can do,' someone mumbled. 'I know a dead person when I see one.' But they went. Jesus went over to Hannah's bed, and took her hand.

'Get up, little girl,' he said. And to the great amazement and joy of Susie and Jairus, Hannah's eyes opened.

'Hello,' she smiled, 'who are you?'

'My name's Jesus,' answered Jesus. 'What's yours?'

'Hannah,' she replied, 'and it's nice to meet you.'

Jairus and Susie rushed over to hug Hannah, who liked that very much, but wasn't really sure what was going on. 'Are you really all right?' asked Susie.

'Yes, Mother, of course I am,' answered Hannah, kindly. 'What on earth's the matter?'

'We can't thank you enough, Jesus!' Susie said.

'It was my pleasure,' said Jesus, 'but you'd better give her something to eat.'

Hannah looked very surprised. 'Eat?' she said. 'No time for that! It's a beautiful day – can't I go out to play?'

Our Story

Jesus understood Hannah – because he loves to enjoy life, as well! Draw attention to the display, and talk about how good God wants life to be for everybody.

Prayers

We're Glad

Thank you, Jesus,
for wanting us to be happy.
It's good to be alive,
especially when people love us
and care about us.
Help us to love life even more!

We're Sad

Forgive us please, Jesus,
for the times we've hurt people.
Sometimes, we've spoiled things,
made life hard for them,
because we've been selfish.
Whenever someone needs you,
you want to help them.
Help us to do the same.

Let's Pray for People

Let's pray for people who don't enjoy life.
Some people are lonely,
or perhaps they're ill.
Maybe they knew someone who has died.
Even when they're sad,
help them to know that life's worth living,
and help us to show them
that you care.

Songs

God knows me
He's got the whole world in his hand
If I were a butterfly
I'm gonna click
Kum ba yah
Morning has broken
Out to the great wide world we go

Wake Up, Little Girl
God's Story

Narrator   Jairus was a very important man in the synagogue. He was married to Susie, and they had a lovely daughter called Hannah aged about twelve. One day, Hannah didn't seem very well.

Hannah   I was going out to play, but I think I'll just have a quiet day at home.

Susie   You never have quiet days at home. Are you ill?

Hannah   *(Angrily)* I'm all right! Why can't you leave me alone?

Narrator   And what do you think she did then?

- She *clenched her fists*
- She *screwed up her face*
- She *waved her fists in the air*

And then she stamped off to her room, leaving Susie standing with her mouth open in amazement. A bit later, Jairus came home.

Susie   I'm terribly worried about Hannah. She's been really unwell all day. And this afternoon, she actually shouted at me.

Jairus   You're joking! Hannah never shouts at anybody.

Susie   I'm *not* joking. Hannah shouted at me, stamped her foot, and went off her room, and she hasn't come out since.

Narrator   Jairus knocked on the door of Hannah's room and went in. Straight away, he knew she was ill. So Susie hurried out and came back with the doctor, who hurried in to see Hannah.

Doctor   I'm afraid Hannah's very ill, and there's nothing I can do. What she needs is a miracle.

Susie	Of course! We know someone who can work miracles.
Jairus	Yes, Jesus does. But some people at the synagogue have been very unkind to him.
Susie	Jesus is too good a person to say 'no' just because of that.
Narrator	Jairus hunted everywhere, until he found Jesus. But just as he was explaining about Hannah, one of his neighbours arrived and said it was too late. Jesus didn't agree.
Jesus	What do you mean, 'Too late'? With God, it's *never* too late!
Narrator	When they got to the house, Jesus asked them to leave, and then went over to Hannah's bed and took her hand.
Jesus	Get up, little girl.
Narrator	Then, to the amazement of Susie and Jairus, Hannah's eyes opened, and she sat up!
Hannah	Hello, who are you?
Jesus	My name's Jesus. What's yours?
Hannah	Hannah, and it's nice to meet you.
Narrator	Jairus and Susie rushed over to hug Hannah, who liked that very much, but wasn't really sure what was going on.
Susie	Are you really all right?
Hannah	(*kindly*) Yes, Mother, of course I am. What on earth's the matter?
Susie	Jesus, we can't thank you enough!
Jesus	It was my pleasure. But you'd better give her something to eat.
Hannah	(*Looking very surprised*) Eat? No time for that! It's a beautiful day – can't I go out to play?

Speechless, but Not Dumb!

Based on Mark 7:31-37

BEFORE THE DAY

Try to collect information from organisations for disabled people. Study it with the children and write or draw their reactions to it. Display some of the information and the reactions at the assembly.

• Think about the actions for all the children to join in during the story.

ON THE DAY

Introduction

We're going to think about disability today. First, we'll say our 'Thank you' prayer.

'Thank you' Prayer

Thank you, God, for all you give us,
thank you for the earth and sea;
thank you, God, for special people,
thank you, God, for making me.

God's Story

Thaddeus was fed up with being talked about as if he weren't there. Although he was deaf, Thaddeus always knew when that was happening by the way people glanced at him and the looks on their faces. Because he was deaf, he'd learnt to use his eyes better than most people, and he was always very clued up about what was going on. The trouble was, because he couldn't hear, he'd never been able to speak, either. And because of that, he had never been able to have a job. Everyone just thought that because he couldn't hear or talk he must be completely stupid and useless. And that was really silly, because:

• His *hands were fine (click fingers)*
• he could *see perfectly well (point to eyes)*
• and he had a *really good brain (point to head)*

So Thaddeus had to beg for a living, and that was really hard. His friend Sue had made him a sign to show to people saying that he couldn't speak or hear and asking if they could spare any cash. Some people were nice about it and gave him a bit of money; others would occasionally buy him some food, or get his clothes washed for him. Other people, though, would brush him aside. Some would call him names, thinking he couldn't understand: names like 'layabout' and 'scrounger'. A lot of people didn't even think he really was disabled, and they would do and say horrible things to try and make him talk. Altogether, it was a terrible life.

Sue and her husband Dan were really worried about Thaddeus, and did all they could to help him, but they knew it wasn't enough.

'Perhaps we could do a sponsored camel-ride to buy him some new clothes?' suggested Dan.

'Been there, done that,' replied Sue, gloomily. 'Anyway, how d'you think Thaddeus feels, being a charity case all the time?'

'I agree,' said Dan. 'I wish I'd got half the brain he has, but he just never gets the chance to use it.'

'What we really need,' said Sue, 'is a miracle.'

'In that case, you want Jesus,' came a voice from behind them.

Sue turned round and saw a stranger standing there. 'How long have you been eaves-dropping?' she asked.

'Couldn't help overhearing,' came the reply. 'Now, you can make of this what you will, but I've got a friend who can cure things like deafness.'

'You wouldn't be winding us up, by any chance?' Dan queried.

'I don't wind people up,' the stranger answered. 'They work better if you don't. Look, d'you want to know more or not?'

'I'm not sure,' Sue said. 'If we raise Thaddeus's hopes and then nothing happens . . .'

'He'd be even worse off than before,' concluded Dan. 'I'm not sure it's a good idea.'

It was happening again! Thaddeus was standing right there, and even his best friends were talking about him as if he were their pet poodle!

'Well, it's up to you,' said the stranger, 'but just don't say I never gave you the chance. Jesus is in town at the moment, but he won't be by tomorrow. So make your mind up.'

The stranger turned to walk off, stopped and came back. 'I should warn you, though,' he said, 'that if you meet Jesus your life won't be the same again. I was a fisherman on Lake Galilee, working with my brother Simon, before Jesus came along. Now, I never know from one day to the next where I'm going to be or what I'm going to be doing.'

'Well, Thaddeus *always* knows that,' thought Sue, 'and a lot of good it does him!'

So it was that they brought Thaddeus to Jesus.

Jesus took Thaddeus's hand and said, 'It must be like being in prison – I bet you hate it, don't you?'

Thaddeus couldn't understand what Jesus was saying, but he knew that he was being talked *to*, and not about. And that was enough to make him think that Jesus might be worth knowing better, so he smiled and nodded in appreciation.

Of course, Jesus was famous as a healer, and most people knew Thaddeus; so a crowd started to gather immediately.

'This won't do,' said Jesus. 'Miracles are my business, not circus stunts! Andrew, you and Simon keep these folk occupied while we find somewhere private.'

There was an alleyway nearby where Simon and Andrew could easily keep the crowd back, and Jesus took Thaddeus there. First, he put his fingers into Thaddeus's ears. Next, he licked his finger and placed it on Thaddeus's tongue; not exactly clinically hygienic, perhaps, but Thaddeus didn't mind. At least he was being taken seriously for a change!

'Yes,' Jesus murmured, 'just like a prison. Well, there's only one thing to do with prisons.' Then his voice became stronger as though he was giving an order. 'Be opened!'

Suddenly, Thaddeus had a completely new experience. His head was filled with a jumble of sounds: people's voices, babies crying, dogs barking, hooves and wheels clattering past in the square. His eyes lit up, and he said, 'Is that the "music" Sue and Dan have told me about?' Then he looked completely shocked: 'I can talk!'

Jesus smiled, and took Thaddeus back to his friends. People were amazed and delighted, and couldn't stop saying what a wonderful thing had happened. And the best part of all for Thaddeus was that they were saying it *to* him. He wouldn't need to be left out of things any more!

Our Story

Talk about the display material and the children's reactions to it. Are there things we can learn about the way we treat people who have disabilities?

Prayers

We're Glad

Thank you, God, for sending Jesus
to show us how much you love *all* people.
Help us to be like him,
and to value everyone we meet
as a human being.

We're Sad

Please forgive us, God,
if we've ever treated people badly
just because they're disabled.
Help us not to take our own fitness
and our abilities for granted,
and teach us to look out for positive qualities
in the people we meet.

Let's Pray for People

We pray for people who are disabled
by other people's attitudes
more than their own difficulties.
Please, God, give them strength
and confidence in themselves
and in you.

Songs

Brother, sister, let me serve you
Father, I place into your hands
Jesus had all kinds of friends
When I needed a neighbour

Speechless, but Not Dumb!

God's Story

Narrator Thaddeus was fed up with being talked about as if he weren't there. Everyone thought that just because he couldn't hear or talk he must be completely stupid and useless. And that was really silly, because:

- His *hands were fine (click fingers)*
- he could *see perfectly well (point to eyes)*
- and he had a *really good brain (point to head)*

So Thaddeus had to beg for a living, and that was really hard. Some people called him names like 'layabout' and 'scrounger', thinking he couldn't understand. His friend Sue and her husband Dan did all they could to help him.

Dan Perhaps we could do a sponsored camel-ride for him?

Sue Been there, done that. Anyway, how d'you think Thaddeus feels, being a charity case all the time?

Dan I agree. I wish I'd got half the brain he has!

Sue What we really need is a miracle.

Andrew In that case, you want Jesus.

Sue How long have you been eavesdropping?

Andrew Couldn't help overhearing. Andrew's the name. Now, I've got a friend who can cure things like deafness.

Dan You wouldn't be winding us up, by any chance?

Andrew I don't wind people up – they work better if you don't. Look, d'you want to know more or not?

Sue I'm not sure. If we raise Thaddeus's hopes and then nothing happens . . .

Dan He'd be even worse off than before. I'm not sure it's a good idea.

Narrator It was happening again! Thaddeus was standing right there, and even his best friends were talking about him as if he were their pet poodle!

Andrew Well, it's up to you. I should warn you, though, that if you meet Jesus your life won't be the same again. I was a fisherman on Lake Galilee, with my brother Simon, before I met Jesus. Now, I never know from one day to the next where I'm going to be or what I'm going to do.

Sue Thaddeus *always* does, and a lot of good it does him!

Narrator So it was that they brought Thaddeus to Jesus.

Jesus It must be like being in prison – I bet you hate it.

Narrator Thaddeus couldn't understand what Jesus was saying, but he knew that he was being talked *to*, and not about. And that made him think that Jesus might be worth knowing better, so he smiled and nodded. Of course, Jesus was famous as a healer, and most people knew Thaddeus; so a crowd started to gather immediately.

Jesus This won't do! Miracles are my business, not circus stunts! Let's find somewhere private.

Narrator There was an alleyway nearby where Simon and Andrew could easily keep the crowd back, and Jesus took Thaddeus there. First, he put his fingers into Thaddeus's ears. Next, he licked his finger and placed it on Thaddeus's tongue; not exactly clinically hygienic, perhaps, but Thaddeus didn't mind. At least he was being taken seriously for a change!

Jesus *(Thoughtfully)* Yes, just like a prison. Well, there's only one thing to do with prisons. *(Loudly and firmly)* Be opened!

Narrator Suddenly, Thaddeus had a completely new experience. His head was filled with a jumble of sounds: people's voices, babies crying, dogs barking, hooves and wheels clattering past in the square.

Thaddeus Is that the 'music' Sue and Dan have told me about? Hey! I can talk!

Narrator People were amazed and delighted, and couldn't stop talking about what had happened. And the best part of all for Thaddeus was that they were saying it *to* him. He wouldn't need to be left out of things any more!

Speechless with Surprise

Based on Luke 1:5-25, 57-64

BEFORE THE DAY

Ask the children for the titles of some of their favourite films, videos, books, etc. Choose a varied selection and write them down on a flipchart in large letters. Write them also on small cards.

• Think about the actions for all the children to join in during the story.

ON THE DAY

Introduction

In a few minutes we'll hear a story about someone who had a big surprise; such a surprise that he was completely speechless – for a very long time! First, we're going to say our 'Thank you' prayer.

'Thank you' Prayer

Thank you, God, for all you give us,
thank you for the earth and sea;
thank you, God, for special people,
thank you, God, for making me.

God's Story

Zechariah couldn't believe what was happening to him! It had started just like any ordinary Sabbath day, with him going to lead worship. It was a very special honour, and only priests could do it. He had to go right into the 'holy of holies' as it was known, behind a curtain. No one could go there unless he was a priest – I say 'he' because only men could become priests, then. And you couldn't just decide to become a priest, either – you had to be born into the 'right' family! So Zechariah was very proud of the special job he did, and always tried to do it as well as possible.

This particular morning, though, he was a little bit distracted. You see, he and his wife, Elizabeth, were very unhappy because they didn't have any children. And they were even more unhappy because everybody seemed to think it was Elizabeth's fault. She must have upset God in some way, they thought, so that he had made her 'barren'. It simply never seemed to occur to them that it might be her husband who had the problem! Anyway, that was on Zechariah's mind a bit, as he began the ceremony in the holy of holies.

As he began to light the incense, Zechariah realised that he wasn't alone in the sanctuary – and he should have been! Out of the corner of his eye, he could see a figure standing by his shoulder. 'Whoever you are, you'd better go,' he said. 'You know only the duty priest is allowed in here.' Still the figure didn't move. 'Look,' said Zechariah, 'if you've got a problem see me afterwards and I'll make you an appointment to consult me – but it won't be until the week after next, mind you, and even then it'll only be an hour because I've got a lot of forms to fill in for the High Priest. Now I'd go if I were you before God strikes you dead or something.'

'Oh, I don't think he'll do that,' said the visitor. 'He doesn't often strike angels dead, you know. We've had the odd one that's fallen from grace, but that's quite another story.'

Zechariah was startled. He looked around, and sure enough the Archangel Gabriel himself was there.

'Well, knock me down with a feather!' said Zechariah.

'Not right now,' said Gabriel. 'I want a word with you. It's just to say that God's going to give you and Elizabeth a son. You're going to call him John, and he's going to be a really great man – he's going to prepare the way for the Messiah you've all been waiting for.'

'Is that what you've come here for?' asked the indignant Zechariah. 'Have you come just to tease an old man? Look, my wife's old. So am I, of course, but we men don't show it as much, do we? Anyway, we're too old to have children and that's it. And if we did have a child, he wouldn't be called John in any case. There've been Zechariahs in my family for generations, and no one has ever had a common old name like John!'

'Have you finished?' asked Gabriel. 'I hope you have, because that's the last word you're going to say for a bit. This is me you're talking to – Gabriel – Supreme Archangel, and trusted ambassador of God himself. I've taken more messages for God than your entire family's had hot dinners, and no one – no one, I tell you – has ever called me a liar before. No, it's no good trying to protest, because you can't talk – so for once you're going to have to listen. It's time you priests learned to do that anyway. As I said, you're going to have a son. You'll call him John, and he'll be a great preacher who will prepare the way for the Messiah. Got it? Oh, sorry, you can't speak can you? Well, that will give your congregation a bit of a break. Toodle-oo!'

Suddenly, Zechariah was alone again. The archangel had gone, and just as he had said Zechariah was completely unable to speak. Outside, the congregation were getting impatient because he should have started the service, and Zechariah had to try to signal to them that he'd lost his voice.

'He must have seen a vision,' said one of the worshippers.

'Rubbish!' said another. 'It's that incense that's got to him. I've said it before and I'll say it again, worship should be plain and simple without all that 'high synagogue' nonsense.'

Elizabeth had two shocks when Zechariah went home: to begin with he couldn't speak, and then he wrote her a note saying she was going to have a baby. She was overjoyed, and even more so when she found that her cousin Mary was pregnant as well.

By the time the baby was born, the whole neighbourhood was excited. Everyone was talking about it – well, everyone except Zechariah. And when the birth was announced the neighbours came round and they all sang hymns to celebrate – well, all except Zechariah. Then one of the neighbours asked, 'What are you going to call him?'

'We're going to call him John,' Elizabeth answered.

They were all amazed. 'Why John?' they asked 'You're supposed to call him after one of Zechariah's family. You can't call him John!'

Zechariah got a bit cross with the neighbours for laughing about it.

- He *picked up a pen*
- and he *dipped it in the ink*
- and he *wrote a note*

The note said, 'His name's John, and that's an end to it.'

'All right,' said Sam, his next-door neighbour. 'No need to be stroppy.'

'I'm not being stroppy!' roared Zechariah. 'Hey, I can talk!'

Everyone laughed, and the celebrations began again. They went on well into the night, and this time Zechariah could join in properly.

Our Story

What must it be like not to be able to talk?

Invite children from other classes present at the assembly to take a card and try to communicate the title without speaking (or mouthing). The rest of the group have to guess, from the list on the flipchart, which title each child is miming.

Prayers

We're Sad

We're sorry, God, for not listening.
Sometimes we're so full of our own ideas
that we don't pay attention.
Then we don't hear what you want to say.

We're Glad

Thank you, loving God,
for speaking to us in lots of different ways.
Thank you, also, for people who listen well.
They show how much they care,
and how much you love us.

Let's Pray for People

There are people who can't hear at all,
and some of them can't speak.
Please, God, help them to take part
in the world we share.
Teach us how to communicate,
and help us make the world
more friendly towards them.

Songs

A still small voice
Make me a channel of your peace
Out to the great wide world we go!
Peace, perfect peace
Rabbles, babbles (SS)

Speechless with Surprise

God's Story

Narrator   Zechariah couldn't believe what was happening to him! It had started just like any ordinary Sabbath day, with him going to lead worship. He had to go right into the 'holy of holies', behind a curtain. No one could go there unless he was a priest – I say 'he' because only men could become priests, then. As he began to light the incense, Zechariah realised that he wasn't alone in the sanctuary – out of the corner of his eye, he could see a figure standing by his shoulder.

Zechariah   Whoever you are, you'd better go – before God strikes you dead or something.

Gabriel   Oh, I don't think he'll do that. He doesn't often strike angels dead, you know. Gabriel's the name.

Zechariah   Well, knock me down with a feather!

Gabriel   Not right now; I want a word with you. God's going to give you and Elizabeth a son. You're going to call him John, and he's going to be a really great man – he's going to prepare the way for the Messiah.

Zechariah   Is that what you've come here for – just to tease an old man? Look, my wife's old. So am I, of course, but we men don't show it as much, do we? Anyway, we're too old to have children and that's it. And if we did have a child, he wouldn't be called John. There've been Zechariahs in my family for generations, and no one has ever had a common old name like John!

Gabriel   This is me you're talking to – Gabriel – I've taken more messages for God than your entire family's had hot dinners, and no one – no one, I tell you – has ever called me a liar before. No, it's no good trying to protest, because you can't talk – so for once you're going to have to listen. It's time you priests learned to do that anyway. As I said, you're going to have a son. You'll call him John, and he'll be a great preacher who will prepare the way for the Messiah. Got it? Oh, sorry, you can't speak can you? Well, that will give your congregation a bit of a break. Toodle-oo!

Narrator Then the archangel had gone, and just as he had said Zechariah was completely unable to speak. Outside, the congregation were getting impatient because he should have started the service, and Zechariah had to try to signal to them that he'd lost his voice.

Worshipper 1 He must have seen a vision.

Worshipper 2 Rubbish! It's that incense that's got to him. I've said it before and I'll say it again, worship should be plain and simple without all that 'high synagogue' nonsense.

Narrator By the time the baby was born, the whole neighbourhood was excited. Everyone was talking about it – well, everyone except Zechariah. The neighbours came round and they all sang hymns to celebrate – well, all except Zechariah.

Neighbour What are you going to call him?

Elizabeth We're going to call him John.

Neighbour Why John? You're supposed to call him after one of Zechariah's family. You can't call him John!

Narrator Zechariah got a bit cross with the neighbours for laughing about it.

- He *picked up a pen*
- and he *dipped it in the ink*
- and he *wrote a note*

The note said, 'His name's John, and that's an end to it.'

Neighbour All right, no need to be stroppy.

Zechariah *(Shouts)* I'm not being stroppy! Hey, I can talk!

Narrator Everyone laughed, and the celebrations began again. They went on well into the night, and this time Zechariah could join in properly.

The Women's Story

Based on Luke 1:26-40

BEFORE THE DAY

Ask the children to think of 'special' people they know. Guide them away from choosing famous people such as film stars, politicians, royalty, etc; or their school friends or family. They might think of a neighbour who shows them kindness, or perhaps a favourite babysitter. The children can draw and/or write about them, to make up a display with the heading 'Special People'.

• Think about the actions for all the children to join in during the story.

ON THE DAY

Introduction

We're going to think about special people in a few minutes, but first we'll say our 'Thank you' prayer.

'Thank you' Prayer

Thank you, God, for all you give us,
thank you for the earth and sea;
thank you, God, for special people,
thank you, God, for making me.

God's Story

This is the story of Mary. She lived a very long time ago in a town called Nazareth. Yes, that's right – that Mary. She wasn't very old – perhaps sixteen or thereabouts, but in those days girls got married very young, and people were beginning to talk. 'What about Mary?' they used to say. 'She's on the shelf you know – should be married and have a family by now.'

The trouble was that even people who didn't say that kind of thing sometimes still thought it, deep down. Where Mary came from, women weren't thought to be very important – and if they hadn't got a husband then they weren't important at all. But God was about to change all of that, as we shall see later.

Mary used to get upset, sometimes, about the cruel things people said about her, but the person she was really sorry for was her cousin Elizabeth. Elizabeth was much older than Mary, and married, and yet she didn't have any children. So of course, when people weren't gossiping about Mary they were being unkind to Elizabeth. 'Not much of a wife, is she?' they used to say. 'Can't even give her husband a baby.'

Mary was very sad about that, and every time she prayed she asked God to help her cousin Elizabeth to have a baby.

One day, Mary was doing some work around the house. There was a broken chair and she knew that if she waited for her father to mend it then it would never be done, so she went and found some tools and some glue and settled down to work.

• She *opened the jar*
• she *dipped in the brush*
• and she *brushed on the glue*

Just as she got to a very tricky part of the job, she heard a voice say, 'Hello, Mary.'

'That's strange,' thought Mary, 'I'm not expecting any visitors.' She didn't want to look up in case she let her hand slip and ruined her work, so she just kept her head down and carried on working. 'It must have been the wind,' she thought to herself.

Then the voice came again: 'Mary.' This time Mary knew it must be real, but she didn't want to lose track of her work. So she kept her eye on what she was doing, and said, 'Hello. Who's that?'

'I'm the archangel Gabriel,' said the voice.

Mary was just about to say, 'Yes, and I'm the queen of Sheba,' when something made her look up, and there he was! Mary was speechless at first. I mean, what do you say to an angel? Normally, she would have offered any visitor a seat and some food and drink, but she didn't know whether angels needed those things or not. Anyway, she hadn't finished mending the chair, yet.

When Mary eventually found her voice, all the words just fell over one another.

'Very pleased to meet you, I'm sure,' she said, 'I'm sorry that I ignored you just now, but I've just got to the tricky bit. If you want my parents, I'm afraid they're both out but if you come back about six you can see them, or of course you can talk to me but I'm sure you want someone more important. The Rabbi lives just down the road, and . . .'

'Mary! Mary!' said Gabriel. 'Let me get a word in edgeways. It's you I've come to see. I've been sent to tell you that God's very pleased with you. He thinks you're a really special person.'

'Oh, it's nothing,' said Mary. 'Anyone can mend a chair if they really want to.'

'Not that,' said Gabriel. 'You're going to have a baby. He's going to be a great ruler and save the world. He'll be known as the Son of God, and he'll rule for ever.'

Now if Mary hadn't known he was an angel she'd have laughed, but instead she just said, 'Me? Have a baby? That's a bit difficult for a single girl, isn't it?'

'Not for God,' said Gabriel. 'If God's decided to use you in a special way, why should he need a man to help him?'

'Well, it's usual,' said Mary. 'At least where having babies is concerned.'

'Nothing's impossible for God,' said Gabriel. 'You know your cousin Elizabeth, who's never been able to have a baby?'

'Yes,' said Mary. 'Everyone thinks she's no good because of that.'

'It's certainly a very unfair world, isn't it?' said Gabriel. 'Women seem to get the blame for everything. Anyway, she's going to have a baby as well – she's six months pregnant. So don't you go saying that anything's impossible where God's concerned.'

Mary was a bit lost for words. Obviously something absolutely stunning was happening, and all she could think of to say was, 'Well, God's the boss – whatever he wants is OK by me.'

'Good,' said Gabriel. 'That's what he hoped you'd say.'

As soon as Gabriel had gone, Mary threw away the chair she was mending and all the bits fell apart again, but she was too excited to bother with mending a silly old chair! After all, any man can do that, but they can't have babies, can they! Mary went to get her coat and scarf, and then she ran out of the house and all the way to her cousin Elizabeth's place. They

were so happy – they hugged one another, and they danced and sang, and were completely overjoyed. God had chosen both women for a special purpose, and no one could ever look down on either of them any more. It had always been a silly thing to do, anyway – hadn't it!

Our Story

Some people think that you have to be rich or famous to be special, but we know better! God uses ordinary, everyday people like us.

Prayers

We're Sad

Forgive us, please God, for silly prejudices:
for saying, 'That's a man's job',
or, 'That's women's work',
or even worse, 'That's a woman's place'!
Help us to give each other all the scope we need
to play a proper part in your work.

We're Glad

Thank you, God, for not being stuck
in the moulds we make!
Thank you for showing us
how silly they are!
Thank you for letting us be ourselves.

Let's Pray for People

Some people can't be themselves;
they always have to be
what other people expect them to be.
Please, God, set us all free from prejudice,
and help people to live in ways that please you,
and not just each other.

Songs

God turned darkness into light
He's got the whole world in his hand
I'm black, I'm white, I'm short, I'm tall
Jesus had all kinds of friends
Out to the great wide world we go!
Stand up! Walk tall
Thank you, O God, for all our friends (SS)

The Women's Story

God's Story

Narrator   This is the story of Mary. She lived a very long time ago in a town called Nazareth. Yes, that's right – that Mary. She wasn't very old – perhaps sixteen or thereabouts, but in those days girls got married very young, and people were beginning to talk.

Gossiper 1   What about Mary? She's on the shelf you know – should be married and have a family by now.

Gossiper 2   After all, having babies is what women are for, isn't it? And if she can't get a husband there's no way she can do that.

Narrator   One day, Mary was doing some work around the house. There was a broken chair and she knew that if she waited for her father to mend it then it would never be done, so she went and found some glue.

- She *opened the jar*
- she *dipped in the brush*
- and she *brushed on the glue*

Just then, she heard a voice.

Gabriel   Hello, Mary.

Mary   Hello. Who's that?

Gabriel   I'm the archangel Gabriel.

Mary   Very pleased to meet you, I'm sure. I'm sorry not to look up, but I've just got to the tricky bit. If you want my parents, I'm afraid they're both out but they'll be back about six. If you want the Rabbi, he lives just down the road, and . . .

Gabriel   Mary! Mary! Let me get a word in edgeways. It's you I've come to see. I've been sent to tell you that God's very pleased with you. He thinks you're a really special person.

Mary   Oh, it's nothing. Anyone can mend a chair if they really want to.

Gabriel Not that! You're going to have a baby. He's going to be a great ruler and save the world. He'll be known as the Son of God, and he'll rule for ever.

Mary   Me? Have a baby? That's a bit difficult for a single girl, isn't it?'

Gabriel If God's decided to use you in a special way, why should he need some man to help him?

Mary   Well, it's usual, at least where having babies is concerned.

Gabriel Nothing's impossible for God. You know your cousin Elizabeth, who's never been able to have a baby?

Mary   Yes. Everyone thinks she's no good because of that.

Gabriel It's certainly a very unfair world, isn't it? Women seem to get the blame for everything. Anyway, she's going to have a baby as well – she's six months pregnant. So don't you go saying that anything's impossible where God's concerned.

Mary   Well, God's the boss – so it's OK by me.

Gabriel Good! That's what he hoped you'd say.

Narrator As soon as Gabriel had gone, Mary threw away the chair she was mending and all the bits fell apart again, but she was too excited to bother with mending a silly old chair! After all, any man can do that, but they can't have babies, can they! Mary got her coat and scarf, and then she ran out of the house and all the way to her cousin Elizabeth's place. They were so happy – they hugged one another, and they danced and sang, and were completely overjoyed. God had chosen both women for a special purpose, and no one could ever look down on either of them any more. It had always been a silly thing to do, anyway – hadn't it!

There's a Baby in My Dinner

Based on Luke 2:1-20

BEFORE THE DAY

Have any of the children recently acquired a new baby brother or sister? Discuss with them the pros and cons of having a baby arrive in the house. List them in two columns on a large sheet of paper.

• Think about the actions for all the children to join in during the story.

ON THE DAY

Introduction

We've got a story to tell you about a baby who got in the way – and still does. First, we'll say our 'Thank you' prayer.

'Thank you' Prayer

Thank you, God, for all you give us,
thank you for the earth and sea;
thank you, God, for special people,
thank you, God, for making me.

God's Story

Why are human beings so obsessed with numbers? They count everything! You wouldn't find us self-respecting donkeys wasting all our time counting things. Life's too short for that. Humans, though, well they'll count anything. I know a person, not very far away, who has lots of bags full of little bits of gold. I can't see the fascination, personally – when you've seen one bit of gold you've seen them all. But he spends hours every night counting them.

Now let me see, what was I working up to? Oh, yes – the census. That's how we came to be in the silly situation I'm in now. Apparently, the government had the bright idea of counting all the people. I mean, can you imagine it? How can you count people when they won't stand still for ten minutes at a time? Well, they decided to tell all the people to go back to the town where they were born and register their names, and my master, Joseph, comes from Bethlehem. Now, make no mistake, Bethlehem is a wonderful place to come from – a lousy place to go to, but wonderful to come from. Trouble was, we had to go to it. And now we're here.

To make matters worse, Joseph's wife Mary was nine months pregnant, and seemed to think that gave her the right to ride on my back everywhere. Now that's all very well, but when did you last see a pregnant donkey being given a piggyback by a human? Never. Precisely. It's species discrimination and I intend to make a complaint about it.

Anyway, that's how we came to be here. We had a terrible journey – not a service area in sight the whole way, and the road's been neglected for years. My feet are killing me – and I've got twice as many as you have! Still, we eventually got here, and I was really looking forward to a warm stable, some soft straw and a good square meal. Well, you'll never guess. All the rooms in the hotels were full – I told Joseph he should have booked, but would he listen? The first I knew about the problem was when I was just about to lie down on the straw and in came the innkeeper and offered Joseph and Mary my room. I don't know what the world's coming to. Not only that, but when the baby was born they put it to bed in my dinner! No kidding! Slapped it straight into the manger without so much as a 'by your leave'! Human beings really are an undeveloped species you know. I mean, we donkeys think nothing of having babies. We just get on with it, without fuss and bother, and when it's born it has to stand on its own feet – literally – straight away. These humans, though, you never saw such a carry-on. Still, I must admit there's something very special about a human baby – they're sweet little things. So naturally I wanted to have a look. I wandered over to the manger – it was meant to be for me, after all – and had a look inside. As I looked in I caught the smell of the hay, and thought I'd just get a quick nibble while I was there. You'd have thought I was doing something dreadful! Mary screamed, and

Joseph got hold of my collar and started to drag me away. I tell you I'd just about had enough. What with the walk, the invasion of my privacy, and now I wasn't even allowed to eat a bit of my own food. So maybe I overreacted, I don't know, but I did something that comes very naturally to us donkeys. I dug my hooves into the earth floor and refused to move an inch. Even though my feet were hurting, it was worth it.

- Poor Joseph *pulled*
- and he *pulled*
- and he *pulled*!

I didn't know Joseph even knew some of the words he used! Very soon, the innkeeper and his wife came over to see what the fuss was about and I had a real live audience to play to, but they didn't stay long. The wife disappeared to the house and came back with a bucket of the most delicious-smelling oats you ever saw in your life. 'Well,' I thought. 'Somebody cares about me.' Then she went and put it the other side of the stable. Of course, I knew what the game was, but I decided I'd made my point. After all, donkeys are stubborn but we're not stupid. So I walked over to the bucket and had a good feed and pretended not to notice Joseph tying me up.

Anyway, things have improved a bit now. We've got some visitors, and Mary's letting them hold the baby which gives me a chance for a good look. Mind you, I'm not too happy about the visitors – they've got a distinct smell of sheep about them, and little bits of wool all over their clothes. They *say* they're shepherds, and they're telling some incredible story about angels coming to them and saying that a baby had been born. They *say* that they were so excited they left their flocks in the fields and came rushing over to see the baby. They certainly look and smell like shepherds, but I know their game. I mean, what shepherd who's any good leaves the sheep in the field at night without protection? Even if they did, they wouldn't admit it to strangers.

No – I've got their number. Oh, I'll admit they're playing the part very well, right down to the grass stains on their clothes and the mud on their sandals, but I've got them rumbled. I know travelling salesmen when I see them.

You mark my words, before those people leave, Mary and Joseph will have spent money they can't afford on pretty little bootees and silly cardigans with lambs all over them – now donkeys I could understand.

(Do you think the donkey's right about the visitors?)

Our Story

Look at the lists. Like all good things, babies can inconvenience us somewhat. God's like that, too. He comes to love us, but he changes things, and sometimes we find him quite difficult to live with. But he's worth making the effort for!

Prayers

We're Glad

Thank you, God,
for making life such an adventure.
Thank you for the unexpected times
when what seemed like terrible problems
turn out to be your opportunities.
Help us to be more open to you.

We're Sad

We'd like to say 'sorry'
for always wanting to be comfortable
when you are trying to disturb us!
Sometimes you ask us to do things
we would rather not do,
or not to do things which we like.

Let's Pray for People

Some people only ever see the hard side of life,
and don't notice the good things
all around them.
That's very sad.
Please, God, help people who are unhappy
to find something to smile about,
something to give them hope.

Songs

God was born on earth
Hee haw! Hee haw!
See him lying on a bed of straw
We wish you a merry Christmas

There's a Baby in My Dinner

God's Story

Donkey Why are human beings so obsessed with numbers? They count everything! You wouldn't find us self-respecting donkeys wasting all our time counting things. Life's too short for that. Anyway, the government had the bright idea of counting all the people. Joseph and Mary weren't pleased.

Joseph We've been told we've got to go to Bethlehem.

Mary Whatever for?

Joseph To be counted. We've all got to go back to the town we first came from.

Mary Oh, great! And me about to have a baby!

Donkey I'm not surprised Mary wasn't thrilled. Bethlehem is a wonderful place to come from – but it's a lousy place to *go to*. And now we're here. Mary rode the whole way here on my back. Now that's all very well, but when did you last see a pregnant donkey being given a piggyback by a human? Never. Precisely. It's species discrimination and I intend to make a complaint. But it got worse. I was just settling down in my stable when Mary and Joseph came in with the innkeeper.

Innkeeper I'm sorry, but this is simply all I have available.

Joseph Well, it's not good enough.

Mary Oh, do lay off, Joseph. I'm too tired to argue. This will just have to do.

Donkey I tell you, I didn't believe it! I told Joseph right from the start he should have booked, but would he listen? And it got worse. When the baby was born they put it to bed in my dinner! No kidding! Slapped it straight into the manger without so much as a 'by your leave'! Still, I must admit there's something very special about a human baby – they're sweet little things. Naturally, I wanted to have a look, so I wandered over to the manger.

Mary   AAAAH! Get that dreadful animal away!

Donkey   She didn't say that when she was using me as a four-wheel drive on the way here! Joseph got hold of my collar and started to drag me away. I tell you I'd just about had enough. Maybe I overreacted, I don't know, but I dug my hooves into the earth floor and refused to move an inch.

- Joseph *pulled*
- and he *pulled*
- and he *pulled*

But I just stood there. Boy, was he mad! Very soon, the innkeeper came to see what the fuss was about.

Innkeeper   Leave this to me. If I put this bucket of oats over here . . .

Donkey   Of course, I knew what the game was, but I'd made my point. After all, we donkeys are stubborn but we're not stupid. So I walked over to the bucket and pretended not to notice Joseph tying me up. Then, just as I thought we might all get some sleep, we had visitors. I ask you – at that time of night!

Shepherd 1   We don't want to be a nuisance.

Donkey   That means they're going to be.

Shepherd 2   We're shepherds, and while we were minding the sheep an angel told us this was a special baby.

Donkey   Oh, that's a good one! I haven't heard that one before. I mean, what shepherd who's any good leaves the sheep in the field at night unprotected? Even if they did, they wouldn't admit it.

Joseph   Oh, please come in. How kind of you!

Donkey   Easily taken in – that's his trouble. But I've got them rumbled. I know salesmen when I see them. You mark my words, before those people leave, Mary and Joseph will have spent money they can't afford on pretty little bootees with lambs all over them – now donkeys I could understand.

(Do you think the donkey's right about the visitors?)

Questions! Questions!

Based on Luke 2:41-end

BEFORE THE DAY

Teach the class about different kinds of food, and prepare cards with 'You are a banana' etc. on them, along with a few facts to jog the children's memories on the day. Keep the cards safe until the assembly.

• Think about the actions for all the children to join in during the story.

ON THE DAY

Introduction

We're going to play a game of questions in a few minutes, but first we'll say our 'Thank you' prayer.

'Thank you' Prayer

Thank you, God, for all you give us,
thank you for the earth and sea;
thank you, God, for special people,
thank you, God, for making me.

God's Story

Joseph wasn't happy. He was tired, his head ached and his feet were sore. 'I don't know,' he said to Mary. 'Perhaps we ought to live a little nearer Jerusalem.'

'Oh, don't start that again,' said Mary. 'We like living in Nazareth, and it *is* only once a year we have to do it. Anyway, you must admit it was a great celebration, and Jesus loved it.'

It had been Jesus' first time at the annual festival. He'd certainly had a wonderful time, seeing all the sights of Jerusalem – such as the Temple and the Governor's Palace – and watching the big parades.

'Speaking of Jesus,' said Joseph, 'where is he?'

'Oh, he's with Zebedee and Rachel,' replied Mary. 'You remember, he spent most of his time with them in Jerusalem.'

'Well,' said Joseph, 'he's not with them now. Look, there they are – and there's no sign of Jesus.'

Mary and Joseph weren't really worried, but they thought they'd better check, so they hurried around, trying to find Jesus. Gradually they realised that he simply wasn't there.

'We'll have to go back to Jerusalem,' said Joseph, 'and me with these feet.'

'Well, you can't very well go without them, can you?' said Mary, a little crossly because she was a lot more worried about Jesus than about Joseph's feet.

So they walked all the way back again to Jerusalem. They could really have done with a good rest, but they were too worried to stop. On and on they walked, right through the night, with wolves howling around them and the moonlight making frightening shadows, and what with all that and being so worried about Jesus, Joseph almost forgot about his feet!

In the morning, they got to Jerusalem. 'Now where do we start looking?' wondered Joseph. It seemed like a hopeless job. For three days, Joseph and Mary hunted around the city and couldn't find Jesus anywhere.

• They *looked to the left*
• they *looked to the right*
• they turned and *looked behind them*

They went into the hotels and the amusement centres; they searched around the market stalls and checked all the stables, because Jesus loved animals. The only place they hadn't tried was the Temple.

So they made their way into the Temple, and straight away they noticed that quite a crowd was gathering in one of the courtyards. They pushed their way through the crowd, thinking that they might find a Temple guide who could help them to search, and guess what they saw!

In the middle of the crowd was a little circle of priests and teachers, all sitting around discussing religion (as you know, when people of that kind get together today, they tend to talk about religion – and use all kinds of long words to make themselves seem important – and things weren't much different then) and the little group were so engrossed in their talking that they didn't see Mary and Joseph pushing their way through. But Mary and Joseph had seen someone, though. Can you guess who?

There, sitting in the middle of the priests and teachers, was Jesus. He was listening very carefully to them, and asking questions. And they weren't just any old questions, either, but he was really making the wise people scratch their heads and think! Mary was embarrassed – rather like other parents often are when they think their children are being a nuisance – but was too relieved at finding Jesus safe and well to worry too much about that.

'There you are!' she said. 'What d'you think you're doing, making your father and me so worried about you? Four days we've been searching for you – and him with his feet as well!'

Jesus looked at her, and said, 'Why did you worry – you should have known where I'd be.'

Joseph was about to say something very stern to Jesus for being cheeky to his mother, when one of the teachers spoke to Mary.

'He's your son, is he?' he said. 'Well, he's a bright lad, and he's going to go a long way.'

Yes,' said Joseph, grumpily. 'All the way back to Nazareth, and I hope his feet hurt as much as mine do.'

The teachers assured Mary and Joseph that Jesus had not been a nuisance. 'Never discourage him from asking questions,' they said. 'That's how bright children like him get even brighter.'

Mary and Joseph took Jesus home. They always remembered what the teachers had said, and encouraged Jesus to ask questions – even ones that sounded silly. And sure enough, he learned, and he became even wiser, and everyone said what a great man he was going to be one day.

Our Story

Call a few children from the class to the front, and give them each a card. The rest of the children must work out what each of them is by asking questions. You can then make the point that asking questions is a good way of learning.

Prayers

We're Sad

Sometimes we cause people who love us to get anxious,
all because we don't think before we act.
Please, God, forgive us,
and make us more considerate.

We're Glad

Thank you, God, for people who care.
Sometimes we complain about it,
tell them not to make a fuss,
or that they worry too much,
but we're glad they care enough to worry.
Thank you, God.

Let's Pray for People

Every day, people get lost,
and other people worry.
Sometimes it ends happily,
sometimes it doesn't.
Sometimes it seems as though
it will never end at all.
Please God, be specially close to people
who are separated from one another;
give them comfort, and hope,
and if there is bad news
give them people to comfort them
and love them,
the way you do.

Songs

Jesus had all kinds of friends
Out to the great wide world we go!
Questions! Questions! (SS)
Stand up! Walk tall

Questions! Questions!

God's Story

Narrator	Joseph wasn't happy. He was tired, his head ached and his feet were sore.
Joseph	I don't know, Mary. Perhaps we ought to live a little nearer Jerusalem. At this rate we'll be ages getting home to Nazareth.
Mary	Oh, don't start that again. We like living in Nazareth, and it *is* only once a year we have to do it. Anyway, it's always worth the effort. You must admit it was a great celebration, and Jesus loved it.
Narrator	Jesus was twelve years old, and he'd certainly had a wonderful time, seeing all the sights of Jerusalem – such as the Temple and the Governor's Palace – and watching the big parades.
Joseph	Speaking of Jesus, where is he?
Mary	Oh, he's with Zebedee and Rachel. You remember, he spent most of his time with them in Jerusalem.
Joseph	Well, he's not with them now. Look, there they are – and there's no sign of Jesus.
Narrator	Mary and Joseph weren't really worried, but they thought they'd better check, so they hurried around all the other families who were walking with them, trying to find Jesus. Gradually they realised that he simply wasn't there.
Joseph	There's nothing for it, we'll have to go back to Jerusalem – and me with these feet.
Narrator	So they turned round and walked all the way back again to Jerusalem.
Joseph	Now where do we start looking? It's a big town, and it's full of visitors!

Narrator   For three days, Joseph and Mary scoured the city.

- They *looked to the left*
- they *looked to the right*
- they turned and *looked behind them*

But they couldn't find Jesus anywhere. The only place they hadn't tried was the Temple.

Mary   He won't be in there. There are lots of things going on here that he'll find more exciting than religion.

Narrator   Even so, they thought they might as well try. So they made their way into the Temple and noticed a crowd in one of the courtyards gathered around a group of priests and teachers, and in the middle of them was Jesus, listening very carefully and asking questions.

Mary   There you are! What d'you think you're doing, making your father and me so worried? Four days we've been searching for you – and him with his feet as well!

Jesus   Why worry? You should have know where I'd be.

Narrator   Joseph was about to say something very stern to Jesus for being cheeky to his mother, when one of the teachers spoke to Mary.

Teacher   He's your son, is he? Well, he's a bright lad, and he's going to go a long way.

Joseph   Yes, all the way back to Nazareth, and I hope his feet hurt as much as mine do.

Teacher   Never discourage him from asking questions. That's how bright children like him get even brighter.

Narrator   Mary and Joseph took Jesus home. They always remembered what the teachers had said, and encouraged Jesus to ask questions. And sure enough, he learned, and he became even wiser, and everyone said what a great man he was going to be.

Poor Ebenezer!

Based on Luke 12:16-21

BEFORE THE DAY

Organise a shop. Get the children to bring in a variety of goods for display, and make a list of their prices. Have other things without prices on the stall, too: a bottle of politeness, a box of love, a packet of friendship.

• Think about the actions for all the children to join in during the story.

ON THE DAY

Introduction

Most of us know the prices of some things, but do we know the *value* of what's really important? We'll think about that in a moment, but first we're going to say our 'Thank you' prayer.

'Thank you' Prayer

Thank you, God, for all you give us,
thank you for the earth and sea;
thank you, God, for special people,
thank you, God, for making me.

God's Story

Ebenezer was a very careful little boy. He had decided that when he grew up he'd be rich. He always saved his pocket money; he never spent it on what he thought were silly things like sweets or comics. And if someone was collecting for charity they never got anything from Ebenezer: 'People should learn to look after themselves,' he used to say.

Ebenezer never had any real friends. No one seemed to want to be friends with him. Sometimes he used to be sad about that, but then he'd say to himself, 'Friends are no use. Friends don't make you rich. I'm going to be richer than all of them.'

When he was a teenager, he never seemed to have any girlfriends, either. His parents got quite worried about it. 'Why don't you ask Rachel from down the road to go to the theatre with you?' his mother asked one day.

'What?' said Ebenezer. 'Have you seen the price of theatre tickets?' And he went to his bedroom to count his money. Ebenezer had quite a lot of money by now, but somehow it never seemed like very much. The trouble was that he'd got used to it. He didn't know what being rich really meant. He just thought that it meant having more than he had then, and so he was always trying to get richer!

Gradually, the people Ebenezer had been at school with got married and started families. He would have liked some children of his own to play with, but he knew that families cost money. None of those people looked like ever being rich. So instead, he bought a farm and started growing crops. 'People will always need food,' he told himself. 'I'll get really rich selling my produce to them.' And he did. But he never *felt* rich, because 'rich' always means 'better off than I am now'!

Then one year he had a really big crop. Everything seemed to go right for Ebenezer that year. There was just the right amount of sunshine and rain, not too many slugs and snails and Ebenezer's home-made scarecrow kept the birds away. So when it came to harvest he had so much produce that he didn't know what to do with it! He had bags of wheat grain stacked up to the ceiling of his biggest barn, and so many apples, oranges and pomegranates that the greengrocers couldn't sell them fast enough. What was he to do with all this extra food?

While Ebenezer was wondering, the Mayor was on his way to see him.

- He *walked up the path*
- and he *knocked on the door*
- and he gave Ebenezer *a big smile*

Ebenezer was really pleased. The Mayor must have come to tell him that he'd been made Businessman of the Year. This would show them! All those people who'd never wanted to be his friend would wish they'd been nicer to him, now. When he became Businessman of the Year everyone would want to be his friend, but he wouldn't let them of course. 'Too late!' he would say. 'Go away and leave me alone.'

How he would enjoy seeing them squirm!

'I expect you know why I've come to see you,' the Mayor began. Ebenezer was very careful. He didn't want to look conceited.

'No,' he answered, 'I really can't imagine.'

'Well,' said the Mayor, 'you've had a really terrific crop, haven't you? You must be about the most successful businessman in the town.'

'What d'you mean, "about"?' thought Ebenezer. 'I'm *absolutely* the most successful businessman within a hundred miles!' He didn't say it, though, because he didn't want to sound conceited. So he just smiled modestly and nodded his head.

'So,' said the Mayor, 'we wondered whether you would consider . . .'

'Here it comes,' thought Ebenezer. 'Now I must try to look surprised.'

The Mayor continued, '. . . whether you'd consider helping out the poor people by giving some of your crops away.'

Ebenezer was just about to smile and say, 'Of course, my dear Mr Mayor! I would be honoured to accept the award,' when he realised what the Mayor had said.

'What!' he bellowed, 'You want me to give my food away? How will I ever become rich if I go doing silly things like that?'

'B-b-but you *are* rich,' said the Mayor.

'Nonsense!' roared Ebenezer. 'I've got to be a lot better off than I am now, before I'm rich.'

'What are you going to do with that food, though?' asked the Mayor. 'You haven't got big enough barns to store it.'

'Then I'll build bigger ones!' cried Ebenezer. 'I'll store up all the food so that I can get rich without having to work for it!' 'Just fancy,' he thought, 'suggesting that I should give my food away. Just because those silly people chose to have families, and wasted money on their friends, they expect me to help them when they're poor!'

That night, Ebenezer had a terrible shock. He died. No one was there to hold his hand, and no one came to his funeral. Poor, sad Ebenezer died as he'd lived – alone. He never got to enjoy all that lovely food, and although he had more money than everyone else in the town put together, he never thought he was rich, because to him 'rich' always meant 'better off than I am now'.

Poor, sad Ebenezer!

Our Story

Draw attention to the 'shop'. Ask the children if there is anything they would like to buy, and then carefully check the price list. 'That would cost you 10p', etc. When it comes to the other 'goods' (perhaps with a bit of prompting) look very puzzled: 'There doesn't seem to be a price for this one.' You can then make the point that there are some ('priceless'?) things that money can't buy.

Prayers

We're Sad

Loving God,
we're sorry for the times we've been greedy,
when we've kept more for ourselves
than we really needed
and neglected other people.
Help us to remember that it's love
that makes us truly rich.

We're Glad

God, you are our friend.
Thank you for giving us
the most important thing of all.
Thank you for your love;
help us to share it with others.

Let's Pray for People

People like Ebenezer
will never be truly happy,
because however much they have
they just want more.
Please God, help people to be happy
with just enough,
and help us all to discover
the joy of friendship.

Songs

I come like a beggar
It's me, O Lord
Jesus can make us truly rich (SS)
Love is like a circle
Out to the great wide world we go!
Thank you, O God, for all our friends (SS)
When I needed a neighbour
You shall go out with joy

Poor Ebenezer!

God's Story

Narrator	Ebenezer was a very careful little boy. All he wanted was to be rich. So he always saved his pocket money.
Ebenezer	After all, if you look after the pennies, the pounds will look after themselves.
Narrator	He would never lend anything to the other children.
Ebenezer	Neither a borrower nor a lender be.
Narrator	And he never gave his pocket money to charity.
Ebenezer	People should learn to look after themselves.
Narrator	Ebenezer never had any friends – but he didn't mind.
Ebenezer	Friends are no use. Friends don't make you rich.
Narrator	When he was a teenager, he never seemed to have any girlfriends, either. His parents got quite worried.
Mum	Son, why don't you ask Rachel to the theatre with you?
Ebenezer	What? Have you seen the price of theatre tickets? No, I'll just stay in and count my money.
Narrator	Soon, Ebenezer had quite a lot of money, but he always thought that being rich meant having more! Gradually, his friends got married. He used to see them in their gardens, playing with their children.
Ebenezer	I'd like some children, but families cost money.
Narrator	So Ebenezer just had to resign himself to never having a family of his own. Instead, he bought a farm.
Ebenezer	People will always need food – and they'll pay for it!
Narrator	One year, Ebenezer had a big crop. While he was wondering what to do with it all, the Mayor called.

- He *walked up the path*
- and he *knocked on the door*
- and he gave Ebenezer *a big smile*

Ebenezer *(Aside)* Oh, good! I bet he's come to tell me that I've been made Businessman of the Year.

Mayor I expect you know why I've come to see you.

Ebenezer *(Pretending to be casual)* No, I really can't imagine what you'd want with a humble person like me.

Mayor Well, you've had a really terrific crop, haven't you?

Ebenezer Yes, I have.

Mayor You must be about the most successful businessman in the town, so we thought . . .

Ebenezer *(Aside)* Here it comes. I must try to look surprised.

Mayor . . . that you might give some food to the poor people.

Ebenezer What! How will I get rich if I do silly things like that?

Mayor B-b-but you *are* rich, Ebenezer.

Ebenezer Nonsense! I've got to be a lot better off before I'm rich.

Mayor But you haven't got big enough barns for all that food.

Ebenezer Then I'll build bigger ones! I'll store up all the food so that I can get rich without having to work for it! What a cheek! Just because those silly people chose to have families, and wasted money on their friends, they expect me to help them when they're poor!

Narrator That night, Ebenezer had a terrible shock. He died. No one was there to hold his hand, and no one came to his funeral. Poor, sad Ebenezer died as he'd lived – alone. He never got to enjoy all that lovely food, and he never enjoyed being rich, because to him 'rich' always meant 'better off than I am now'. Poor, sad Ebenezer!

Airs and Graces

Based on Luke 14:7-11

BEFORE THE DAY

It's fantasy time. Let the children make themselves some simple fancy dress, based on a character they would like to be, whether from the real world or fiction. Keep it simple – a cardboard crown for the queen, coronet for lesser royals, a mask for Batman, etc. Then on the morning itself, place some chairs in a prominent position, each labelled discreetly with a child's real name.

• Think about the actions for all the children to join in during the story.

ON THE DAY

Introduction

We'll be hearing a story soon about someone who thought he was more important than he really was, but first, we're going to say our 'Thank you' prayer.

'Thank you' Prayer

Thank you, God, for all you give us,
thank you for the earth and sea;
thank you, God, for special people,
thank you, God, for making me.

God's Story

Tom was really excited. He had been invited to the wedding of the famous concert pianist, Roland F. Sharpe, and the operatic soprano, Edwina G. Flatte. They were a very loving couple, and everyone said how natural they were together.

• Tom *combed his hair*
• and he *tied his tie*
• and he *straightened his buttonhole flower*

'I've got to look smart,' he said. 'After all, I'm bound to be on the top table; I was an old college friend of Roland's during my Academy days when I was a violinist.'

'Your "Academy days"?' said his mother. 'You're exaggerating a bit, aren't you? And you weren't a violinist, either.'

'Yes I was,' Tom insisted.

'You worked in the canteen,' said his mother.

'I'd have been a student,' Tom protested, 'but they just didn't seem to recognise my talent.'

'Couldn't seem to find it, more likely!' his mother corrected him. 'Now, Tom, you're not going to go giving yourself airs and graces are you? Without listening to any more that his mother was saying, Tom put on his coat and went out.

Meanwhile, in a different part of the town, Richard was also getting ready to go. He couldn't understand why he'd been invited. He used to work at the Academy, too, as the caretaker. Although he loved music, he'd never really been able to master an instrument, but he used to sit in his office at the college listening to music on the radio and loving every note of it. A lot of the students had very expensive instruments, and – although it wasn't really part of his job – Richard used to look after them for them sometimes, to save them carrying them around all the time. Roland never used to ask him to look after his piano for him. So he couldn't imagine why he'd been invited.

It was a lovely wedding; of course, the music was wonderful! All the most famous musicians were there, and after the service, Tom went around slapping them on the back, and talking about 'old times'. He thought it strange that such clever people had such bad memories, but he didn't mind reminding them who he was. Tom eventually decided to get off early to the reception.

Richard enjoyed the ceremony, too. He sat at the back, and thought how wonderful it was to be with all these famous people. Then after the ceremony he slipped quietly out to his car and drove to the hotel for the reception.

When Tom arrived at the reception, he went to the top table and sat down near to where the couple would be. 'Better leave room for their families,' he thought. 'Don't want to be pushy.' So he chose a place a few seats away from where Roland and Edwina would sit. Soon, he saw the happy couple approaching. Tom had his arm around someone – oh yes, it was that caretaker fellow, Richard. Tom remembered him from his 'Academy days'. Quite a nice man, but no musician – all he did was listen to it. Tom used to say, 'Any fool can *listen*. What's really hard is *playing* it.' You can see now why Tom never got accepted as a student.

Roland caught sight of Tom and came up to him, still with his arm around Richard's shoulders. 'Hello,' he said. 'I'm sorry, but I don't think we've met.'

Tom thought it was a wonderful joke! He roared with laughter, stood up and slapped Roland on the back. 'Hi there, Roly baby!' he shouted.

'Oh, yes,' said Roland, frowning. '*Now* I remember you. Look, I'm sorry – this is rather embarrassing – this place is for Richard here. You remember Richard, don't you. We always thought the world of him; he was so helpful – and *such* a musician! There's a place for you over there. Would you mind showing him, Richard – it's the one you were in before I found you.'

As Richard showed him to his seat, Tom didn't hear a word he was saying. He just had those words of Roland's ringing around inside his head '. . . and *such* a musician'. Roland must have got confused. Yes, that was it. Poor Roland – all the pressure of fame must have got to him. Then Tom noticed that the people around him seemed to be enjoying a joke. As he passed they started giggling and whispering to one another. Tom couldn't imagine what they were laughing at.

When he sat down, Tom watched Richard returning to the place he had wanted, and he noticed something very strange. Everyone seemed to know Richard, and to like him, and to want to talk to him. Although Richard was very shy, and found it a little embarrassing, people were grabbing his hand as he went past and smiling as they greeted him. Tom couldn't understand it, but then that was poor Tom's whole trouble, you see. He just couldn't understand what was really important in life, and what wasn't.

Our Story

Invite the children to put on their fancy dress and come forward to take the place prepared for them. As they come forward, ask them who they are, and then try and find their fantasy name on one of the VIP chairs. It won't be there, of course, so you can say, 'I'm terribly sorry, there's a chair here for . . . (the child's real name), but that's not you, is it?' Do the whole thing in a light-hearted way as the children learn that they have to 'be themselves' in order to get the places of honour.

Prayers

We're Sad

It's tempting to try and pretend
that we're something we're not.
Please forgive us, God,
when we give ourselves airs and graces,
and help us just to be ourselves.

We're Glad

God, we thank you
for making us as we are.
This is how you have made us;
and you love us.
Why should we want to be anything else!

Let's Pray for People

Some people are never satisfied with themselves,
and are always pretending,
trying to impress others.
Please God, help them to know
that you love them the way you made them.
And help us always to be kind,
and not to make people feel small
just so that we can look big.

Songs

Be yourself! (SS)
God turned darkness into light
I come like a beggar
I'm glad I'm alive
It's me, O Lord
Stand up! Walk tall

168

Airs and Graces

God's Story

Narrator Tom was really excited. He had been invited to the wedding of the famous concert pianist, Roland F. Sharpe, and the operatic soprano, Edwina G. Flatte. They were a lovely couple, and everyone said how natural they were together.

- Tom *combed his hair*
- and he *tied his tie*
- and he *straightened his buttonhole flower*

Tom I've got to look smart. After all, I'm bound to be on the top table; I was an old college friend of Roland's.

Mother That's the first I knew of it. When was that?

Tom You know, Mother. During my Academy days when I was a violinist.

Mother Your 'Academy days'? You're exaggerating a bit, aren't you? And you weren't a violinist, either.

Tom Yes I was.

Mother You worked in the canteen.

Tom I'd have been a student, but they just didn't seem to recognise my talent.

Mother Couldn't seem to find it, more likely! Now, Tom, you won't give yourself airs and graces, will you?

Tom I told you, we're real mates, old Roly and me.

Narrator Meanwhile, in a different part of the town, Richard was also getting ready to go. He couldn't understand why he'd been invited. He used to work at the Academy, too, as the caretaker. Although he'd never learnt to play, he loved to listen to music on his office radio. A lot of the students had very expensive instruments, and – although it wasn't really his job – Richard used to look after them for them. Well, it was a wonderful wedding service, and afterwards Tom went around slapping everyone on the back, and talking about 'old times'.

Tom It's strange that such clever people seem to have such bad memories, but I don't mind reminding them who I am. Well, better get to the reception.

Narrator When Tom arrived at the reception, he was really pleased that he was such a special friend of Roly. There were so many tables!

Tom I'm glad I got here early. Ah, this must be the top table. Better leave a couple of seats for their families – don't want to be pushy.

Narrator Very soon, the room started filling up and Tom saw the happy couple approaching. Roly had his arm around someone – it was that caretaker fellow, Richard.

Tom I remember him from my Academy days. Quite a nice man, but of course not one of the 'in' set. He was no musician – all he did was listen to it. Any fool could do that. What's really hard is *playing* it.

Narrator You can see why Tom never got accepted as a student.

Roland Hello. I'm sorry, but I don't think we've met.

Tom Hi there, Roly baby! Love the sense of humour!

Roland Oh, yes. *Now* I remember you. Look, I'm sorry – this is rather embarrassing – this place is for Richard here. You remember Richard, don't you. He was always so helpful – and *such* a musician! There's a place for you over there near the entrance.

Narrator Tom couldn't believe what he was hearing. Everyone also seemed to start giggling as he walked past. Then Tom noticed something else that was strange. They all seemed to know Richard, and to like him, and to want to talk to him. Tom couldn't understand it. But then, that was poor Tom's whole trouble, you see. He just couldn't understand what was really important in life, and what wasn't.

Let's Have a Party!

Based on Luke 14:15-24

BEFORE THE DAY

Talk with the children about parties: what do they eat? Do they play games? Make a list of the important ingredients of parties – and whatever you do, don't forget to include guests!

• Think about the actions for all the children to join in during the story.

ON THE DAY

Introduction

Today we're going to hear a story about a really special party. But first we'll say our 'Thank you' prayer.

'Thank you' Prayer

Thank you, God, for all you give us,
thank you for the earth and sea;
thank you, God, for special people,
thank you, God, for making me.

God's Story

Mike and Sarah were a couple who loved to throw parties. The table would be loaded with food, and decorated with flowers, and they always had a band. Their parties were the talk of the neighbourhood, and people used to say that only a very special kind of fool would ever refuse an invitation from Mike and Sarah.

One evening, they decided to have another party. They invited their friends Joe and Elizabeth, and some others called Tim and Anna, as well as Eli who was a newcomer. They all said they would come.

So Mike and Sarah started getting the food ready. 'We'll have a fruit punch,' said Sarah.

'Yes,' said Mike, 'But be careful – not everyone's used to your punches!'

Well, the food was ready, and the table was set out, and the 'Bethany Blues Band' was playing gently at one end of the room.

• One of them was *playing a trombone*
• One was *playing a piano*
• Another was *playing the drums*

Mike and Sarah were really excited – but gradually when no-one came, they started getting worried.

'I hope they haven't forgotten,' said Sarah.

'I'll go and check,' said Mike.

So he went to Joe and Elizabeth's place. Elizabeth looked very embarrassed.

'I'm sorry,' she said. 'But we've just bought that bit of land next door to our garden, and it's full of weeds! We'll have to weed it.'

Mike wasn't pleased. 'I wish you'd told us before,' he said. 'We've gone to a lot of trouble.' Then he went to find Tim and Anna.

'I really am sorry,' said Tim, 'but we've just bought this lovely new puppy, and we can't leave him all on his own, can we? I hope you haven't gone to too much trouble.'

'Yes,' replied Mike, '*much* too much trouble!'

And he went on to find Eli. 'Eli's probably forgotten,' he thought to himself. 'I expect he'll come back with me.' But when he got to Eli's house, no-one was in. Then one of the neighbours called out, 'Eli's off on his honeymoon – he got married this morning.'

Sarah was as angry as Mike was. 'D'you mean to tell me that they let us do all this work, and didn't really want to come at all?' she said. 'Well, someone's got to eat this food; it mustn't be wasted.'

'I know!' said Mike. 'If the people who were invited don't appreciate our cooking, let's invite those who will! Let's go into the streets, and invite all the homeless people – all the people nobody wants!'

'What a wonderful idea!' exclaimed Sarah. 'They'll appreciate a party, even if our boring friends don't!'

So that's what they did, and before long the house was full of people eating, and laughing, and singing and dancing. 'Well!' said Sarah. 'This is a bit different from our usual parties. No airs and graces – just people who appreciate a good party.'

'Yes!' said Mike. 'Even the band are enjoying it more than usual – just listen to how they're playing!'

Just then, Joe and Elizabeth arrived. 'We felt so sorry for you,' said Joe, as they swept in, 'that we put off the weeding and came. After all what are friends for?' Before Mike could answer, they had arrived in the dining room.

'Good grief!' screeched Elizabeth. 'What are all these people doing here?'

'Enjoying themselves, actually,' said Sarah. 'They really know how to get stuck in to a good party. Why don't you join them?'

'Not likely!' replied Elizabeth. 'Come on Joe, we're going home!'

The party continued well into the night. No-one wanted it to end. As they left the guests all said, 'When's the next party going to be?'

'As soon as possible,' smiled Sarah.

'Too right!' said Mike. 'I've never enjoyed anything so much!'

Our Story

Draw attention to the display. The food and other things are wonderful – but they're a lot better when there are people to share them with!

Prayers

We're Glad

Loving God,
thank you for fun,
for our family
and the things we enjoy together.
Help us to make each other happy.

We're Sad

Sometimes people go to a lot of trouble
to make us happy,
and we hurt them.
We're sorry, Jesus,
help us to be more careful
about other people's feelings.

Let's Pray for People

Some people are so sad,
and never really enjoy life.
They don't notice
the good things others do.
Other people spend lots of time
trying to make others happy,
and then feel let down.
We pray for them.
Help them to know that you care,
and that we care.
Show us how to make them feel
that all their work is worthwhile.

Songs

All things bright and beautiful
Come on and celebrate!
I'm black, I'm white, I'm short, I'm tall
Jesus had all kinds of friends
Jesus turned the water into wine
Thank you, O God, for all our friends (SS)
When I needed a neighbour

Let's Have a Party!

God's Story

Narrator   Mike and Sarah decided to have a party. They invited their friends Joe and Elizabeth, and some others called Tim and Anna, as well as Eli, who was a newcomer. They all said they would come. So Mike and Sarah started getting the food ready.

Sarah   We'll have a fruit punch.

Mike   Yes, but be careful – not everyone's used to your punches!

Narrator   Well, the food was ready, and the table was set out, and the 'Bethany Blues Band' was playing gently at one end of the room.

- One of them was *playing a trombone*
- One was *playing a piano*
- Another was *playing the drums*

Narrator   Mike and Sarah were really excited – but no-one came.

Sarah   I hope they haven't forgotten.

Mike   I'll go and check.

Narrator   First Mike went to see Joe and Elizabeth.

Elizabeth   I am really sorry but we've just bought a bit of land and we've got to weed it.

Mike   I wish you'd told us before.

Narrator   Then Mike went to find Tim and Anna.

Tim   I really am sorry but we've just bought this lovely new puppy, and we can't leave him all on his own, can we?

Narrator When Mike got to Eli's house, no-one was in. Eli had got married and gone off on his honeymoon! Sarah was angry.

Sarah   Well, someone's got to eat this food; it mustn't be wasted.

Mike   I know! Let's invite all the homeless people, all the people nobody likes! They'll appreciate a party, even if our boring friends don't!

Narrator Before long, the house was full of people having a wonderful time.

Sarah   Well! This is a bit different from our usual parties. No airs and graces – just people who appreciate a good party.

Narrator Just then, Joe and Elizabeth arrived.

Elizabeth We felt so sorry for you that we put off the weeding and came. After all what are friends for?

Narrator Before Mike could answer, they had swept into the dining room.

Elizabeth *(horrified)* Good grief! What are all *these* people doing here?

Sarah   Enjoying themselves, actually! Why don't you join them?

Elizabeth *(snobbishly)* Not likely! Come on Joe, we're going home!

Narrator The party continued well into the night. No-one wanted it to end. And I hear they're planning another – very soon!

What A Silly Sheep!

Based on Luke 15:1-7

BEFORE THE DAY

Think of the people on whom we rely to help us if we're in difficulties – even when it's our own silly fault! Perhaps the children could draw pictures of nurses, firemen, doctors etc. If some were able to dress up for the assembly, so much the better.

If using the drama, prepare some placards saying:

> This Way to Adventure

> Juicy Grass Over Here

• Think about the actions for all the children to join in during the story.

ON THE DAY

Introduction

In a few minutes, we're going to hear a sheep telling a story! But first we'll say our 'Thank you' prayer.

'Thank you' Prayer

Thank you, God, for all you give us,
thank you for the earth and sea;
thank you, God, for special people,
thank you, God, for making me.

God's Story

I never meant to cause trouble. I just wanted some excitement. Being a sheep isn't easy, you know – we spend most of our time travelling about looking for decent grass. The only view we get is the back of the sheep in front, and take it from me, that's not very exciting!

But we're lucky in one way – our shepherd's good. Joshua's his name. Not all the *people* like him, but then people are funny that way, aren't they? He's very popular with the sheep. He really cares about us – and a good thing too, or I would have got myself in big trouble by now!

I was always a bit of a rebel – always wandering off looking for excitement. My mum used to get so mad! 'One day,' she used to say to me, 'you'll get into real trouble!' I never believed her. I just longed to be big enough to go off on my own without her fussing over me. Then one day we'd stopped for a feed on some juicy grass, and I could see some that was even greener, just up the hill. So off I went, and no-one noticed. It was good stuff. Then I went further, and it was even better. The trouble was that I soon got lonely. I missed my mum and dad, and all my sisters and my cousins and my aunts in the flock. But when I tried to get back, I must have taken a wrong turning. It was all different. I thought I'd better try in another direction. But then I got completely lost!

I was getting frightened (but don't tell my mum I said that, will you, because she'd only say, 'I told you so!') and I began to think that I'd never get back. All this excitement was getting me down – and walking along looking at the rear view of another sheep seemed like a wonderful idea! As night fell, I thought I'd better try and find a cave to shelter in. So I tried to turn around and had the fright of my life. Somehow, I'd wandered onto the side of a cliff. I was standing on a ledge so narrow there was no way I could turn round. Now I was *really* frightened!

• I couldn't *fly* up to the top,
  'cos sheep can't *fly*
• I couldn't *climb a rope,*
  even if I'd had one!
• I couldn't *hang glide,*
  'cos I didn't have the gear!

Then, I heard a whistle; Joshua's special whistle he used when we wandered off. If I hadn't been standing where I was, I'd have jumped for joy. As it was, I just gave out a little 'Baa' and I heard the whistle again – this time closer than before. So I gave him another 'Baa!' And that's how we went on – whistle . . .

'Baa' . . . whistle . . . 'Baa' until he was at the cliff top above me.

'You wait there,' he called – as if I'd do anything else – 'and I'll be down to you.' He scrambled down to where I was. 'I don't know how you got here,' he said, 'but I'll get you safe.' And he picked me up, slung me across his shoulders and climbed up. I tell you, I closed my eyes and hung on. That was another thing my parents found embarrassing about me – a sheep that's scared of heights, I ask you!

When we got to the top, I thought Joshua was going to carry me all the way home on his shoulders, but he put me down. 'Come on,' he said. 'You walked here, you can walk home. But don't worry, I'll be right with you all the way.' And he was, too.

Since that day, I've been more careful. It's not so bad, travelling – in fact, we see some pretty exciting places. All I have to do is turn my head to the side – can't imagine why I didn't think of it before!

Our Story

Draw attention to the display. All those people will help us, because they care – even if it is our own fault! Of course, we should be careful not to waste their time, but everyone does silly things sometimes and it's good to know that someone will help us. Jesus told us that God is even more loving!

Prayers

We're Glad

Thank you, God, for caring for us.
Thank you for telling us that wherever we go,
and whatever we do, you won't forget about us

We're Sad

We know you care about us, Jesus,
and we know we should follow you.
But sometimes, other things seem more exciting,
and we wander off, do our own thing,
then complain when we get into trouble!
Help us to enjoy life, to have fun,
but to stay with you.

Let's Pray for People

People get lost sometimes,
and then others worry about them.
Loving God,
be very close to anxious people:
children who are lost,
parents who are worried about them,
people who have lost their way.
Thank you for people who help:
the police,
the Salvation Army,
and many other organisations.
Help them to go on showing
that you care.

Songs

Come on and celebrate
He's got the whole world in his hand
Out to the great wide world we go!
Thank you, O God, for all our friends (SS)

What A Silly Sheep!

God's Story

Sheep   I never meant to cause trouble. I just wanted some excitement. Being a sheep isn't easy, you know – we spend most of our time following Joshua around (Joshua's our shepherd), looking for decent grass. I suppose I was always a bit of a rebel – always wandering off looking for excitement. My mum used to get so mad!

Placard holders   Over here! – No, over here! – Come this way! (*As they call, the Sheep starts towards each one*)

Mum   One day, you'll get into real trouble!

Sheep   See what I mean? Parents! I just longed to be big enough to go off on my own without her stopping me.

Placard holders   Over here! – No, over here! – Come this way!

Mum   You'll learn the hard way – you just mark my words!

Sheep   Yeah, yeah! Now where was I? Oh yes . . . One day I saw some juicy grass, just up the hill.

Placard holders   Over here! – No, over here! – Come this way!

Sheep   So off I went, and no one noticed. It was good stuff. And further on, it was even better. But I forgot to keep an eye on the others, and soon I was completely lost! I was very frightened (but don't tell my mum I said that, will you, because you know what she'd say . . .)

Mum   I told you so! I don't like to say it, but . . .

Sheep   See what I mean? But I must admit that all this excitement was getting me down – and walking along back with the rest of the flock seemed like a wonderful idea! Then I had the fright of my life. Somehow, I'd wandered onto the side of a cliff and I was standing on a narrow ledge. Now I was *really* frightened!

- I couldn't *fly* up to the top, 'cos sheep can't *fly!*
- I couldn't *climb a rope*, even if I'd had one!
- I couldn't *hang glide*, 'cos I didn't have the gear!

Then, I heard something.
(*'Joshua' blows a whistle from the back of the hall*)
That was Joshua's special whistle he used when we wandered off. If I hadn't been standing where I was, I'd have jumped for joy. As it was, I just gave out a little 'Baa' and I heard the whistle again – this time closer than before. So I gave him another 'Baa!' And that's how we went on – whistle . . . 'Baa' . . . whistle . . . 'Baa' (*'Joshua' progresses gradually towards the front, still blowing the whistle when appropriate*) until he found me.

Joshua   You wait there.

Sheep   I ask you! As if I'd do anything else! He scrambled down to where I was and then he carried me up. I tell you, I closed my eyes and hung on. That was another thing my parents found embarrassing – a sheep that's scared of heights, I ask you! When we got to the top, Joshua put me down.

Joshua   Come on! You walked here, you can walk home. But don't worry, I'll be right with you all the way.

Sheep   He was, too. I'm more careful now. It's not so bad staying with the flock – in fact, we see some pretty exciting places. All I have to do is turn my head to the side – can't imagine why I didn't think of it before!

Keep Your Wig on, Judge!

Based on Luke 18:2-5

BEFORE THE DAY

Take the class to a suitable part of the school, and tell them to be very quiet and listen. Get them to draw what they hear: traffic on the road outside; footsteps in the corridor; lessons going on in other classes; kitchen staff preparing the school lunch; telephones ringing – and how many will notice the sound of pencils on paper right next to them? How long can the silence creatively be maintained? Collect in the drawings and make a display.

• Think about the actions for all the children to join in during the story.

ON THE DAY

Introduction

Some of the children have been doing some careful listening this week, and they're going to tell us about it. But first, we're going to say our 'Thank you' prayer.

'Thank you' Prayer

Thank you, God, for all you give us,
thank you for the earth and sea;
thank you, God, for special people,
thank you, God, for making me.

God's Story

Gabriella's husband had died and she was left alone with her daughter, Becky. In those days women's jobs were not very well paid, and anyway, Gabriella couldn't leave Becky on her own while she went to work. So how were they going to pay the rent?

Sam, the landlord, was one of those people who was always very nice to anyone who had money to spend, but changed completely if they fell on hard times. 'It's not my fault your husband's dead, is it?' he said, nastily. 'I've still got to live you know. I've got to pay my butler, and the man who prunes my roses, and of course I only drink the very best wine. So I can't go reducing people's rent or I might end up poor and pathetic like you.'

Gabriella didn't know what to do. For a time she got a job fig picking, but she knew that once the season was over that would come to an end. Then she heard about a job as a cleaner at the local tailor's. The work was quite hard – Gabriella was always getting hurt by needles and scissors that were left lying around – and it was very badly paid. Also, she had to take Becky along with her, and she didn't think that was either safe or fair.

One day Becky said to her mother, 'If you didn't have to pay so much rent, you wouldn't need to earn so much money.'

Gabriella smiled. 'The trouble is,' she explained, 'that Sam owns most of the houses in the town and can charge what he likes.'

That afternoon, when they were out for a walk, they saw a man who was wearing really funny clothes, and a wig. 'Hasn't he got any hair of his own?' asked Becky.

'Yes,' laughed Gabriella, 'but he's a very important person. He's a judge.'

'Oh,' said Becky. 'Does that mean that the more important people are, the more silly they have to look?'

Gabriella thought that Becky might have a point, but she was teaching her daughter to be polite, so she said, 'You mustn't talk like that about people. He probably thinks that your clothes are silly, but he hasn't said so.'

'What does a judge do, then?' asked Becky.

'Oh,' said her mother, 'he settles arguments between people. If someone's being unfair to someone else then he can tell them to stop.'

Before Gabriella could stop her, Becky was running over to the judge.

'Hey, Mister Judgy Person,' she called out. 'Can you help my mum, please, and stop her landlord charging her so much rent? – and I promise I won't say your wig looks silly ever again.'

The judge stopped. 'Is this abominable child your responsibility?' he shouted. 'Take her home and punish her – and teach her to be polite to important people, you disgusting, scruffy woman.'

'She's not abominable,' said Gabriella, 'and if I'm scruffy it's because I do an honest job. Anyway, I'd rather be scruffy than rude and arrogant. Come on, Becky.'

Gabriella was surprised at herself. 'I shouldn't have done that,' she said to Becky. 'We must always be polite. Just because someone's rude to you doesn't mean you can be rude back.'

'You weren't rude,' said Becky. 'You were just standing up for yourself. Anyway, I think he should help you.'

Gabriella started thinking about what Becky had said. Perhaps she should go and see the judge.

'Why should I help you?' said the judge. 'You're the rude woman with the horrible child, aren't you?'

'I'm sorry if you think I was rude,' Gabriella answered, 'but you weren't very polite, either. Anyway what you think of me doesn't alter the case. I'm being charged too much rent.'

'Go away,' said the judge. 'Sam is a good respectable citizen. And he's very rich. We need rich people in this town a lot more than we need poor spongers like you.'

That did it. Gabriella decided the judge was going to do the right thing. Every day, she went to his house and knocked on his door, but he wouldn't see her. Then she made a big poster saying 'Sack the unjust judge' and stood outside his courtroom with it. Soon she was joined by other women, and every time the judge went past they started chanting.

- *Fair rents for all!*
- *Fair rents for all!*
- *etc.*

Eventually, it all got too much for the judge, and he called Sam to see him.

'You'll have to lower your rents,' he said.

'Not me,' said Sam. 'Anyway, if I do that I'll have less to give to you.'

'Shut up!' hissed the judge. 'D'you want the whole town to know that you bribe me? Look, either you reduce your rents or we'll get the inspectors in to check your houses over.'

'Oh, don't do that!' said Sam, hastily. 'I'll cut the rents.'

The judge went and told the women. 'Now will you leave me alone?' he asked.

'Well,' replied Gabriella, 'we're very pleased about the rents, but we think we ought to talk to you about fair wages for cleaners.'

Our Story

Draw attention to the display and show the children what a range of noises is around them all the time. Life is a lot more interesting if we learn to listen!

Prayers

We're Sad

Sometimes, we're a bit like that judge:
we know what we should do,
but we try to get out of it.
Please forgive us, God,
and make us more willing to help people.

We're Glad

Thank you, God, for not having to be pestered.
Thank you for listening to us,
and for caring about us.

Let's Pray for People

There are lots of people like Gabriella,
who have to fight for fair treatment.
Loving God, please help us to care more,
to listen better,
and to make the world more fair
without waiting to be pestered into it.

Songs

I come like a beggar
Life for the poor was hard and tough
Lord of the dance
Out to the great wide world we go!
Stand up! Walk tall

Keep Your Wig on, Judge!

God's Story

Narrator	Gabriella's husband had died and she was left alone with her daughter, Becky, and with no money. Sam, the greedy landlord, wasn't very nice about it.
Sam	It's not my fault your husband's dead. If I reduce the rent I might end up poor and pathetic like you.
Narrator	Gabriella didn't know what to do. Then she got a job as a cleaner. The work was quite hard and very badly paid. Becky thought it was all Sam's fault.
Becky	If you paid less rent, you'd need less money.
Gabriella	Sam owns all the houses, so he can set his own rents.
Narrator	That afternoon, when they were out for a walk, they saw a man who was wearing really funny clothes.
Becky	Why's he wearing a wig? Hasn't he any hair?
Gabriella	Yes, but he's a very important person. He's a judge.
Becky	Oh, do important people have to look silly?
Gabriella	You mustn't talk like that about people.
Becky	What does a judge do, then?
Gabriella	He settles arguments and makes people behave fairly.
Becky	Hey, Mister Judgy Person, can you help my mum, and stop her landlord charging so much rent? – and I promise I won't say your wig looks silly ever again.
Judge	Take this abominable child home and teach her to be polite to important men, you dreadful, scruffy woman.
Gabriella	She's not abominable, and I work for my living. I'd rather be scruffy than rude. Come on, Becky.
Narrator	Gabriella was surprised at herself.

Gabriella	I shouldn't have done that. Just because someone's rude doesn't mean it's right to be rude back.
Becky	Well, I think he should help you.
Gabriella	You may be right. I'll go and see him one day.
Judge	Why should I help you? You and your horrible child!
Gabriella	That's not the point. Sam's charging too much rent.
Judge	Go away, Sam is a good respectable citizen. And he's very rich. We need rich people in this town a lot more than we need poor spongers like you.
Narrator	Gabriella decided the judge was going to do the right thing, whatever it took. Every day, she went and hammered on his door. Then she stood outside with a big poster saying, 'Sack the unjust judge'. Soon other women joined her and started chanting,

- *Fair rents for all!*
- *Fair rents for all!*
- *etc.*

Eventually, the judge called Sam to see him.

Judge	You'll have to lower your rents.
Sam	If I do that you'll have to reduce your cut.
Judge	Shut up! D'you want the whole town to hear? Look, I've had enough of being pestered by this woman. Either you reduce your rents or we'll get the inspectors in to check your houses over.
Sam	Oh, don't do that! I'll cut the rents.
Judge	Now will you women leave me alone?
Gabriella	Well, we're very pleased about the rents, but we think we ought to talk to you about fair wages for cleaners.

Representation and Reality

Based on Luke 18:9-14

BEFORE THE DAY

Ask the children to write some letters to God; simple little notes containing just one sentence either of praise or perhaps to pray for someone who is unwell. Pin the letters up, where appropriate, on a display board.

• Think about the actions for all the children to join in during the story.

ON THE DAY

Introduction

This morning we're going to think about ways of praying. First, we'll say our 'Thank you' prayer.

'Thank you' Prayer

Thank you, God, for all you give us,
thank you for the earth and sea;
thank you, God, for special people,
thank you, God, for making me.

God's Story

'Oh, dear, it's Sunday again,' thought Tony, and he felt guilty straight away because everyone kept telling him that Christians should enjoy Sundays: going to church, worshipping God, seeing other Christian people. *Real* Christians, Tony thought, enjoyed all of that – so what was wrong with him?

He expected that Harry Snooks would be there, as usual. Harry was a Real Christian: a fully paid up, card-carrying member of the Perfectly Pious True Believers' Club. He was so good it hurt! Everyone knew how good Harry was, because Harry was always telling them. Every year he sat down and worked out how much money he'd earned, and gave exactly one tenth of it to the church. Each week, he was at the Prayer Meeting, the Bible Study, the Praise Meeting and the 'Let's Spread the Gospel' Club – known among a few irreverents as Bible Bashers Anonymous, which would have infuriated Harry if he'd ever found out.

What Tony most dreaded about going to church was the slot in the service where anyone could pray out loud. Of course, Harry *always* prayed, and sounded so eloquent, using long words and mysterious phrases like 'substitutionary atonement'. Tony always felt he ought to pray like that, but he could never compete. Not that he hadn't tried, though. There was that Sunday when he'd joined in. He'd spent most of Saturday writing his own prayer out, going over it again and again and changing the words to make it flow better. He'd even used a dictionary to find out what 'substitutionary atonement' meant, but he still didn't understand it so he left it out. After the service, Harry came over to him and told him off for reading his prayer. 'Prayer,' Harry told him, 'has to come straight from the heart.'

'But it did,' protested Tony. 'I meant every word of it.'

'Real prayer,' said Harry, 'doesn't need to be thought about. You just know what to say.'

You can understand why Tony didn't enjoy going to church. He actually thought that to be a Real Christian, you had to say Real Prayers and be just like Harry. Perhaps it would help if he attended the midweek meetings like Harry did, but it was terribly difficult. Apart from his family commitments, he used to collect money for 'Save the Children' and go to visit people who were in hospital and in prison. Those people liked him as he was, and didn't want him to be like Harry. What was he to do? He was sure that going to church was important, but he didn't like feeling so guilty all the time.

Tony couldn't understand why God was so concerned about the kind of prayers he used but not about the other things he thought were important. Didn't God care about the people he visited? Harry didn't seem to think so.

• He *shook his head*
• then he *shrugged his shoulders*
• then he *pointed his fingers* at Tony

'Shouldn't have got themselves sick or in trouble in the first place,' he said. Tony couldn't believe that that was how God really felt, but he knew that Real Christians didn't have doubts or ask difficult questions. Well, the only answer was that he wasn't a Real Christian and probably never would be. And that frightened him very much.

So on this particular Sunday, when Tony arrived at the church, he found a seat just inside the door, right at the back, and sat there. When they came to the 'Open Prayer Time', Tony was beginning to feel ill. Harry started his usual prayer. He thanked God for helping him to be a Real Christian. He said he could never have given four thousand pounds to the church if God hadn't strengthened him. And he thanked God for helping him say such wonderful prayers, and guaranteeing him a good place in heaven.

By the time Harry got to the end, Tony was feeling worse than he ever had before! Without thinking about it, he said, in an embarrassingly loud voice, 'God, forgive me for being such a terrible person!'

There was a deathly silence. No one else prayed aloud, and Tony just sat there, wondering what was going to happen at the end of the service. He didn't hear the sermon, and he couldn't bring himself to join in the hymns. He just sat there, thinking what a fool he had made of himself.

When the service ended, a group of people gathered around Tony. He thought he was in for a telling off for spoiling the service, but they all seemed to like him! They said it was the best prayer they had heard in their lives. 'Simple and to the point,' said one person. 'Absolutely sincere,' said another. Tony found that he had a lot of friends in the church, and that they actually thought very highly of him.

'Why d'you think you're so bad?' asked Joan, who was a Pillar of the Church. 'Everyone in the town loves you because of the way you help people.'

Tony noticed Harry standing all alone in a corner of the room and looking lonely. 'I'd better go and talk to him,' he thought.

The two men walked home together, and Harry seemed a lot quieter and less sure of himself than usual. 'Are you all right?' Tony asked.

'Oh, I'm all right,' said Harry. 'I just wish I could be a bit more like you.'

Our Story

Read out some of the prayers, or get the children themselves to do it if they're willing. Point out how few words were needed just to express what was felt. Then use some of the prayers as part of a prayer slot in the assembly.

Prayers

We're Sad

It's sad when religion is misused
to make people feel bad.
Please forgive us, God,
if ever we have done that.

We're Glad

It's wonderful to know you love us, God!
Thank you for finding so many ways
of showing us just how much you care,
and how important all people are to you.
Thank you for being so loving.

Let's Pray for People

We pray for all people who feel guilty,
or who feel pushed out of things
because of the way religion has been used.
Please, God, help us all to know
that true religion
is about love and acceptance.
Help us to love and accept one another,
the way you love and accept us.

Songs

God doesn't want (SS)
I'm black, I'm white, I'm short, I'm tall
Out to the great wide world we go!
Stand up! Walk tall
Thank you, O God, for all our friends (SS)
When I needed a neighbour

Representation and Reality

God's Story

Narrator	It was Sunday again, and Tony felt guilty. Everyone kept telling him that Christians should enjoy Sundays.
Tony	*Real* Christians enjoy worship. What's wrong with me? I bet Harry Snooks will be there today, as usual.
Narrator	Harry was a Real Christian: he was so good it hurt! Everyone knew how good Harry was, because Harry was always telling them. Every week, he was at the Prayer Meeting, the Bible Study and the 'Let's Spread the Gospel' Club – known among a few irreverents as Bible Bashers Anonymous.
Tony	What I really dread is the Open Prayer slot in the service. One week, I spent most of Saturday writing a prayer out, and plucked up courage to use it on Sunday. Afterwards, Harry told me off for reading it.
Harry	Real Prayer has to come straight from the heart.
Tony	But it did. I worked really hard at getting it right.
Harry	Real Prayer doesn't need to be thought about. You just know what to say.
Narrator	Perhaps it would help if Tony attended the midweek meetings like Harry did, but it was terribly difficult. Apart from his family commitments, he used to collect money for 'Save the Children' and go to see people who were in prison – and he couldn't let all those people down. Tony had even begun to ask questions about how true it all was.
Tony	If there's a God, why's he so concerned about the kind of prayers we use but not about the other things I'm doing? Doesn't God care about the prisoners?
Narrator	<ul><li>Harry *shook his head*</li><li>then he *shrugged his shoulders*</li><li>then he *pointed his finger* at Tony</li></ul>

Harry   They shouldn't have got in trouble in the first place.

Narrator   When Tony arrived at the church this Sunday he found a seat just inside the door, right at the back. The service started and they sang some very jolly songs, but that just made Tony feel worse. Then they came to the 'Open Prayer Time', and Tony was feeling ill.

Harry   Thank you, God for helping me to be a Real Christian. I could never have given four thousand pounds to the church if you hadn't strengthened me. And I thank you for making me so good with words, so that I always say such great prayers. And thank you, God, for reserving me a good place in heaven.

Narrator   By the time Harry got to the end, Tony was feeling worse than ever. Suddenly he did an amazing thing.

Tony   (*Loudly*) God forgive me for being such a bad person!

Narrator   There was a deathly silence. Tony just sat there, thinking what a fool he had made of himself. When the service ended, a group of people gathered around him. Tony thought he was in for a telling off for spoiling the service, but they all seemed to like him!

Worshipper 1   What a wonderful prayer! Simple and to the point.

Worshipper 2   Absolutely sincere.

Narrator   Tony found that he had a lot of friends – including Joan, who was a Pillar of the Church.

Joan   Why d'you think you're so bad? Everyone in the town loves you because of the way you help people.

Narrator   Tony couldn't believe it. Then he noticed Harry standing all alone in a corner of the room, and felt sorry for him. The two men walked home together, and Harry seemed a lot quieter and less sure of himself.

Tony   Are you all right?

Harry   Yes – but I just wish I could be a bit more like you.

A Stranger On The Road

Based on Luke 24:13-35

BEFORE THE DAY

What do the children do when they're unhappy? Do they go to a special person, or place? Perhaps their bedroom provides a retreat, or maybe they have a special toy which serves as a 'security blanket'. You could make a list (probably without names on it) or get the children to draw, or just prepare a short talk on the basis of what you have done.

• Think about the actions for all the children to join in during the story.

ON THE DAY

Introduction

This story is about a wonderful surprise that happened to two sad people when they least expected it. But first we'll say our 'Thank you' prayer.

'Thank you' Prayer

Thank you, God, for all you give us,
thank you for the earth and sea;
thank you, God, for special people,
thank you, God, for making me.

God's Story

Cleopas and his wife Joanna lived in a village called Emmaus, about seven miles from Jerusalem. They had gone to Jerusalem for a big festival, and to see Jesus. But when they got there, they heard that Jesus had been captured by some bad people, and had been killed. What they didn't know was that God had brought Jesus back to life.

'Let's go home,' said Joanna, 'I don't like it here, any more.'

'Neither do I,' said Cleopas, 'the place is full of terrible memories.'

So they set out to walk the seven miles home. It was beginning to get dark when a stranger started to catch up with them. Joanna was saying, 'I can't understand how it happened. Jesus had so many friends, you'd have thought they'd have stopped it.'

'Stopped what?' asked the stranger, who had drawn level with them. 'What's happened?'

'You must have been walking around with your eyes closed!' said Cleopas. 'Jesus was killed – just because some powerful people were jealous of him.'

'Oh, that!' said the stranger. 'If you'd been reading your Bible, you'd have expected it. People like Jesus always get on the wrong side of powerful people.'

'We did hear a rumour that God had brought him back to life,' said Joanna.

'Yes,' said Cleopas impatiently, 'but that was just some silly women – we men knew it wasn't true!'

Cleopas and Joanna did not know that this stranger was Jesus himself! The 'silly women' had been right! But they didn't recognise him, and he walked with them talking about the bible, and how it said that God's special helper was going to get himself into trouble. By the time they got home to Emmaus, they were feeling better.

'It's a dreadful shame that Jesus was killed,' said Cleopas. 'But perhaps God's at work in all this somewhere.'

'Oh, yes, I think he is,' said the stranger mysteriously. 'God doesn't like bad things happening, but sometimes he can do amazing things with them!'

By this time, they were at the door of Cleopas' and Joanna's house. 'Boy, am I glad to be home!' exclaimed Joanna. 'Here we can feel safe. Nothing exciting happens here, and we always know where we stand.'

'Really?' said the stranger. 'I wouldn't bank on that, if I were you. Goodnight.' And he started to move on.

'Just a minute,' called Cleopas. 'It's late. Please come and stay with us.'

'Thank you,' said the stranger, and followed them in to the house. They soon had a warm fire going, and put some bread on the table. Just as Cleopas was about to offer the food round, the stranger did a very odd thing. Instead of being waited on by Cleopas and Joanna, like a guest, *he served them!*

- He *picked up* the bread
- He *broke it* into pieces
- He *handed it round*

'That's strange,' thought Cleopas, 'he's our guest, but he's serving us.'

'Good heavens!' Joanna exclaimed suddenly. 'It's Jesus!'

'So it is!' cried Cleopas, joyfully, and they both went to hug Jesus at the same time. But he wasn't there! He'd gone!

'Come on!' said Cleopas. 'We've got to get back.' They scurried back to Jerusalem and burst into the room where Jesus' other friends were.

'Guess what!' panted Joanna.

'No,' said Philip, 'you guess what! Jesus is alive again – it's true. We know it's true, because Simon told us.'

Joanna nearly said, 'Oh, so you believe a man, do you?' but she didn't want to spoil the evening. Everyone was wonderfully happy. They kept on telling the stories to each other of how they had found out.

'Just think,' said Cleopas to Joanna, 'a few hours ago, Jerusalem was a terrible place, and now it's the best!'

'Yes,' said Joanna. 'That often seems to happen when Jesus is around.'

Our Story

Talk about retreats. Use the display if you have one; otherwise tell the whole group about the kinds of things your group discussed. This story shows us that, when we need to get away, Jesus understands. He doesn't try to stop us, or turn us back, but he goes with us and gives us the confidence to go back when we are ready.

Prayers

We're Glad

Thank you, Jesus,
for being our friend.
Thank you for always being with us,
wherever we are,
and whatever we're doing.
Thank you for never leaving us
to cope on our own.

We're Sad

Sometimes, we run away,
just when people need us.
We don't want to face up to things,
or do difficult jobs.
We're sorry, Jesus,
help us to be brave.

Let's Pray for People

Please, God, help people who are frightened,
and who want to run away.
Help them to know that you're still there,
still caring.
And if they can't recognise you,
because they're confused or unhappy,
show us the best way to help them

Songs

I'm black, I'm white, I'm short, I'm tall
Jesus had all kinds of friends
Jesus took a piece of bread
Thank you, O God, for all our friends (SS)

A Stranger On The Road

God's Story

Narrator Cleopas and Joanna lived in a village called Emmaus, about seven miles from Jerusalem. They had gone to Jerusalem for a big festival, and to see Jesus. But Jesus had been captured by some bad people, and had been killed.

Joanna Let's go home! I don't like it here any more.

Cleopas Neither do I; the place is full of terrible memories.

Narrator So they set out to walk the seven miles home. It was beginning to get dark when a stranger caught up with them, and heard what Joanna was saying.

Joanna I can't understand how it happened. Jesus had so many friends, you'd have thought they'd have stopped it.

Stranger Stopped what? What's happened?

Cleopas You must have been walking around with your eyes closed! Jesus was killed – just because some powerful people were jealous of him.

Stranger Oh, that! If you'd been reading your Bible, you'd have expected it. People like Jesus always get on the wrong side of powerful people.

Joanna We did hear a rumour that God had brought him back to life.

Cleopas Yes, but that was just some silly women – we men knew it wasn't true!

Narrator Cleopas and Joanna did not know that this stranger was Jesus himself! The 'silly women' had been right! He walked with them talking how the Bible said that God's special helper was going to get himself into trouble. By the time they got home, they were feeling better.

Cleopas   It's a dreadful shame that Jesus was killed, but perhaps God's at work in all this somewhere.

Stranger   Oh, yes, I think he is. God doesn't like bad things happening, but sometimes he can do amazing things with them when they do!

Joanna   Well, this is our house. Boy, am I glad to be home! Here we can feel safe. Nothing exciting happens here.

Stranger   Really? I wouldn't bank on that, if I were you. Goodnight.

Cleopas   Just a minute. It's late. Please come and stay with us.

Stranger   Thank you.

Narrator   The stranger followed them in to the house. They soon had a warm fire going, and put some bread on the table. Then the stranger did a very odd thing. Instead of being waited on like a guest, *he served them!*

- He *picked up* the bread
- He *broke it* into pieces
- He *handed it round*

Joanna   Good heavens! It's Jesus!

Cleopas   So it is!

Narrator   They both went to hug Jesus. But he wasn't there!

Cleopas   Come on! We've got to get back.

Narrator   They scurried back to Jerusalem to tell their story. Philip said they already knew Jesus was alive because Simon had told them so. Everyone was wonderfully happy, and kept on telling the stories to each other.

Cleopas   Just think: a few hours ago, Jerusalem was a terrible place, and now it's the best!

Joanna   Yes. That often seems to happen when Jesus is around.

The Biggest Picnic in History

Based on John 6:1-14

BEFORE THE DAY

Ask the children to identify their favourite foods. Try to get a variety of things - sweet and savoury, fresh and processed. You could create a very interesting display, using food items, packets, wrappers, cooking utensils etc.

• Think about the actions for all the children to join in during the story.

ON THE DAY

Introduction

We're going to hear a story about a great big picnic shortly, but first we'll say our 'Thank you' prayer.

'Thank you' Prayer

Thank you, God, for all you give us,
thank you for the earth and sea;
thank you, God, for special people,
thank you, God, for making me.

God's Story

Sam was well known in his neighbourhood, with his uncombed curly hair, freckles and a big, permanent grin. He also loved listening to stories. It didn't really matter what they were about – he just enjoyed listening to them. So of course when he heard that Jesus was in the area, he wanted to go and listen. No-one could tell a story quite the way Jesus did – they were all about the kind of people and places everyone knew well; and the way he told them, you just couldn't help listening. So Sam was really excited.

'Mum! Mum! Jesus is here! Can I go and listen to him?'

Well, Mum knew that she wouldn't get any peace until she said 'Yes', but she didn't let Sam go just like that. 'Take some food with

you,' she said. 'Once you start listening to that Jesus fellow, you're likely to be there all day!' She was right. Once Sam got listening to a good story, he'd forget about everything – including going home for tea!

Jesus wasn't actually planning on telling any stories that day; he really wanted to rest. So he took his disciples away into the hills, and didn't tell anybody where they were going. Unfortunately, it was about as hard to keep a secret, where Jesus lived as it is in X*, so it wasn't long before just about everyone knew where Jesus was! And before long, the 'quiet place' was full of people – about five thousand of them! 'Well,' said Jesus, 'that's our peace and quiet done for!'

Jesus spent a lot of time talking to people, and as time went by he knew that they would be hungry – he always remembered about what people needed, even when they forgot about it themselves! So he said to Philip, 'Can we buy these people any food?'

'We can't afford all that!' said Philip.

Sam thought he'd better try to help – so he went to see Andrew, another of Jesus' friends. 'Look,' he said. 'I've got five bread rolls, and a couple of fish.'

Andrew didn't think that would be very helpful, but he didn't want to be unkind. 'Let's see what Jesus says,' he suggested.

'Well,' said Jesus, 'I think we can do something with this. Tell everyone to sit down, and we'll share out the food we have.'

Jesus' friends didn't think there would be enough, but they knew that Jesus usually turned out to be right. 'Come on,' said Andrew, 'let's do it. James, you start over there, and John go to that side.'

So the people sat down and shared the food.

• They *broke up the bread*
• They *shared it out*
• They *ate* as much as they needed

And can you guess what happened? Everyone had enough to eat! Not only that – when they picked up all the bits that had been dropped, they had another twelve baskets full of food.

Everyone thought Jesus was just the person

---

* The name of your town or village

they'd been waiting for. 'He ought to be our king,' they said. 'He'd be a lot better than Herod.'

Jesus didn't want that at all. Palaces, fancy clothes and servants bowing and scraping weren't his cup of tea! So he turned to his friends, and said, 'I think it's time to find that quiet place we were looking for!' And as Jesus and his friends slipped away, Sam went home.

'Well?' asked Mum, when he got back, 'What stories did Jesus tell today?'

'Oh,' said Sam, 'he told a few good ones, but what was really exciting was what Jesus *did*!'

Don't you agree?

Our Story

Draw attention to the display, and get the children talking about their favourite foods. How would they feel if they couldn't get them – or even their second favourite? Is it fair that we can pick and choose while others can't even get the basic necessities? Are there ways we can help?

Prayers

We're Glad

Thank you, God,
for our food.
We like lots of different things,
and we know that they all come
from you.
Thank you for our food.

We're Sad

Sometimes, we're greedy.
We eat more than we need.
Other times, we throw food away;
we waste it.
We know some people are hungry,
and we could help them
more than we do.
We're sorry.

Let's Pray for People

Jesus, give us the things we need,
and help us not to be greedy,
or wasteful.
Bless all the people who grow our food
or pack it
or bring it to us,
and help us to care for others
who don't have enough.

Songs

God knows me
Kum ba yah
Thank you, O God, for all our friends (SS)
When I needed a neighbour

The Biggest Picnic in History
God's Story

Narrator Sam was well known in his neighbourhood, with his uncombed curly hair, freckles and a big, permanent grin. He also loved listening to stories. It didn't really matter what they were about – he just enjoyed listening to them. So of course when he heard that Jesus was in the area, he wanted to go and listen. No one could tell a story quite the way Jesus did – they were all about the kind of people and places everyone knew well; and the way he told them, you just couldn't help listening. So Sam was really excited.

Sam Mum! Mum! Jesus is here! Can I go and listen to him?

Mum Well, I suppose I'll get no peace if I say 'no'! But you'd better take some food with you - once you start listening to that Jesus fellow, you're likely to be there all day!

Narrator She was right. Once Sam got listening to a good story, he'd forget about everything – including going home for tea! Now Jesus wasn't actually planning on telling any stories that day; he really wanted to rest. So he took his disciples away into the hills, and didn't tell anybody where they were going. Unfortunately, it was about as hard to keep a secret where Jesus lived as it is in - - - - - - - - - - - - -*, so it wasn't long before just about everyone knew where Jesus was! And before long, the 'quiet place' was full of people – about five thousand of them!

Jesus Well, that's our peace and quiet done for! But these people must be hungry. Andrew, can we buy them any food?

Andrew We can't afford all that!

Narrator Sam thought he'd better try to help – so he went to see Andrew.

* The name of your town or village

Sam   Look, I've got five bread rolls, and a couple of fish.

Andrew   Hmm . . . Well, let's see what Jesus says.

Jesus   I think we can do something with this. Tell everyone to sit down, and we'll share out the food we have.

Andrew   It doesn't look very hopeful to me, but if you say so, Jesus, we'll give it a go. James, you start over there, and John go to that side.

Narrator   So the people sat down, and shared the food.

- They *broke up the bread*
- They *shared it out*
- They *ate* as much as they needed

And can you guess what happened? Everyone had enough to eat! Not only that – when they picked up all the bits that had been dropped, they had another twelve baskets full of food. Everyone thought Jesus was just the person they'd been waiting for. They wanted to make him king – after all, he'd be a lot better than Herod! But Jesus didn't want that at all. Palaces, fancy clothes and servants bowing and scraping weren't his cup of tea!

Jesus   I think it's time to find that quiet place we were looking for – before things get out of hand.

Narrator   As Jesus and his friends slipped away, Sam went home to Mum.

Mum   Well? What stories did Jesus tell today?

Sam   Oh, he told a few good ones, but what was really exciting was what Jesus *did*!

Narrator   Don't you agree?

I Can See!

Based on John 9:1-39

BEFORE THE DAY

Ask the children what they would miss most if they couldn't see. How would they attempt to make up for lack of sight? Prepare a tactile display, using objects with very different surfaces.

• Think about the actions for all the children to join in during the story.

ON THE DAY

Introduction

We're going to think about different kinds of blindness in a few moments. But first we'll say our 'Thank you' prayer.

'Thank you' Prayer

Thank you, God, for all you give us,
thank you for the earth and sea;
thank you, God, for special people,
thank you, God, for making me.

God's Story

Let me tell you about Tim. He was very clever. Some people said he could have been a good lawyer if he'd had the chance, but he never did. Instead, every day, he sat in the streets hoping people would put some money in the bowl beside him.

Tim's problem was that he'd been born blind. And in those days, that meant he couldn't go to school, or get a job. The rest of him worked well – his ears could hear, his nose could smell, his mouth could talk. It was just that his eyes couldn't see. And because of that one thing, everyone thought he was useless. Poor Tim!

One day, as Tim sat in the streets begging, Jesus and his friends walked past. Matthew said, 'I wonder why he's blind; his parents must have done something dreadful, and God's punishing them.'

'Perhaps he's the one who's being punished,' said John. 'After all, he's the one who's blind.'

'You don't really think God would do that, do you?' Jesus said. 'But as the man is blind, we can use him to show how much God loves people.'

Then Jesus did something very strange. He made some mud from the dust on the ground, and went over to smear it on Tim's eyes.

'Hey!' Tim shouted. 'What do you think you're doing – leave me alone – GERROFF!'

'Don't worry,' said Jesus, 'I'm not trying to hurt you. My name is Jesus, and I want to help you to see.' Then he told Tim to wash in a pond nearby. Tim didn't need to be told twice, and hurried to wash his face.
When he got to the pool . . .

• He *washed his face*
• He *blinked* in amazement
• He *jumped* for joy

'Hey, everybody,' he shouted, 'I can see! I can see people, and houses, and this must be a tree . . .'

Some important people heard the noise and came to see what it was all about. 'What's going on?' asked Paul, who was a lawyer, and a council member. 'What's all the fuss about?'

'I can see! I can see!' shouted Tim, excitedly.

'Don't be silly,' said Paul. 'You're blind – I've seen you begging.'

'Yes,' said Tim, 'but I can see now! Look, I can see a donkey over there, and there's a camel, and . . .'

'All right, calm down,' said Paul. 'How did this happen?'

'Well, it was the funniest thing,' explained Tim. 'This man called Jesus put some mud on my eyes and told me to wash. I thought he was barmy, I don't mind telling you – but now I can see!'

'That troublemaker Jesus again!' thought Paul. 'If this goes on, people will think that Jesus is more important than I am.' Then he turned to Tim. 'You're a liar,' he said. 'You just pretended to be blind to get easy money.'

'Don't be silly!' said Tim. 'The amount of money I got that way, I'd rather have worked.'

'All right, I believe you,' said Paul, 'but this is the day of rest. So if Jesus healed you today he must be an evil man.'

'Evil?' yelled Tim. 'How can someone who helps people be evil?'

Then some other lawyers said, 'Jesus can't have come from God, or we'd have known about him. We don't know who he is.'

'Well, there's a funny thing,' said Tim, laughing at them. 'You don't know who he is! Even I can see who he is. You clever lot can't see what's right in front of your noses – and to think, people used to say that *I* was blind!'

So Tim believed that Jesus was a special good person, from God, but the lawyers just carried on saying what a dreadful, wicked person he was. But then, as Tim used to say, there's none so blind as those who will not see!

Our Story

Would any children volunteer to be blindfolded, and see whether they can identify display items by touch alone? *If it can be done safely*, you might like to move some things around after the blindfolds are on, and then see if the children can find their way round the room.

Talk about things we sometimes don't see even when we do have our eyes open, like whether people are worried or unhappy.

Prayers

We're Glad

It's good to be able to see.
We can see flowers, and trees, and pictures.
Best of all, we can see each other.
We can see when people need us,
and that they love us.
Thank you, Jesus,
for helping us to see.

We're Sad

We don't always see things.
Sometimes people are worried or upset,
and we just don't notice.
We just carry on as though everything's fine,
and we don't see
that for some people it's not.
Jesus, when we're happy,
remind us about others.
And when we're sad,
don't let us forget that others are, too.

Let's Pray for People

We pray for people who can't see.
Help them to use other ways
– like hearing, or touching,
and help us to know
when they need a bit of help.

Songs

Jesus put this song into our hearts
Morning has broken
Out to the great wide world we go!
Think of a world without any flowers
Who put the colours in the rainbow?

I Can See!

God's Story

Narrator   Tim was very clever. But every day he sat in the streets begging. Tim had been born blind, which in those days meant he couldn't go to school, or get a job. The rest of him worked well – he could hear, smell, talk. It was just that he couldn't see. And because of that one thing, everyone thought he was useless. Poor Tim! One day Jesus and his friends walked past and Matthew asked Jesus a question.

Matthew   Why's he blind, Jesus? Did his parents do something dreadful, and God's punishing them, or is he the one who's being punished?

Jesus   You don't really think God would do that, do you?

Narrator   Then Jesus did something very strange. He made some mud from the dust on the ground, and smeared it on Tim's eyes. Tim wasn't impressed at first!

Tim   Hey! Leave me alone – GERROFF!

Jesus   Don't worry. My name is Jesus, and I want to help you to see. Now go and wash in the pond over there.

Tim   You bet I will – fancy doing a thing like that!

Narrator   When Tim got to the pool . . .

- He *washed his face*
- He *blinked* in amazement
- He *jumped* for joy

Tim   Hey, everybody, I can see!

Narrator	After a little while, some important people heard the noise and came to see what it was all about.
Tim	I can see! I can see!
Paul	Don't be silly! You're blind – I've seen you begging.
Tim	Yes, but I can see now! Look, I can see a donkey over there, and there's a camel, and . . .
Paul	All right, calm down! How did this happen?
Tim	Well, it was the funniest thing. This man called Jesus put some mud on my eyes and told me to wash. I thought he was barmy, I don't mind telling you – but now I can see!
Paul	*(Aside, to audience)* That troublemaker Jesus again! If this goes on, people will think that Jesus is more important than I am.
	(To Tim) You're a liar. You just pretended to be blind to get easy money.
Tim	Don't be silly! I'd be better off working!
Paul	All right, I believe you. But this is the day of rest. So if Jesus healed you today he must be an evil man.
Tim	Evil? How can someone who helps people be evil?
Paul	Jesus can't have come from God, or we lawyers would have known about him. We don't know who he is.
Tim	Well, there's a funny thing! You clever lot can't see what's right in front of your noses – and to think, people used to say that I was blind!

Jesus Wins the Battle

Based on John 18:28-19:30

BEFORE THE DAY

Get the children to write some headlines for the Jerusalem newspapers: 'INNOCENT MAN CRUCIFIED'; 'JESUS INNOCENT, SAYS MOTHER', etc. Write them in large bold letters, with some squiggles underneath to represent normal print. Post the 'cuttings' up on a board.

• Think about the actions for all the children to join in during the story.

ON THE DAY

Introduction

Soon, we'll be hearing the story of how people tried to hurt Jesus. First, we'll say our 'Thank you' prayer.

'Thank you' Prayer

Thank you, God, for all you give us,
thank you for the earth and sea;
thank you, God, for special people,
thank you, God, for making me.

God's Story

Hello! My name's Caiaphas, and I'm the High Priest in Jerusalem. We'd been worried for a long time about this Jesus character, because he seemed like a troublemaker. Now let's be clear: he wasn't a priest, and he'd never been to theological college, but he did seem to know what he was talking about. And that sort are always dangerous. He went around telling people that God loves them even if they're not good. And he also told people who were not important – people like women and children, and disabled people – that they were as important as *we* were! Of course, we just couldn't allow it to go on. Once people like that start getting big ideas anything could happen – and then things might get nasty.

So we decided it would be best to get rid of him. That's why we arrested him and put him on trial.

Now the trouble was that he hadn't done anything wrong, so we had to twist things a bit – things he'd said that were really harmless, but we could make them sound worse than they were. Eventually, we managed to get him up for trial in front of the local Governor – a thoroughly untrustworthy politician called Pontius Pilate – and said Jesus was likely to start a revolution. Yes, all right, it was a long shot because we knew we couldn't make it stick, but we had another card up our sleeve. Pontius Pilate isn't a very good Governor. He's done some very silly things in the past few years, and given us excuses for starting riots – of course, we've always been careful to get other people to do the actual rioting so that *we* aren't caught. Anyway, all it would need would be one more truly awesome riot and he'd lose his job. So, while I reminded Pilate about that, and told him what a trouble-maker Jesus was, some of my priests were outside stirring up the crowd. Before he knew what had happened, Pilate had a group of very clever people in his palace telling him that if he knew what was good for him he'd kill Jesus; and at the same time he could hear the crowd outside getting more and more worked up.

Eventually, Pilate agreed to having Jesus crucified – nailed to a wooden cross until he died. I thought that would be the end of the matter. We'd get rid of Jesus, and at the same time we could convince the people that he'd been a fake all along. You see, Jesus was always preaching love and peace, and saying that you should turn the other cheek – all that kind of stuff – and I was looking forward to hearing him get angry – you know the sort of thing: shout and swear a bit, so that we could say he was all talk, and a hypocrite. Well, he talked all right, but you'll never guess what he said!

'Father, forgive them,' he said.

'They don't know what they're doing,' he said.

Here was this man, actually praying for for-giveness for us as the nails went in. I still can't get over it. There he was, hanging there in the heat, in horrible pain, and he really seemed to care more about others than himself. We tried everything to make him lose his cool.

- We *pulled faces*
- we *stuck out our tongues* (on second thoughts, put them back!)
- we even . . . *

But nothing worked. There were two rebels crucified, one on each side of him. One of them turned to him and asked for forgiveness. I was most upset, I can tell you – asking some perishing upstart for forgiveness when there were perfectly good priests there! Anyway, Jesus spoke really kindly to him. 'You'll be with me in paradise today,' he said. Rotten cheek if you ask me, but you've got to admire his courage. Then he looked down and saw his mother and a very special friend standing near the cross and started comforting them and telling them to look after each other. I tell you, I don't understand it at all!

Then, when he actually died, he said the most amazing thing. 'It's complete,' he said, with real satisfaction in his voice, as though he'd achieved something. And I hate to admit it (and don't tell a soul I said this) but I think he had. After everything that had happened to him – all the people who had let him down or turned against him – he really did seem to love us all. I don't mind telling you I'm very upset by the whole thing. Why couldn't he just have yelled at us once? Why did he have to be so good all the time?

I was very worried by all this. I went away thinking that Jesus might be more trouble dead than alive. Now that *was* tempting Providence! You'll never guess what happened next. Just when I thought nothing could get any worse, the whole city started buzzing with rumours that he was alive again. It ruined everything. We'd just got rid of him, and got his friends nice and scared so they wouldn't cause any more trouble, and all of a sudden they were out there, full of confidence, telling everyone they met that Jesus was alive. And they really believed it! We couldn't frighten them any more. We tried threats, we tried blackmail – we even tried torture. No good. These people simply weren't afraid of us any longer.

Whatever we did to them, they just kept on celebrating because Jesus was alive!

I don't mind telling you it's got me really rattled. Still, I'm sure it'll all blow over in a few days . . .

Won't it?

Our Story

Look at the headlines. Because Jesus suffered injustice, and later rose from the dead, that means that he still cares about it. And whenever people are bullied, cheated, taunted, or wrongly punished, he feels it too. So how about we try to care just a little more?

Prayers

We're Glad

Thank you, God, for Jesus' victory.
Thank you for all the people
he has given courage
to help them stand up for what is right.

We're Sad

We're sorry, Jesus, if ever
we've bullied people,
or taken advantage of them.
Help us to treat all other people
as if they were you.

Let's Pray for People

We pray for all who suffer for being good:
people who stand up against injustice,
and are accused of 'being political';
people who love others so much
that they get hurt badly themselves.
Please God, give them courage and hope.

Songs

From heaven you came
Jesus, remember me
There is a green hill
What kind of man was this

* Put thumbs to side of head and waggle fingers.

Jesus Wins the Battle

God's Story

Narrator*   Hello! My name's Caiaphas, and I'm the High Priest in Jerusalem. We'd been worried for a long time about this Jesus character. He said the most ridiculous things!

Jesus   Of course God likes you to be good, but he won't stop loving you if you're not.

Narrator   See what I mean? What sort of way is that to keep the rabble in their place?

Jesus   And the people who are counted least important in this world are most important to God.

Narrator   Now he's *really* gone too far! Once people like women and children and disabled people start getting big ideas, anything could happen. So we decided to get rid of him. Eventually, we managed to get him up for trial in front of the local Governor – Pontius Pilate.

Pilate   What's the problem?

Caiaphas   He's going to start a rebellion.

Narrator   All right, so it was a long shot, but we had another card to play. Some priests were outside stirring up the crowd.

Caiaphas   Hear that? It's starting already.

Pilate   Oh, no!

Caiaphas   You've got to get rid of him. You know your boss isn't happy about all the recent riots. You don't want another.

Pilate   All right, all right. I'll have him crucified.

Narrator   I thought that would be the end of the matter. You see, Jesus was always preaching love and peace, and saying that you should turn the other cheek – all that kind of stuff – and I was sure we could make him shout

* Caiaphas and Narrator are the same person. As 'Caiaphas' he engages in the dialogue with other characters; as 'Narrator' he addresses the audience.

and swear a bit, so that we could say he was all talk, and a hypocrite. Well, you'll never guess what he said!

Jesus Father, forgive them. They don't understand.

Narrator Here was this man, actually praying for forgiveness for us as the nails went in. I still can't get over it. There he was, hanging there in the heat, in horrible pain, and he really seemed to care more about others than himself. We tried everything to make him lose his cool.

- We *pulled faces*
- we *stuck out our tongues* (on second thoughts, put them back!)
- we even . . .*

But nothing worked. Then, when he actually died, he said the most amazing thing.

Jesus It's complete. Everything is achieved.

Narrator I hate to admit it (and don't tell a soul I said this) but I think he *had* achieved something. After everything that had happened to him – all the people who had let him down or turned against him – he really did seem to love us all. I don't mind telling you, I'm very upset by the whole thing. Why couldn't he just have yelled at us once? Why did he have to be so *good* all the time? I went away thinking that Jesus might be more trouble dead than alive. Now that *was* tempting Providence! You'll never guess what happened next. Just when I thought nothing could get any worse, the whole city started buzzing with rumours that he was alive again. It ruined everything. His friends were so full of it we couldn't frighten them any more. We tried threats, we tried blackmail – we even tried torture. No good. These people simply weren't afraid of us any longer. Whatever we did to them, they just kept on celebrating because Jesus was alive!

I don't mind telling you it's got me really rattled. Still, I'm sure it'll all blow over in a few days . . .

Won't it?

* Put thumbs to sides of head and waggle fingers.

Wait for the Power

Based on Acts 2:1-21

BEFORE THE DAY

What do the children think they might be when they grow up? Write a list of examples, and/or get the children to draw themselves as they expect to be when they are older.

• Think about the actions for all the children to join in during the story.

ON THE DAY

Introduction

This morning, we're going to learn about waiting, but first, we'll say our 'Thank you' prayer.

'Thank you' Prayer

Thank you, God, for all you give us,
thank you for the earth and sea;
thank you, God, for special people,
thank you, God, for making me.

God's Story

The friends of Jesus were waiting, all together, in a secret meeting room. When Jesus had gone back to heaven, he had said, 'Stay in Jerusalem until you get the power you need.' Peter was getting impatient, though. 'It's all very well,' he said, 'but the city is full of people. We should be telling people about Jesus.'

'Jesus told us to wait,' said Matthew, who used to be a tax collector before he met Jesus. 'I know all about waiting – people used to keep me waiting for months.'

'It's no good, anyway,' added James. 'The visitors are from all over the world – we'd need to know dozens of different languages if we were going to tell them about Jesus.'

'Let's be honest,' said Thomas. 'We don't really want to go out there. There are people who want to kill us, and I'm too young to die – come to think of it, I always will be.'

As usual, Thomas was the most honest one of the group; he was saying what the others were afraid to say. In their hearts, everybody knew that he was right. That was why they'd bolted the doors and not told anyone else where they were. The friends of Jesus were good people, and good friends – but they had reason to be afraid; the people who had killed Jesus were now looking for his followers, and they weren't going to invite them to tea! Most people would be just as frightened as they were if they had to face that kind of thing.

The problem was, though, how were they ever going to get the courage to do Jesus' work? They had seen him several times after he had risen from the dead, and yet they still seemed to be frightened of being killed themselves. How could that ever be changed? No wonder they were a little bit glum!

Just as they were beginning to get desperate, and thinking what dreadful, useless disciples they were, they heard a strange sound. 'Close the window, Andrew,' said John. 'Sounds like the wind's getting up.'

'It's already closed,' said Andrew. 'We barred it up to keep the religious leaders out so that they can't hurt us.'

'Well, you didn't do it properly,' grumbled Peter. 'That's the trouble with you – you can't be trusted.'

'Ooh! Look who's talking!' Andrew responded, and he would have said a lot more but Thomas stopped him. He didn't think it was the wind at all.

• He *licked his finger*
• and he *held it up in the air*
• and he *shook his head*

He couldn't feel any draught at all. And all the disciples sat very quietly and listened. Sure enough, the noise got louder and louder, but they couldn't feel the wind. Thomas was just thinking that it was a bit like the burning bush – when Moses had seen the flames, but the bush didn't actually burn – when he noticed flames as well.

'Hey, Peter!' he said. 'Your hair's on fire!'

'Don't be daft!' said Peter, 'I'd know if *my* hair was on fire. You're the one who's got that problem.'

Then they realised that there seemed to be flames over everybody's head. 'It *is* like the burning bush!' thought Thomas. 'Something special's happening.'

'Come on!' shouted Peter. 'Let's go outside and . . .' But he was too late. They'd gone. They'd unbolted the door and gone rushing out into the street and started telling everyone that Jesus was alive – and all of a sudden they were language experts! Andrew was speaking in Persian to a group of carpet merchants, while Philip had cornered a couple of soldiers and was talking in Latin, and Thomas – who had always doubted the importance of learning languages – was busy winning an argument with some philosophers, in Greek.

Then Peter realised what he was doing. 'This is silly,' he thought. 'We could get ourselves into serious trouble doing this.' He realised he was still quite frightened, but then he thought, 'Well, some things are worth getting into trouble for – and there's nothing more important than doing this.'

That morning, thousands of people heard the good news that Jesus was alive. The religious authorities didn't like it. 'What will happen to all our power and our privileges,' they asked, 'if ordinary people start being listened to?' So they went around saying that Peter and his friends were drunk.

'Do me a favour!' laughed Peter. 'At this time of the morning? This is the power of God at work, but you're too bothered about yourselves to recognise it.'

Then the disciples realised that this was the 'power' Jesus had promised them. They knew there would still be hard and dangerous times ahead, because Jesus had told them that, too. But they knew it was worth it. Now they understood that, whatever happened, Jesus would always be with them and God wouldn't let their lives or their work be wasted.

Now that's what I call power!

Our Story

Point out the display which your class prepared and describe a few of the ambitions.

'Stephanie wants to be an airline pilot', or whatever. Then ask why they can't be those things now, and the answers may be many and varied but will probably amount to the fact that they are not yet ready. In just the same way, the disciples were not ready for what they had to do. Sometimes, waiting in patience can be very hard!

Prayers

We're Sad

Sometimes it's difficult to understand
people who are different from us,
but that's no reason not to try.
Please, God, forgive us
for letting differences keep us apart.

We're Glad

Holy Spirit,
you break down all the barriers
between different people.
Thank you for making it possible
for us to listen to one another.

Let's Pray for People

We pray for the world,
full of many different kinds of people,
speaking different languages,
and even using the same words differently.
Please, God, give us the gift of understanding,
and stop us being afraid of each other.

Songs

Hang on
I'm black, I'm white, I'm short, I'm tall
One more step
Out to the great wide world we go!
Peace is flowing like a river

Wait for the Power

God's Story

Narrator   Jesus had gone back to heaven, leaving his friends to carry on his work. He'd told them not to start straight away but to stay in Jerusalem until he gave them the power they needed. Peter was getting impatient.

Peter   It's all very well, Matthew, but the city is full of people. We shan't have another chance like this for nearly a year. We should be telling people about Jesus.

Matthew   Jesus told us to wait. I know all about waiting – when I was a tax man, people kept me waiting for months. Anyway, we'd need to know dozens of different languages – wouldn't we, Thomas?

Thomas   Let's be honest. We don't really want to go out there, anyway. There are people who want to kill us, and I'm too young to die – come to think of it, I always will be.

Narrator   As usual, Thomas was the most honest one of the group. In their hearts, everybody knew that he was right. That was why they'd bolted themselves in.

Peter   Close the window, Andrew. Sounds like the wind's getting up.

Andrew   It's already closed. We nailed it up for security.

Peter   Well you didn't do it properly.

Narrator   Thomas didn't think it was the wind, anyway.

- He *licked his finger*
- and he *held it up in the air*
- and he *shook his head*

Thomas   It's not the wind. I can't feel any draught at all.

Narrator   All the disciples sat very quietly and listened. The noise got louder, but the air was still.

Thomas   Hey, Peter! Your hair's on fire!

Peter   Don't be daft! I'd know if my hair was on fire. You're the one who's got that problem.

Narrator   Then they realised that there seemed to be flames over everybody's head. Suddenly, they unbolted the door and went rushing out into the street and started telling everyone that Jesus was alive – and all of a sudden they were language experts! Andrew was speaking in Persian to a group of carpet merchants, while Philip had cornered a couple of soldiers and was talking in Latin, and Thomas – who had always doubted the importance of learning languages – was busy winning an argument with some philosophers, in Greek.

Peter   This is silly. We could get ourselves into serious trouble doing this. Still, some things are worth getting into trouble for – and this is important.

Narrator   That morning, thousands of people heard the good news that Jesus was alive. The religious authorities didn't like it because they were afraid of losing their power. So they went around saying that Peter and his friends were drunk.

Peter   Do me a favour! At this time of the morning? This is the power of God at work, but you're too bothered about yourselves to recognise it.

Narrator   Then the disciples realised that this was the 'power' Jesus had promised them. They knew there would still be hard and dangerous times ahead because Jesus had told them that, too. But they knew it was worth it. Now they understood that, whatever happened, Jesus would always be with them and God wouldn't let their lives or their work be wasted. Now that's what I call power!

Song Section

Be yourself!

To the tune of *Three blind mice*

Be yourself!
Be yourself!
That's all you need!
That's all you need!
You needn't pose as a superstar,
or say that a Porsche is your other car,
for better or worse, you're the person you are,
so be yourself!

Be yourself!
Be yourself!
That's all you need!
That's all you need!
So don't go putting on fancy airs
by posing as princes or millionaires
or one day you'll find yourself caught unawares,
so be yourself!

Be yourself!
Be yourself!
That's all you need!
That's all you need!
Life's not intended to be a test,
you don't have to struggle to beat the rest;
God says that you're special, and he should know best,
so be yourself!

Dry bones

Dem bones, dem bones, dem dry bones,
dem bones, dem bones, dem dry bones,
dem bones dem bones, dem dry bones,
I hear de word of de Lord.

Ezekiel connected dem dry bones,
Ezekiel connected dem dry bones,
Ezekiel connected dem dry bones,
I hear de word of de Lord.

Toe bone connected to de foot bone,
foot bone connected to de ankle bone,
ankle bone connected to de leg bone,
leg bones connected to de knee bones,
knee bone connected to de thigh bone,
hip bone connected to de back bone,
back bone connected to de shoulder bone,
shoulder bone connected to de head bone,
I hear de word of de Lord.

Dem bones, dem bones, g'on walk a-roun',
Dem bones, dem bones, g'on walk a-roun',
Dem bones, dem bones, g'on walk a-roun',
I hear de word of de Lord.

God doesn't want

Based on Amos 5:21-24
To the tune of *Here we go round the mulberry bush*

God doesn't want our fancy prayers,
fancy prayers,
fancy prayers,
God doesn't want our fancy prayers,
if we cannot love our neighbours!

God doesn't want our hymns and songs,
hymns and songs,
hymns and songs,
God doesn't want our hymns and songs,
if we cannot love our neighbours!

God will enjoy our simple prayers,
simple prayers,
simple prayers,
God will enjoy our simple prayers,
when we also love our neighbours.

God will enjoy our hymns and songs,
hymns and songs,
hymns and songs,
God will enjoy our hymns and songs,
when we also love our neighbours.

Jesus can make us truly rich

To the tune of *Here we go round the mulberry bush*

Jesus can make us truly rich,
truly rich,
truly rich.
Jesus can make us truly rich
when he helps us love each other.

Let it be!

To the tune of *Three blind mice*

'Let it be!
Let it be!'
That's what he said.
That's what he said.
The universe was a dreadful sight
a terrible mess and as dark as night,
then God spoke the word and said, 'Let there be light,
O let it be!'

'Let it be!
Let it be!'
That's what he said.
That's what he said.
'Let's get things sorted without delay,
the earth from the sky and the night from day,
now that's looking better, I'm happy to say,
so let it be!'
'Let it be!
Let it be!'
That's what he said.
That's what he said.
'I'm separating the earth and sea,
the land will be covered in flow'rs and trees,
now that's looking pretty delightful to me,
so let it be!'

'Let it be!
Let it be!'
That's what he said.
That's what he said.
'Let's fill creation with life diverse,
let earth be a gem in the universe,
and now I'll make people for better or worse,
so let it be!'

Questions! Questions!

To the tune of *Twinkle, twinkle, little star*

Questions! Questions! What a lot!
'Who', 'Why', 'Where', 'How', 'When' and 'What'!
They're the tools for finding out
what the world is all about.
Questions! Questions! What a lot!
'Who', 'Why', 'Where', 'How', 'When' and 'What'!

Questions! Questions! What a lot!
'Who', 'Why', 'Where', 'How', 'When' and 'What'!
Keep on asking, never fear,
they're what grown-ups love to hear!*
Questions! Questions! What a lot!
'Who', 'Why', 'Where,' 'How', 'When' and What'!

* OK, so put your tongue in your cheek, or cross your fingers or something!

Rabbles, babbles

To the tune of *Baa, baa, black sheep*

Rabbles, babbles, what's it all about?
people talk and people shout.
Nobody listens, so no one is heard,
for everyone's trying hard to have the last word!

Rabbles, babbles echo all around;
empty vessels make most sound!
Sometimes, to listen in silence is best,
to switch off our wagging tongues and give them a rest.

Ride that camel! Chase that star!

To the tune of *Twinkle, twinkle, little star*

Wise men from a country far,
Ride that camel! Chase that star!
Through the lonely desert night
it will be your guiding light.
Wise men from a country far,
Ride that camel! Chase that star!

Wise men from a country far,
Ride that camel! Chase that star!
Incense, gold and myrrh you bring,
presents for the baby king.
Wise men from a country far,
Ride that camel! Chase that star!

Wise men from a country far,
Ride that camel! Chase that star!
Follow where it goes before,
on the desert myst'ry tour!
Wise men from a country far,
Ride that camel! Chase that star!

Sing a song of weather!

Text: Michael Forster
To the tune of *Sing a song of sixpence*

Sing a song of weather,
of wind and snow and rain;
lovely summer sunshine,
(now and again!).
Changes in the weather can catch us on the hop;
what a pity we can't tell the wind and rain to stop!

Sing a song of weather,
for even rain and snow
keep the garden healthy,
help make things grow:
food for us to eat, and grass where we can play;
what a good thing we can't tell the rain to go away!

Thank you, O God, for all our friends

Text: Michael Forster
To the tune of *Here we go round the mulberry bush*

(Before you sing, what kind of morning is it?)

Thank you, O God for all our friends,
for all our friends,
for all our friends,
thank you, O God for all our friends,
on a *cold and frosty**
warm and murky
damp and rainy
foggy, misty
morning!

Thank you, O God, for flow'rs and trees

Thank you, O God, for animals

*Use whichever is appropriate

We're all going to the promised land

Text: Michael Forster
Music: Christopher Tambling

2. In the desert's heat and dust,
   people grumbled, moaned and fussed,
   Moses said, 'In God we trust;
   let's find the promised land.'

3. Through the desert they were led
   by the cloud and fire ahead,
   then one day the lookout said,
   'We've found the promised land.'